Visualize This

Second Edition

Visualize This

The FlowingData Guide to Design,
Visualization, and Statistics

Second Edition

Nathan Yau

ISBNs: 9781394214860 (Paperback), 9781394214884 (ePDF), 9781394214877 (ePUB)

Library of Congress Control Number: 2024935194

SKY10072215_041124

To Bea, Caleb, and Audrey

About the Author

Nathan Yau has a PhD in statistics from the University of California at Los Angeles, with a focus on visualization for presenting and communicating data to everyone. He was the winner of a FastCompany Innovation by Design Award for Graphic Design & Data Visualization, he has won Information is Beautiful awards, and he was featured in *The Best American Infographics*. He has worked as a researcher and for mainstream publications. His work leans toward practical and has reached millions of people. Since 2007, Yau has written, analyzed, and made graphics for FlowingData, his site on visualization, statistics, and design. Yau's goal is to help people understand data, and he believes visualization—from statistical charts to information graphics to data art—is the best way to get there.

About the Technical Editor

Jan Willem Tulp (TULP interactive) is an award-winning data experience designer from The Netherlands. As an independent data visualization designer with more than 12 years of experience, he has worked for a wide variety of clients, such as World Bank, *Scientific American*, Google News Lab, European Space Agency, the Dutch Railways (NS), and Nielsen. Tulp speaks regularly at international conferences, such as Open VisConf, IEEE VIS in Practice, Visualized, Indo Data Week, and OutlierConf. His work has been published in a number of books and magazines, including *The Functional Art*, *Design for Information*, and *The Book of Circles*. The nature of his projects ranges from interactive exploratory tools to data-driven storytelling to experimental visualizations that push the boundaries. Occasionally, his work is shown in exhibitions. One of his current projects is in the permanent collection for 3 years of Ars Electronica.

Acknowledgments

This book would not have been possible without the work of statisticians, data scientists, cartographers, analysts, and designers before me, who developed and continue to create useful tools for everyone. If you are one of these people, I thank you.

Many thanks to the FlowingData readers who helped me, an introvert who likes to think about data, reach more people than I ever could have imagined. They are one of the main reasons why this book was written.

Thank you to my wife for supporting me and to my parents who always encouraged me to find what makes me happy. Thank you to my kids for their perspective, which makes work more meaningful and life fuller.

Contents

Introduction

Data is everywhere, and one of the best ways to explore a dataset is with visualization. Place the numbers into a visual space and let your brain find the patterns. We're good at that. Discover insights that you wouldn't see in a spreadsheet alone. From here, you can use visualization to communicate to others, from an audience of one to millions.

For a long while, visualization was more of a quantitative and technical exercise. Show data, get out of the way, and let the data speak. This approach works sometimes, but it assumes that data speaks a language that everyone understands and that it always speaks definitively and in absolutes. However, data is not always so straightforward, and the insights are often not so certain.

Over the past 17 years of writing for FlowingData, a site on visualization, statistics, and design, I've seen an evolution. Visualization was mostly an analysis tool when I started my studies but it has developed into a medium to tell stories with data. You can show just the facts, but you can also evoke emotion, entertain, and compel change.

In my own work, visualization is a way to understand data, share what I find, and, most importantly, make sense of what's going on around me. I follow an iterative process of answering questions with data, visualizing the answers, and then asking more questions. Repeat until there are no more questions. While the general analysis and visualization process remained about the same since the first edition of this book, the steps to carry out the process were refined and the tools shifted, varying by the year you asked me.

This is the second edition of *Visualize This*. When I wrote the first edition more than a decade ago, visualization in practice was in a different place. The tools were different (like Flash), people tended to follow stricter design guidance (like ratios between data and ink), the purpose behind visualization was narrower (such as analysis and quantitative insights only), and organizations were still figuring out what data to make public (which feels less open at times these days).

As a reflection of my own evolving process, this edition provides all new examples, explanations, and guidance, with a focus on making charts to communicate. This is how to visualize data from my point of view, and it isn't the only way to do things. For me, it's what works best. My hope is that after working through this book, you'll know the mechanics of chart-making, be able to refine your process to fit your specific needs and form your own opinions about what makes visualization great.

LEARNING DATA VISUALIZATION

I got my start in statistics during my first year in college. It was a required introductory course toward my electrical engineering degree. The professor was refreshingly enthusiastic about his teaching and clearly enjoyed the topic. He quickly walked, nearly running, up and down the stairs of the lecture hall as he taught. He waved his hands wildly as he spoke and got students involved as he whizzed by. His excitement drew me into studying data and eventually led to graduate school, studying statistics four years later.

Throughout my undergraduate studies, statistics was procedural data analysis, distributions, and hypothesis testing. I enjoyed it. It was fun to look at a new dataset to find trends, patterns, and correlations. When I started graduate school, though, my field of vision widened, and things got more interesting. My appreciation for statistics grew.

Statistics became less about hypothesis testing, bell curves, and coin flips. It became more about telling stories with data. You get a bunch of data, which represents the real world, and then you analyze and interpret that data to make sense of what's going on around you. These stories can inform public policy, business, technology, health, happiness, and everyday life.

The ubiquity of data means the process of communicating data comes in handy in many places. However, a lot of people don't have the time or know how to connect data to real life. You can be the bridge between abstract numbers and insight.

How do you learn the necessary skills to visualize data usefully? These days, there are courses and degrees you can earn in data visualization, but you can also learn through practice without a dedicated degree. I've never taken a visualization course.

The first charts I made from scratch were in the fourth grade. They were for my science fair project. My project partner and I pondered, very deeply I am sure, what surface snails move on the fastest. We put snails on rough and smooth surfaces and timed them to see how long it took them to crawl a specific distance. So, the data was clocked times for different surfaces, and I made a bar chart. I can't remember if I had the insight to sort from least to greatest, but I do remember struggling with Microsoft Excel. Charts were easier after that, though. Once you learn the basic functionality and your way around the software, the rest is easier to learn. (By the way, the snails moved fastest on glass, in case you were wondering.)

It's the same process with any software or programming language you learn. As my career extended beyond the fourth-grade science fair project on snails, I learned how to visualize data as I went. I learned R to analyze data in school and more so later for work. I joined a research group using Python for data collection and PHP for web applications, so I learned those languages to not be totally useless. I wanted to make interactive and animated graphics for the web, so I learned Flash, and when Flash died, I learned JavaScript. To prepare for a graphics internship, I studied all the data design books I could, but it wasn't until I struggled making graphics with Adobe Illustrator when I figured out how to make charts for a general audience.

If you've never written a line of code or used a hefty software package, the process can seem intimidating, but after you work through some examples, you start to get the hang of things. This book can help you with that.

HOW TO USE THIS BOOK

This book is example-driven, with practical steps for how to use a mix of visualization tools and understand different types of data. With each example, you start with a dataset and work through the process of asking questions, learning about data, and communicating insights to a wider audience.

Each chapter includes data, code, and files you can download. Download everything at www.wiley.com/go/visualizethis2e or https://book.flowingdata.com/vt2. The files will make it easier to work through examples step-by-step, poke at the data if you are curious, and apply what you learn to other datasets.

You can read this book cover to cover or pick your spots if you already have a dataset or visualization in mind. The chapters are organized by data type and what you want to visualize. The sections within each chapter discuss what to look for in your data and the chart types that can help you and others see relevant patterns.

By the end, you should be able to visualize your own data and design publication-ready graphics. Have fun in the process.

Telling Stories
with Data

Think of the data visualization works that you enjoy—the ones that you see online, that appear in lectures, and that you associate with quality. Most likely the works that popped into your head tell an interesting story. Maybe the story was to convince you of something. Maybe it was to compel you to action, enlighten you with new information, or force you to question your assumptions. Maybe it made you smile. Whatever it is, the best data visualization, big or small, for art or a slide presentation, shows patterns that you could not see otherwise.

MORE THAN NUMBERS

My interest in visualization began as a new statistics student ready to analyze all the datasets. Charts were a tool I could use to understand data better, and I would occasionally export an image to stick in a report. That was about it.

I approached chart-making from a technical point of view, without giving much thought to what type of chart worked best, who was going to look at my work, or how to design around insight and story. I just needed to figure out how to make a chart so that I could move on to the rest of my analysis.

However, the more I worked with data, the more I learned about its complexity, subjectivity, and how it related to the rest of the world. At the same time, we were interacting with data more through computers, phones, and connected devices. Data intertwined with the everyday instead of with just a spreadsheet that analysts opened at work, and I grew interested in how data would play a role in understanding ourselves better.

A couple of years into graduate school, a graphics internship at a major news publication got me thinking about visualization's role in the presentation and communication of data. How did it differ from visualization for exploratory data analysis? Then with FlowingData, I suddenly got a taste of what it was like for a visualization project to communicate data to millions of people. I felt like I was onto something, so I kept going. I was hooked. What started as a side project to keep in touch with classmates became my full-time dream job.

See the classic *Exploratory Data Analysis* by John Tukey (Pearson, 1977), which introduced a novel idea at the time to use visualization to study data.

Over the years, visualization matured beyond just an analysis tool. It became a way to communicate data to nonprofessionals. It could be fun. Visualization grew into a medium to tell stories with data, and like any good medium, it lets you tell different types of stories.

STATISTICALLY INFORMATIVE

Statistical stories probably come to mind for most people when it comes to data and visualization. In a journalistic context, the stories often follow a familiar article format with charts coupled with narrative. The charts show the data, and the narrative, in the form of text and annotations, describe what the data is about and provide context for the numbers. Think data projects by news organizations like the *New York Times*, the *Washington Post*, and *Reuters*.

You can also find statistical stories in a more analytical context, such as in reports, presentations, and analysis results. Maybe these aren't stories in the traditional sense, but the data you work with is about something, and that something is what makes visualization meaningful.

In 1874, the United States Census Bureau published a *Statistical Atlas of the United States*. It provided a graphical summary of the data collected for the 1870 decennial count with maps and charts. In the present day, it's like looking at a snapshot in time that shows what life was like.

Check out the *Statistical Atlas of the United States* from the 1870s at `https://datafl.ws/714`.

More recently, I wondered if I could use the visual forms of the original atlas to take a current snapshot. I used the most recently available data to make a revised atlas. For example, as shown in Figure 1.1, a breakdown of population by state and race was designed using the original 19th century aesthetic and wordage.

This idea of data snapshots that we can look at centuries from now drives most of my work. How do things look now, and how will things look 100 years from now? What do these snapshots look like for individuals using the data they collect (actively and passively) through their phones and devices?

We can use data for insight, and the insight coupled with context gives us stories. This helps people make better informed decisions in both work and everyday life.

ENTERTAINING

Statistics. People would ask me what I studied, and either their eyes would glaze over in disinterest, or they would groan about the introductory statistics course they hated in college. They remembered bell curves and hypothesis tests something or other. Occasionally, someone would feign interest, and while I appreciated the effort, I knew better.

Data can be boring if you don't know how to interpret it. It might as well be gibberish. The fun thing about visualization is that people can see patterns in pictures that are more difficult to understand through equations and text.

Over the years, more people grew to appreciate data, and charts grew into a form of entertainment. People tell jokes with charts, draw comics, explore fun curiosities, and create social media-based businesses under the premise of infotainment.

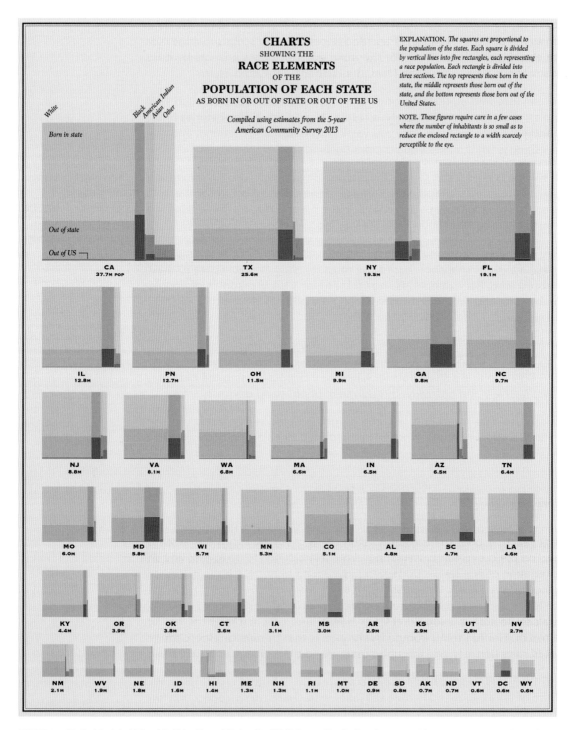

A lot of the projects I publish on FlowingData are for my own entertainment, such as the one in Figure 1.2. A question pops up, and I try to answer it with data. But if I'm interested in something, at least one other person must be curious, too. I think that's one of the foundations of the Internet.

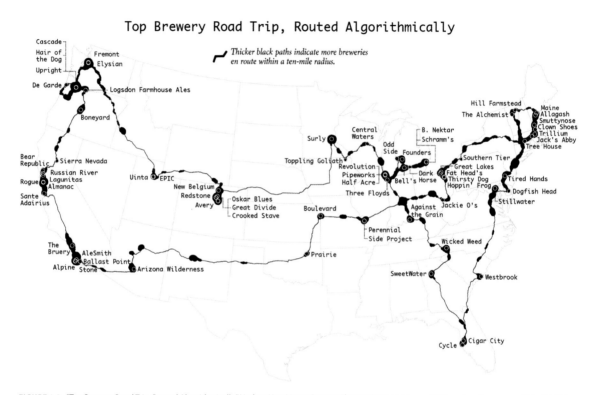

FIGURE 1.2 *"Top Brewery Road Trip, Routed Algorithmically,"* Nathan Yau / 2007-Present FlowingData / `https://flowingdata.com/2015/10/26/top-brewery-road-trip-routed-algorithmically` / *last accessed February 08, 2024.*

Every year, the beer review site RateBeer publishes the top 100 breweries based on preferences and user ratings. With a fascination for road trips and an appreciation of fine beer, I wondered what a road trip through the breweries on the list in the lower United States would look like. And, where there is one excellent brewery, there are usually others nearby, so I also wanted to know the places to stop in between the top breweries. The map shows the way to the top breweries in 2014 routed by travel times and a genetic algorithm, or a set of rules that stepped through possible solutions until it converged to an optimal route.

The visualization might not be optimized for lightning-fast decision-making, but it did seem to entertain a good number of people.

EMOTIONAL

Visualization as a field of study has a tendency toward optimized insights. This makes sense for analysis. You want to explore data quickly and efficiently so that you can evaluate from various angles.

However, if we were always after the most efficient and perceptually accurate visualization, we should just use bar charts most of the time. Or better yet, skip the visualization and just show a table for full accuracy. (I am exaggerating, but not by much.) This is not my favorite path.

Sometimes you want to visualize data in a way that reflects meaning beyond the quantitative insights. In Figure 1.3, I explored what makes people happy.

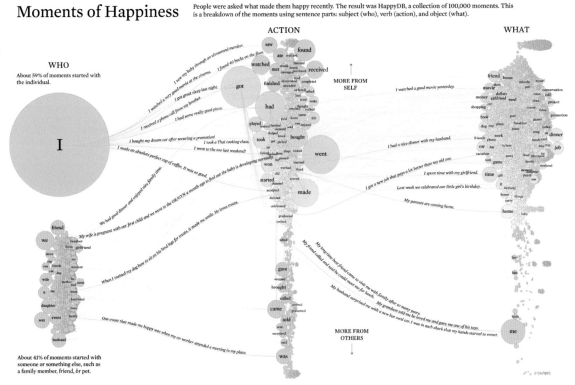

FIGURE 1.3 *"Counting Happiness and Where it Comes From,"* Nathan Yau / 2007-Present FlowingData / `https://flowingdata.com/2021/07/29/counting-happiness` / *last accessed February 08, 2024.*

Researchers asked 10,000 participants to list 10 things that recently made them happy. The result was HappyDB, a collection of 100,000 happy moments. For each moment, I parsed out the subject, verb, and object to better see what makes people happy overall. While the aggregates help you see the big picture, I was most interested in the moments and the individual words used.

How do we use visualization to feel through data? There are lots of examples such as Jonathan Harris and Sep Kamvar's *We Feel Fine* (Scribner, 2009), which examined emotions through connected vignettes; Giorgia Lupi and Stefanie Posavec's *Dear Data* (Princeton, 2016), which was a year-long data drawing project that used unique visual representations to communicate via post cards; and Stamen Design's *Atlas of Emotions* (2016), a collaboration with the Dalai Lama and Paul Ekman, which explored the range of human emotions.

While data can seem dry and concrete, it can also represent less measurable things, and visualization helps bring that aspect of data to life.

See FlowingData for more examples of data art at `https://datafl.ws /art`.

COMPELLING

It's possible for visualization to be more than one thing at a time. When a project is informative, entertaining, and emotional, it can also be compelling.

No one has done this better than the late Hans Rosling, who was a professor of international health and director of the Gapminder Foundation. Using a tool called Trendalyzer, as shown in Figure 1.4, Rosling ran an animation that showed changes in poverty by country. He did this during a talk that first draws you in to the data, and by the end, everyone is on their feet applauding. A standing ovation for data. Amazing.

The visualization itself is straightforward these days. Rosling's presentations compelled many to implement their own versions of Trendalyzer with various tools. Bubbles represent countries and move based on the corresponding country's poverty during a given year. Why is the talk so popular then? It's in Rosling's presentation style and framing. He tells a story. How often have you seen a presentation with charts and graphs that makes you drowsy? Rosling used the meaning of the data to his advantage and found a way to engage his audience. The sword-swallowing at the end of his talk tends to form a lasting impression, too.

Watch Hans Rosling wow the audience with data at `https://datafl.ws /hanstalk`.

As statistician John Tukey wrote in his 1977 book *Exploratory Data Analysis*, "The greatest value of a picture is when it forces us to notice what we never expected to see." Visualization allows you to show data with context, and framed as a story, you can help people understand concepts that are often too complex on their own.

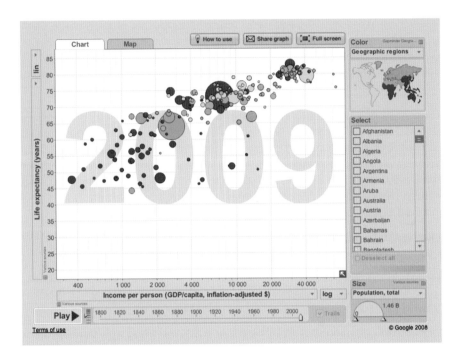

© Google 2008

FIGURE 1.4 *Trendalyzer by the Gapminder Foundation*

What kind of story are you trying to tell? Is it a report or is it a novel? Do you want to convince people that action is necessary?

Every data point has a story behind it in the same way that a character in a movie has a past, present, and future. There are interactions and relationships between the data points. It's up to you to find them.

ASK QUESTIONS ABOUT THE DATA

That's the challenge. You must figure out what the data is about and what stories to tell based on what you find. Some might tell you to just let the data speak, as if you could plug a dataset into your favorite charting software and a magical, visual tale comes out. If that were the case, we could end the book here, but as of this writing, there's still more to the process.

A single dataset, even a small one with a few data points, can be visualized in many ways. Add more data variables and observations, and the possibilities for chart types, geometries, colors, formats, and dimensions multiply. To demonstrate, I visualized a single dataset, life expectancy by country over time, with 25 different charts (see Figure 1.5).

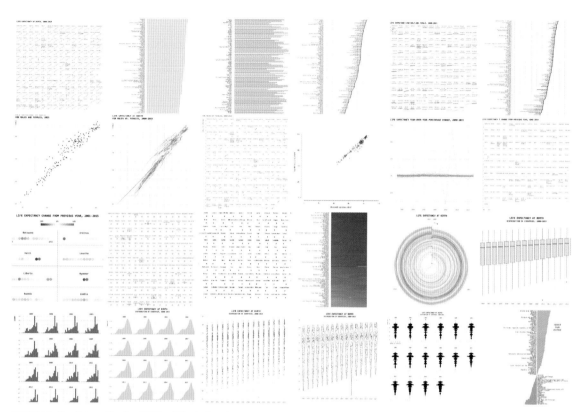

FIGURE 1.5 *"One Dataset, Visualized 25 Ways,"* FlowingData / https://flowingdata.com/2017/01/24/one-dataset-visualized-25-ways / *last accessed 08 February, 2024.*

I could've made a lot more charts by grouping regions, focusing on specific countries, or highlighting a range of time. I could've switched to less traditional visualization methods. I didn't even get to annotating and explaining the data.

Try it yourself. Think of all the ways to visualize two numbers, say 5 and 10. You could draw 10 circles and 5 squares, draw 10 squares and 5 circles, draw a shape that's twice the area of another shape, use a darker shade to indicate a higher number, or use a line that connects the two numbers with a defined axis.

With so much fun to be had, you need a way to filter. Find the relevant parts in the data and work through the noise. This is basically the field of statistics, which I don't have time to detail in its entirety right now, but I've found that the best way to analyze data and to provide focus to your visualizations is to ask questions about it. Use these questions and the resulting answers to verify quality, explore the meaning of the data, and communicate insight.

VERIFICATION

While you're looking for the stories in data, you should always question what you see. Remember, numbers don't always mean truth. Data is subjective in the way it's collected, who collected it, and what is collected.

In my younger days, data checking was my least favorite part of visualizing data. It seemed like a chore when I just wanted to make some charts. However, over the years, I've grown to appreciate verifying data as an important part of the visualization process. Weak data leads to mistakes and misinterpretations, whereas high confidence in your data makes it a lot easier to have high confidence in your visualization.

Basically, what you're looking for is stuff that makes no sense. Maybe there was an error at data entry and someone added an extra zero or missed one. Maybe there were connectivity issues during a data scrape and some bits got mucked up in random spots. Maybe the data was collected in haste and does not represent what you think it does.

Note: *Data scraping* is a way to automate the process of retrieving data on the Web. You'll learn how to do this in Chapter 3.

Data always has its imperfections. You need to work with them if you plan to understand the data. Here are some questions to ask early in the process:

- Does the sample represent the full population?
- Why are there so many gaps in the data, and are those gaps relevant to the existing data?
- Are the outliers errors in measurement or true standouts?
- How reliable is the data?
- Did you make an error in your calculations?
- How does the data hold up against your expectations?

This is not an exhaustive list. Some people spend their entire academic careers figuring out this stuff. But for our purposes, make sure the data is good before you waste all your time analyzing and visualizing junk.

EXPLORATION

Most of my visualization projects stem from an everyday curiosity, which I've learned to note immediately note because I have a terrible memory. They are questions like how people earn an income (https://datafl.ws/7nz), whether I am old or not (https://datafl.ws/7n1), whether it is too late for a career change (https://datafl.ws/7o1), or how much toilet paper I should buy at the store when I restock (https://datafl.ws/7o0). I try to answer these deeply profound questions with data.

Answering these simple questions, or at least trying to, often generates more questions and leads me to various datasets. I make a lot of charts to explore. They are unpolished and made with speed in mind. Figure 1.6 shows a sample from an analysis session.

If I can answer my own questions and more curiosities pop up, it usually means I'm on the right track.

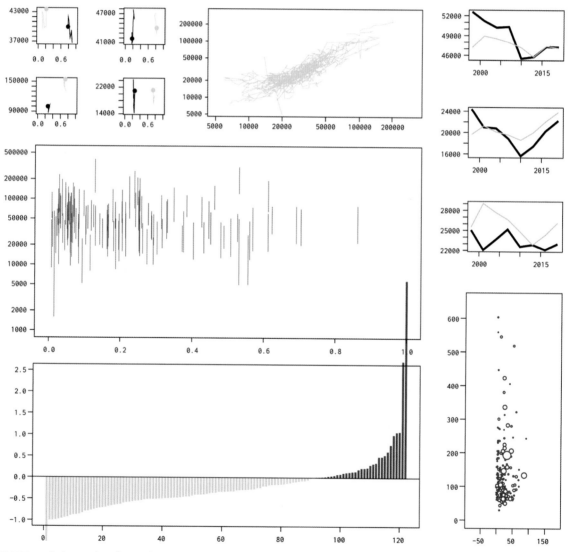

FIGURE 1.6 *Exploratory charts from analysis session*

So, it helps to ask a question first and then look for data that helps you answer those questions. Your work might go the other way, where you have a lot of data and need to form your own questions afterward. Either way, questions can form a path toward worthwhile insights.

Here are general questions to help you get started:

- What is this data about?
- How did things change over time?
- How are these things related?
- Can you explain the shifts over time or across categories?
- What makes one group different or similar to another?
- What's most common? Most rare?
- What if?
- What stands out?
- Is this normal?

Try to form questions that are more specific than "What is the mean?" Of course, you can always calculate the mean, but think about it in the context of the data and what you're studying. Does the mean matter? Is it out of the ordinary? Is the mean heavily influenced by a few data points with high or low values? What does the value of the mean. . .mean?

The best data visualization projects stem from interesting curiosities that the creator spent time digging into. In the end, the story you want to tell is rarely about the data itself and much more about what the data represents.

COMMUNICATION

This brings us to insights. Let's assume you have good data. Let's assume you figured out what your data is about. This leads to questions about how you want to communicate to others.

- Who is the audience?
- What do you want to highlight?
- What details do you have to explain, and which ones can you quickly summarize?
- What is the purpose of the chart?

While visualization for analysis and visualization for an audience share many of the same statistical aspects, they require different approaches because you use them differently. For example, Figure 1.7 is an alluvial diagram using system defaults. The chart type is one my favorites to show how categorical values change over time, and you'll learn how to make one in Chapter 5. This one shows the consumption of dairy foods in the United States over time.

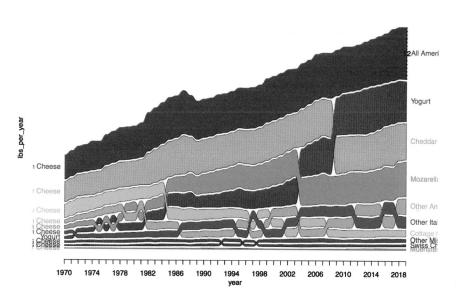

FIGURE 1.7 *Exploratory plot on dairy consumption*

Figure 1.8 is a more polished version with clearer annotation and coloring that more closely resembles the food category. The second chart, part of a data story on food consumption in America, is easier to read because it provides context and explains the data, even with just a few short notes.

When you visualize data for an audience, you explain the data to people while considering what they know and what they need to know for the chart to be useful.

You communicate. Your chart exists to show people specific patterns, comparisons, or trends in data rather than plopping a bunch of numbers in front of readers and expecting them to know what to look for. Otherwise, you force them to become the analyst, and usually, that's not what people are looking for. Even as an admirer of visualization, I have only so much attention span that I can dedicate to interpreting data.

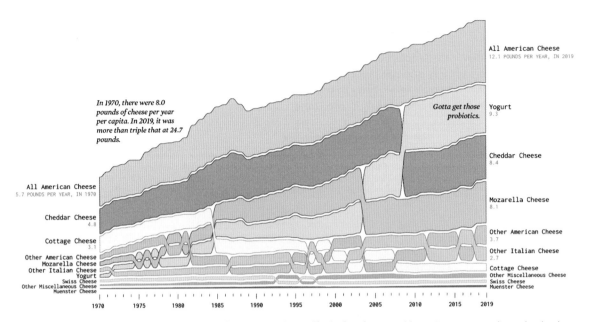

In 1970, there were 8.0 pounds of cheese per year per capita. In 2019, it was more than triple that at 24.7 pounds.

Gotta get those probiotics.

All American Cheese
5.7 POUNDS PER YEAR, IN 1970

Cheddar Cheese
4.8

Cottage Cheese
3.1

Other American Cheese
Mozarella Cheese
Other Italian Cheese
Yogurt
Swiss Cheese
Other Miscellaneous Cheese
Muenster Cheese

All American Cheese
12.1 POUNDS PER YEAR, IN 2019

Yogurt
9.3

Cheddar Cheese
8.4

Mozarella Cheese
8.1

Other American Cheese
3.7

Other Italian Cheese
2.7

Cottage Cheese
Other Miscellaneous Cheese
Swiss Cheese
Muenster Cheese

1970   1975   1980   1985   1990   1995   2000   2005   2010   2015   2019

FIGURE 1.8 *"Seeing How Much We Ate Over the Years,"* Nathan Yau / 2007-Present FlowingData / `https://flowingdata.com/2021/06/08/seeing-how-much-we-ate-over-the-years` / *last accessed February 08, 2024.*

Ask questions about how you want to communicate your findings, who you're communicating to, and what you're communicating for.

You'll ask more questions with concrete examples throughout this book, but keep it in mind as you work through charts and think about how it applies to your own data.

DESIGN

Answering questions about how you want to communicate through visualization leads to design choices. Thoughtful design can help make your data more readable and understandable, which typically leads to good things when you're telling stories.

Some mistakenly classify design in visualization as just a way to make charts look pretty. Anyone who says this either doesn't know what they're talking about or has a very narrow view of visualization.

First, I'm not sure what these people have against pretty charts. A good-looking chart is an indicator that someone cared enough about the data or information to make it look good. In contrast, a chart that looks rough and was made with default settings would indicate a rough analysis, even if it shows the same data as the pretty chart. Second, good chart design can show readers where to look and, at its best, helps people understand and appreciate a dataset as well as you do without the hours of analysis.

When you design for purpose, audience, devices, and clarity, you produce charts that are better than default computer output.

PURPOSE

One of my go-to datasets is survey responses from the American Time Use Survey. It's from the Bureau of Labor Statistics, which asks Americans to recall what they did during the past 24 hours. For each activity, respondents fill in what they did, when the activity started, and when it ended.

Individually, you get a diary of someone's day, such as when they woke up, when they went to work, and when they ate dinner. Put all those diaries together in aggregate, and you get a good picture of Americans' day-to-day schedule. Figure 1.9 shows the percentage of people who were engaged in various activities on a weekday.

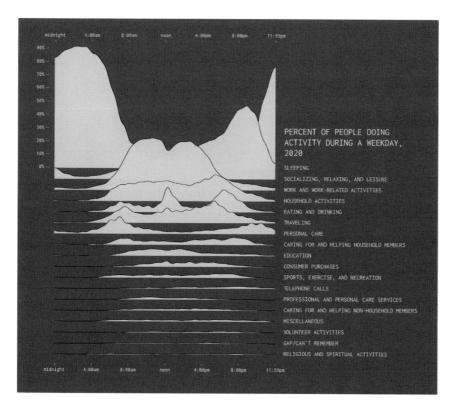

FIGURE 1.9 *"Daily Routine, 2020,"* FlowingData / https://flowingdata .com/2021/08/19/ daily-routine-2020 / *last accessed 08 February, 2024.*

Most people are sleeping during the early morning hours, work peaks around 8 a.m., and meals peak around 12 p.m. and 6 p.m. for lunch and dinner. The chart provides an overview of the day.

However, with a different visualization using the same dataset, I simulated the day of 1,000 individuals and animated their activities over time, as shown in Figure 1.10.

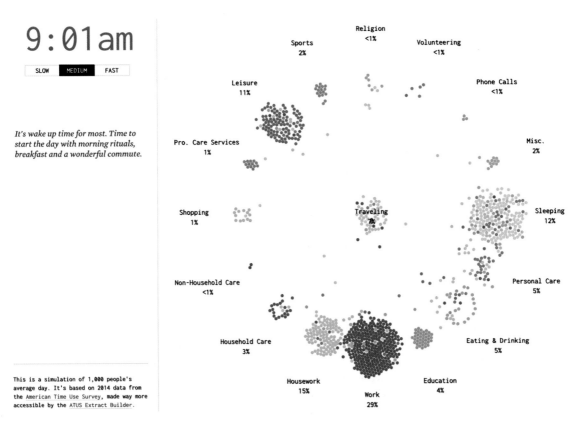

FIGURE 1.10 *"A Day in the Life of Americans,"* FlowingData / `https://flowingdata.com/2015/12/15/a-day-in-the-life-of-americans` / *last accessed 08 February, 2024.*

Both visualizations show the same data. Different goals led to different design choices. The first one is a quick summary, whereas the second one takes longer to play out because it is an animation but better reflects the flow of people from one activity to the next.

Different purpose means different design choices. Use colors, geometries, and charts that best serve or highlight the purpose.

AUDIENCE

Consider who the charts are for. If they're for an auditorium full of people, you might want to avoid going too complex so that the people in the back can read the labels. On the other hand, if you design a large graphic that's meant to be studied on a computer screen by one person at a time, you can include more details.

Maybe you're after engagement on social media in the land where volume is high and attention span is low. Your charts must stand out, perhaps visually or with unique insights or both, but they also must be quick to read.

Are you working on a business report for your boss? Then you probably don't need to create the most beautiful piece of data art the world has ever seen. Instead, create a clear and straight-to-the-point graphic.

Are the charts just for you to analyze data? Then you don't need to spend too much time on aesthetics and readability because you're already familiar with the data. Make the chart and move on to the next to learn more about your data instead of tinkering with label placement.

Imagine who you're telling your stories to and, go from there. In my own work, I like to make charts and write as if I'm talking to an old friend from high school. It forces me to make the data relatable, avoid jargon, and try not to be boring. The more specific your audience, the more focused you can make your charts.

DEVICES

When I wrote the first edition of *Visualize This*, there weren't as many devices to consider as there are now. My research group in graduate school was still wondering if the iPhone was significant enough to study. If we wanted our mobile data collection devices to work for the full day, we had to carry around oversized battery packs. So, if a chart wasn't made for print, it was typically assumed to exist on a computer monitor that sat on a desk.

Now we must consider smaller mobile phones, which have become the default screen size in many cases. Some places design specifically for mobile, some just for desktop, and some accommodate both. I try to do both, which usually means before publishing, I'll make at least two versions of a chart. I test different sizes in the browser, as shown in Figure 1.11.

We can gripe all we want about variable screen sizes (I did for a good while), but if your audience is mostly looking at your work with a phone, it's in your best interest to figure out how to make data readable with limited space.

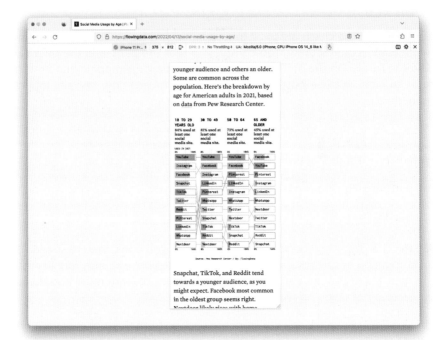

FIGURE 1.11 *"Social Media Usage by Age," mobile version, FlowingData* / `https://flowingdata.com/2022/04/13/social-media-usage-by-age` / *last accessed 08 February, 2024.*

CLARITY AND INSIGHT

There are many types of charts. On FlowingData, I have a growing list of more than 60, shown in Figure 1.12, all of which can be combined and modified slightly to make other types. The options can seem intimidating when you're first figuring out what kind of chart to use for a dataset, but we'll go over many of them in this book.

There's a filtering process. Some chart types lend themselves to a certain type of data, such as a line chart for timeseries data. Some chart types are useful for showing certain aspects of data, such as a histogram to show distributions.

However, the process rarely narrows down your choices to a single option. Instead, you pick among what's available that best fits your purposes. Ideally, clarity and insight are at the top of your reasons for visualizing data, so you choose charts (and visual encodings for the more advanced) that show data patterns honestly in a nonconfusing way.

It's OK to make charts that take a while to understand, but also design them so that the confusing parts are easier to work through visually. At the least, this means you use geometries and colors correctly to represent your data, explain

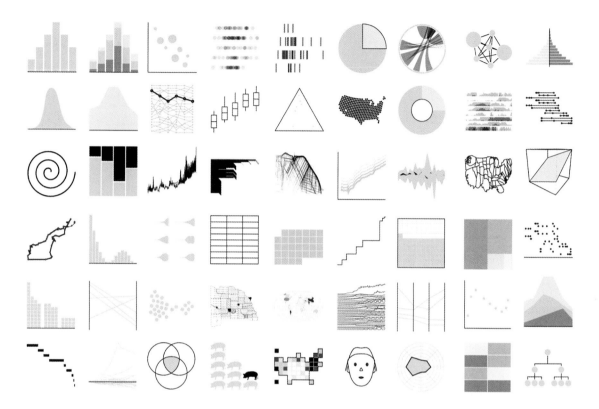

FIGURE 1.12 *Chart types,* flowingdata.com/chart-types/ *with Adapted from Chart Types.*

encodings that might not be obvious to your audience, and label your charts to provide context to the numbers. You'll see more of this in later chapters.

TRADE-OFFS

A lot of visualization design advice would have you believe that there is a fixed set of rules that every chart should follow. Some people act as if there is a checklist, and the visualization is classified as unsuccessful or misleading if there are any missing boxes.

However, in practice, professionals don't work through a checklist or pontificate about the placement of every single element on a chart. There are always limitations at some point in the process. The right data might not be available to answer the original question, an idea might not be technically feasible in a limited amount of time or on the current platform, or the skillset required to understand a dataset in a certain way just isn't there.

Every chart has its trade-offs because of such limitations. So, the goal isn't to follow a certain set of magical rules. The goal is to make the best thing you can with what you have.

WRAPPING UP

In short, start with a question, explore your data with a critical eye, and figure out the purpose of your graphics and who they're for. This will help you design clear graphics that are worth people's time—no matter what kind of graphic it is.

You learn how to do this in the following chapters. You learn how to handle and visualize data. You learn how to design graphics from start to finish. You then apply what you learn to your own data. Figure out what story you want to tell and design accordingly.

The next chapter covers the visualization tools available to help you follow this process. Some like to stick with a single tool, but I like a mixed toolset, which lets you stay flexible to make focused charts that fit your needs.

Ch.2

Choosing Tools
to Visualize Data

In the previous chapter, you learned about asking questions to guide analyses and communicate with data. You could do this by hand with pencil and paper, but my guess is that you'd rather use a computer for some of the work.

Luckily, you have lots of options. Some are point-and-click. Others require programming. Some tools weren't designed specifically for data visualization but are still useful. Some tools are small and are good at helping with visualization tasks. This chapter covers these options to help you decide which tool or set of tools is best for you.

MIXED TOOLBOX

Many people stick with a single tool for all their visualization needs. It helps to streamline your workflow, and you don't have to spend time struggling with a new tool. Instead, you can spend your time analyzing and visualizing data.

Others move with shifts in technology, so they learn how to use new tools before their current toolset falls out of favor. After all, many of the visualization tools listed in the first edition of this book are no longer available or don't work with the current Web.

I go with a hybrid approach. I have a small set of tools that I use to complete most of my work, and I learn new tools when I want to make something that stretches beyond the scope of my current toolset. The approach helps you get things done but lets you work closer to the boundaries of your imagination than the limits of a certain software package.

For the tools I am already comfortable with, I don't have to think too much about how to use them. I try to work without having to stop to debug or read a lot of documentation. It's like learning to type. At first you must think about where each letter is on a keyboard, but when you figure it out, you can just write.

At the same time, there is no single tool that can do everything. Some companies might want you to think their software can do it all, but every tool has its trade-offs. Some are great for analysis but lack in presentation functions. Some are good for static graphics but don't work well if you want interaction and animation. Some work well for the Web but make less sense if you work with print.

In the following sections, you learn the options and the trade-offs. I'll point out the ones that I like to use, but every practitioner has their own preferences depending on what they want to make.

POINT-AND-CLICK VISUALIZATION

Noncoding solutions are the easiest for beginners to pick up. Copy and paste your data or load a CSV file. Then just click the chart type you want, select from options like labels and grid type, and you have a visualization.

Many point-and-click solutions have come and gone over the years, and many solutions promise wonderful insights for minimal effort. Some suggest an automated process. I still have not seen a solution that follows through on those promises.

Of course, there are parts of visualization that can be automated. For example, given a certain data format, you can automatically narrow down options. You probably wouldn't visualize a single-metric, nonproportion time series with a pie chart. However, that still leaves a lot of other options and doesn't even cover the most important insight portion of the analysis. Insight is contextual and specific to a dataset and application, which is what makes great data stories.

So, be wary of any software or service that says it provides automatic insights. Look for software that is flexible enough for you to adapt your visualizations to the data you're looking at.

OPTIONS

The point-and-click tools vary, depending on the application they've been designed for. Some, such as Microsoft Excel or Google Sheets, are meant for basic data management and graphs, whereas others were built for more rigorous analyses, visual exploration, or presentation.

While there are always new tools that try to improve on the current offerings, most tend to fade away (especially the ones that try to do everything). The tools that follow have solidified themselves in the data visualization process and should stick around for a while.

Microsoft Excel

You know this one. You have the familiar spreadsheet where you put your data, such as in Figure 2.1. More buttons and features have been added over the decades since my fifth-grade science fair project, but much of the software still works the same.

You click the button with the little bar graph on it to make the chart you want. You get all your standard chart types (see Figure 2.2) such as the bar chart, line, pie, and scatterplot.

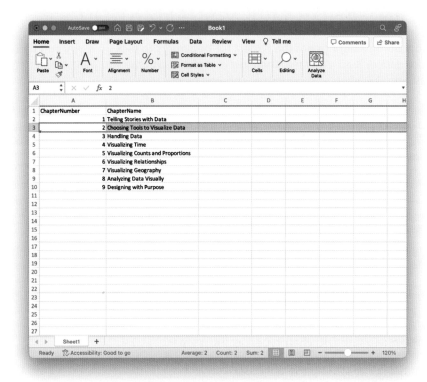

FIGURE 2.2 *Microsoft Excel chart options*

Find more about Microsoft Excel at www.micro soft.com/en-us/ microsoft-365/excel.

Some people scoff at Excel, but it's not all that bad for the right tasks. For example, I don't use Excel for any sort of deep analyses or graphics for a publication, but if I get a small dataset in an Excel file, as is often the case, and I want a quick feel for what is in front of me, then sure, I'll whip up a graph with a few clicks.

Google Sheets

Google Sheets is a browser-based spreadsheet application that is like Microsoft Excel (see Figure 2.3).

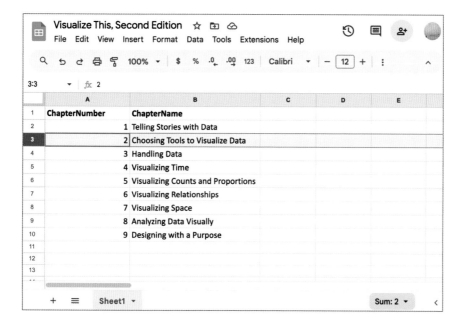

FIGURE 2.3 *Google Sheets*

It also offers standard chart types, as shown in Figure 2.4.

Sheets was previously the only usable online spreadsheet application. Your data would automatically save to the cloud, and you could collaborate in real time with others on a spreadsheet. You could easily share your spreadsheets with different permission levels.

One time, I was looking for a dataset on movie box office numbers. I had the movie names but I didn't have the dollar amounts, so I shared a spreadsheet via Google Sheets and asked readers to fill in the blanks with data from Wikipedia. It was fun to watch the spreadsheet fill out in real time, and the process was much quicker than if I had done it by myself. The online availability felt like a huge advantage at the time.

But Microsoft made an online version of its own, so the collaborative feature of Google Sheets is not much of an advantage anymore. Over the years, Google has tried adding various features to try to automate parts of the analysis, but they never seemed to catch on. So, the choice between Sheets and Excel is mostly a choice between Google and Microsoft products. That and Sheets is free to use compared to Excel's subscription fee.

It's good to use at least one. I go back and forth with both, depending on what I already have open or the original format of the data I'm looking at.

Visit Google Sheets at sheets.google.com.

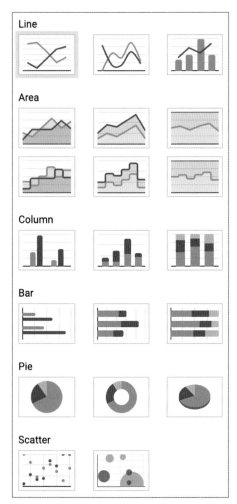

FIGURE 2.4 *Google Sheets charting options*

Find out more about Tableau at `tableau.com`.

Find out more about Looker Studio at `lookerstudio .google.com`.

Learn more about Power BI at `powerbi .microsoft.com`.

Tableau

Tableau has various products, but for the individual, Tableau Desktop, shown in Figure 2.5, remains the point of focus. The software leans more heavily into visual analytics and data exploration than the spreadsheet applications.

The software offers interactive visualization tools and does a good job with data management, too. You can import data from Excel, text files, and database servers. Standard timeseries charts, bar graphs, pie charts, basic mapping, and so on are available. You can mix and match these displays, integrate a dynamic data source for a custom view, or a dashboard, for a snapshot of what's going on in your data.

Tableau also offers Tableau Public, which is a way for you to share your work online. Make interactive dashboards and views in the browser. While the implementation seems more straightforward with a graphical interface instead of code, the browser-based views tend to be sluggish.

The expanded functionality also comes at a cost, which is more expensive than Excel. So, if you don't need all the features, it might be better to stick with the simpler options.

Looker Studio

Looker Studio from Google is an online tool less focused on data analysis and more focused on reports and dashboards. They make it easier to integrate data from various sources so that you can make a quick view into a more complex (business) system. As of this writing, Looker Studio, shown in Figure 2.6, is free to use for individuals. Looker Studio Pro is a paid enterprise version, although there is currently no fixed price.

Power BI

As the name suggests, Power BI from Microsoft is an analytics tool focused on business intelligence. It is not so much a visualization tool as it is a tool to manage data from various sources. You can make charts in the process. There is variable pricing for individuals and enterprise users.

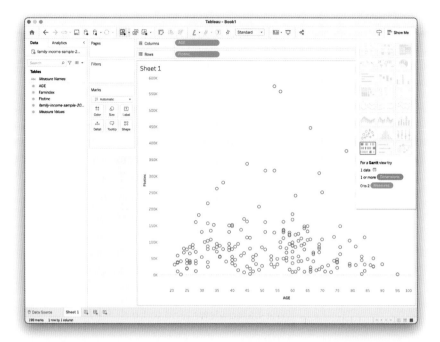

FIGURE 2.5 *Tableau Desktop*

FIGURE 2.6 *Looker Studio*

Datawrapper

Many visualization tools for presentations have come and gone over the years, but they were usually too generalized and tried to do too much at once. The nonspecific tools, mostly targeted toward business, lacked polish and specific purpose, which is essential for telling stories with data.

Datawrapper, as shown in Figure 2.7, is focused specifically on telling stories with data online. You can import data, select your options, and make a wide variety of charts, maps, and tables that work well in browsers and are responsive to screen size. Because of the focus on online presentations, the process of making charts with Datawrapper is straightforward and intuitive instead of filled with a lot of buttons and menus that try to fit every single need. The charts are built for communication.

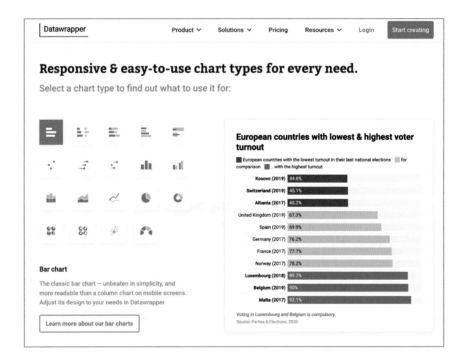

FIGURE 2.7 *Datawrapper*

Make publication-ready charts with Datawrapper at datawrapper.de.

Datawrapper also promises not to sell your data, not track your readers, keep charts private when you want, and, most importantly, in the age of fleeting online things, have pledged to keep your charts online indefinitely. This applies to even the flexible free tier of the application, which is surprising these days but welcome.

Flourish

Flourish is an online application focused on helping you tell stories with data. They aim to make it easier to share visualization online with a library of charts and templates. Upload data, fill in the blanks, and export or embed the charts on your site.

It has a similar premise to Datawrapper's, but Flourish, shown in Figure 2.8, is more open-ended with what you can do using story-centric templates. This provides more ad hoc visualization flexibility, visualization, such as animated bar charts, packed circles, and Sankey diagrams. There are also templates for interactive elements, such as quizzes or visualization that incorporates sliders. These elements used to require code, but Flourish has made such story formats easier to implement.

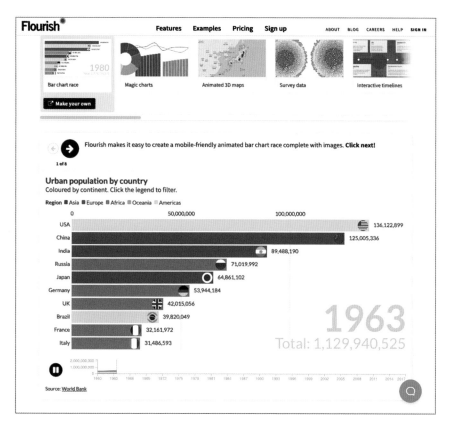

FIGURE 2.8 *Flourish*

This flexibility also adds complexity. You can do more, but there are more options and menus to sift through. That should not be a deterrent though, as Flourish provides a free plan, which is useful for individuals and small groups. For more functionality, Flourish provides paid tiers.

Try making interactive charts with Flourish at flourish.studio.

RAWGraphs

RAWGraphs is an open-source tool aimed at designers who want to make and customize charts. Load your data, pick your chart type, set the variables you want to visualize (like you would with spreadsheet software), and customize. You can export the result as an image or a vector file. Then do what you want with the file: publish it as is or edit in your favorite illustration software.

Use the interactive and open-source RAWGraphs at `rawgraphs.io`.

This is a great option for those who are used to visualizing data with spread-sheets but want more chart options. RAWGraphs, shown in Figure 2.9, provides 31 chart types as of this writing. A point-and-click interface makes it easy to use. If you're a developer, you can also extend the open-source application.

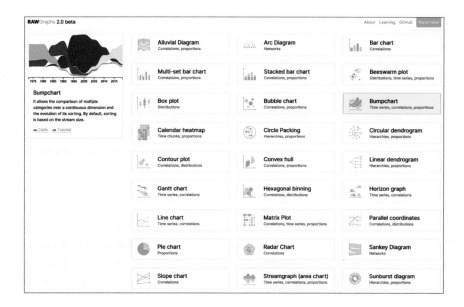

FIGURE 2.9 *Chart options in RAWGraphs*

TRADE-OFFS

Although these tools do not require programming experience, there are draw-backs. In exchange for point-and-click, you give up flexibility in what you can do. You can usually change colors, fonts, and titles, but you're restricted to what the software offers. If there is no button for the chart type you want, you're out of luck.

It can also be a challenge to reproduce analyses and visualizations. While you don't have to learn a new language with point-and-click interfaces, you must learn which buttons to press and which menus to open, and the order of operations isn't always intuitive.

Say you want to make a chart that is like something you've made before but with a different dataset. If you don't save a template, you must remember all the steps. Maybe that's not too bad for advanced users. For beginners, it might be more tedious. In contrast, when you write code to handle your data, it's often more straightforward to reuse code and plug in a different dataset.

Don't get me wrong. I'm not saying to avoid point-and-click software. It can help you explore your data quickly and easily, and the applications continue to improve. But as you work with more datasets, there will be times when the software doesn't fit, and when that time comes, you can turn to programming.

PROGRAMMING

Gain just a little bit of programming skills, and you can do so much more with data than if you stick only with point-and-click software. Again, it's no knock on point-and-click. It's just that programming gives you the ability to be more flexible and more able to adapt to different types of data, because you are not limited to buttons and menus.

If you've ever been impressed by a visualization that looked custom-made, most likely code was involved. With code, you're able to make a visualization specifically for a dataset instead of working within fixed limits of a collection of chart types.

Code can look cryptic to beginners—I've been there. But think of it as learning a new language. You're learning to tell your computer what to do, and like any language, you can't immediately converse fluently. Start with the basics and then work your way up. Before you know it, you'll be coding and visualizing data in a way that more closely resembles your imagination.

OPTIONS

So, you decide to get your hands dirty with code—good for you. A lot of options are freely available. Some languages are better at performing certain tasks than others. Some solutions can handle large amounts of data, whereas others are not as robust in that department but can produce better visuals or provide interaction and animation. The language you use largely depends on the kind of visualization you want to make and what you're most comfortable with.

Some people stick with one language and get to know it well. This is fine, and if you're new to programming, I highly recommend this strategy. Familiarize yourself with the basics and core concepts of code.

As you progress, you might find that what you're using doesn't allow for certain visualization methods or makes what you want to do tedious. In this case, it's worth exploring other options. For me, I have go-to tools that I use for analysis and asking questions about data, but over the years, I've picked up others as I need them, namely, to keep up with the changing requirements of making things for the Web.

R

If you are new to programming but want to learn a language to visualize data, I recommend R. It is free and open-source and typically straightforward to install on your computer. The language was designed by statisticians to help with analysis and statistical graphics, so it's easy to load, explore, and visualize data, which is great for asking and answering questions.

R is also my favorite software for analysis and visualization, so take that as you like. I call R my thinking language. I know it well enough that I don't have to think about the mechanics or syntax, and I can spend more time looking at the data. If I get stuck somewhere, I know where to look for help and how to debug quickly enough to get unstuck more quickly than if I were working with a different tool. Again, that's just me. Different chart-makers have their favorites, although clearly R is the best.

You can make traditional statistical graphics, such as bar charts, line charts, and scatterplots, with just a few lines of code. Customize colors, shapes, and sizes as you like. You'll see how this works in Chapter 4, "Visualizing Time." Figure 2.10 shows a heatmap made in R.

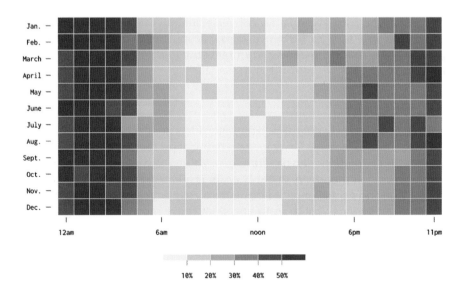

FIGURE 2.10 *Heatmap generated in R*

One of the main advantages of R is that there are lots of packages that extend the basic functionality (also known as base R). Many packages have been added over the years and continue to be maintained and developed. Installing them is also straightforward, which is a big plus when you want to try new visualization types or experiment with your own.

For example, R does not come with a treemap function (to show hierarchical data) out of the box, but you can install the *treemap* package and then you have a new function to use, as shown in Figure 2.11.

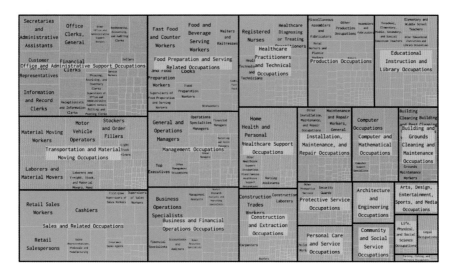

FIGURE 2.11 *A treemap generated in R*

There are packages for alluvial diagrams, streamgraphs, packed circles, geographic maps, calendars, networks, and more. If there's a name for the visualization method, there is probably a package for it.

R Visualization Packages

Packages extend the functionality of R. There are tens of thousands of them in the R repository (called CRAN). Here are general visualization packages and a few chart-specific ones that were used to make the charts you've seen so far in this book. You will see more packages in later chapters.

- **ggplot2:** A flexible visualization package that follows a syntax consistent across a collection of packages known as the Tidyverse. It is based on *The Grammar of Graphics* by Leland Wilkinson.

- **plotrix:** As the name implies, a general package that provides new plot types and functions that follow the same code patterns as base R.

- **animation:** Makes the data move with GIFs.

- **treemap:** Visualizes hierarchical data with a treemap.

- **alluvial:** Shows ranks and absolute values over time.

- **packcircles:** Draws circles that don't overlap.

If there is no package or existing function for what you want to make, R provides base drawing functions. Draw lines, shapes, and colors using the coordinate system and geometries that you want.

R sounds great, right? It's easy to install, useful for analysis, and, most importantly, you can make many charts in a short time. It still doesn't do everything, though. For example, R works on your desktop but not so great online, and while there are solutions for running an instance of R in the browser, they are either clunky or require a complicated setup, or usually both.

R is also not good with interactive graphics on the Web. There are packages that try to make exporting or generating web-native charts, but they are limited in what they provide.

Learn more about R and download it for free at r-project.org. While R comes with its own developing environment, it's grown more common to use RStudio, which you can download at https://datafl.ws/rstudio.

Finally, you might have noticed that the charts in Figures 2.10 and 2.11 lack polish and contextual elements such as titles and annotation. I used default settings on purpose, which often work fine when you're analyzing data for yourself. When it's time to publish, you might want to create a certain aesthetic or improve readability for the audience. You can tighten up the design in R by messing with different options or writing additional code, but there's a lot of trial and error involved. So, my strategy is usually to start charts in R and then edit and refine them in illustration software such as Adobe Illustrator, which is discussed soon.

Python

Now that I've given you the hard sell for R, you might wonder what Python is doing here. But like I said, I mix my tools, and sometimes there are fun-looking libraries that are available only in Python. Mostly though, I use the language for data processing and formatting. Occasionally, I use it to scrape data.

Unlike the statistics-focused R, Python is a general-purpose programming language. Data analysis and visualization are not baked into the language. Instead, there are libraries like pandas and Matplotlib that make working with data more straightforward in Python. If you can make a chart in R, you can most likely make it in Python. For example, Figure 2.12 shows a heatmap made in Python that uses the same data that was used for Figure 2.10, which was made in R.

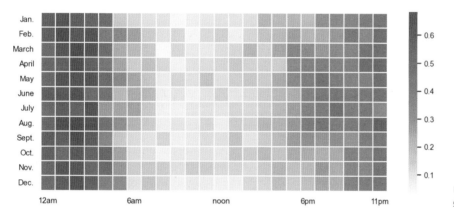

FIGURE 2.12 *A heatmap generated in Python*

Go with what you already know or are required to learn when you start with visualization. If you're one of the many who use Python, then you should make charts with Python. Learn the logic and process of visualizing data in one language and the steps translate to other languages. The upside is that you can spend less time on programming principles and more time learning how to use the relevant libraries.

Find Python documentation on getting started and what's available at `python.org`.

Python Visualization Libraries

Python is a general-purpose programming language, so the approaches to visualization vary across libraries.

■ **Matplotlib** (`matplotlib.org`)**:** Released in 2003; one of the earlier plotting libraries for Python.

■ **Seaborn (`https://seaborn.pydata.org`):** Based on Matplotlib; provides high-level functions to make charts.

■ **pandas (`https://pandas.pydata.org`):** Primarily used for data analysis but has some charts and works with Seaborn.

■ **Altair (`https://altair-viz.github.io`):** Focused on simplicity and consistency with less code.

■ **Plotly (`https://plotly.com/graphing-libraries`):** Interactive charts for the Web. They have both open-source and enterprise offerings that provide functionality for Python, R, JavaScript, and others.

Processing

Processing is an open-source programming language and software sketchbook (see Figure 2.13) originally intended for visual artists who are new to code. It's quick to get up and running, and the programming environment is lightweight.

FIGURE 2.13 *Processing sketchbook*

With just a few lines of code, you can make an animated and interactive visual. It would, of course, be basic, but because it was designed with the creation of visuals in mind, you can draw shapes and work with geometry more easily than if you were to use a general programming language. Load data, draw based on that data, and you've got yourself a visualization.

Processing was originally only Java-based, which is a general programming language, and you get a mini-application, or applet, when you export your project that you can embed elsewhere. However, Processing also now has versions in JavaScript (different from Java) and Python, which make it easier to incorporate with what you know or to use the version that works best for your purposes.

So, this is a great place to start for beginners, especially if you're more interested in custom visualization than in established chart types. If you mostly want to make charts with axes, you might want to try other options first.

Try Processing software with the visual arts in focus at processing.org.

HTML, CSS, and JavaScript

Then there is visualization for the Web. You can always share static images, but if you want interactive and animated visualization that runs in the browser, you need to know a combination of HTML, CSS, and JavaScript. Hypertext Markup Language (HTML) provides structure; Cascading Style Sheets (CSS) sets the way objects appear; and JavaScript lets you dynamically change objects on a web page. This is broadly speaking, as there is overlap in what you can use each for. This also means you change how you use JavaScript, HTML, and CSS together, based on what you want to make.

This route tends to be more complex than the previously mentioned options because the Web serves a broad spectrum of purposes, appears on varied devices, and is used by many people. The technology also changes. For visualization that was interactive and animated on the Web, Flash and its associated programming language, ActionScript, were the default solution. Flash was deprecated in 2017, and many visualization projects were lost to the ephemeral web. You can still find Flash files through the Internet Archive, a nonprofit organization and website that serves as a digital library of all things that appear online, but even then, only some will work with a Flash emulator.

In the first edition of this book, I listed resources for the JavaScript section, and they either went offline, were deprecated, haven't been updated in more than a decade, or are still around but are no longer considered a good solution for visualizing data. So, this branch of visualization tends to update quickly, which can be good or bad, depending on your point of view. That said, most of my favorite JavaScript-based visualization projects still work despite the change.

The upside is flexibility. When you want standard chart types, you can use code libraries that take care of most of the work. Usually, there are functions for specific charts. You just supply the data. When you need more control over each chart element or want a custom visualization, there are also libraries for that. They let you define the parts and how things fit together.

Figure 2.14 shows a visualization that I needed to customize for interaction and layout. I used D3, which is a JavaScript library that doesn't have specific

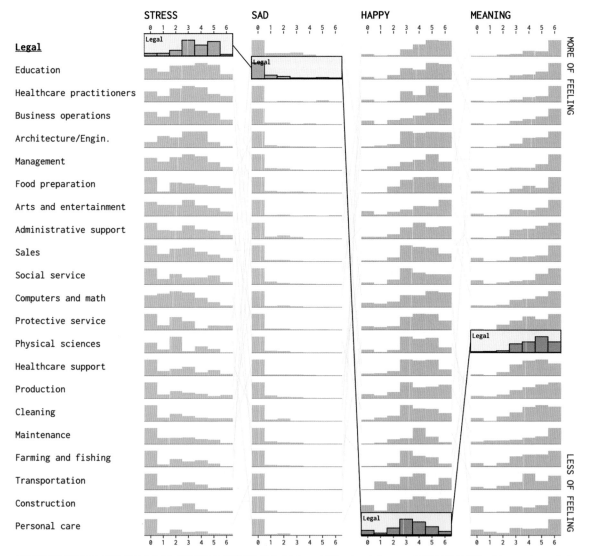

FIGURE 2.14 *"Feelings at Work,"* Nathan Yau / 2007-Present FlowingData /https://flowingdata.com/2022/10/26/feelings-at-work/ *last accessed February 08, 2024.*

charting functions. Instead, it provides methods to load and handle data and to draw geometries and colors based on that data.

People were asked to score stress, sadness, happiness, and meaningfulness at work on a scale from 0 to 6, where 0 is low and 6 is high. There's a bar chart for each occupation group and feeling, and when you hover over an occupation group, all the charts for the group highlight and connect. The result is a combination of bar charts and a bump chart.

It was more straightforward for me to implement the interaction with D3, but there are multiple ways to do the same thing. The specific method you choose will usually depend on your current setup. You also don't have to stick with one library. Sometimes, you just need a quick bar chart, so you go with a high-level library, and sometimes, you need to get creative, so you go with the low-level library. Sometimes, you want a combination of several libraries.

Learn about HTML basics from Mozilla at `https://datafl.ws/whathtml`.

What is CSS? See `https://datafl.ws/whatcss`.

What is JavaScript? See `https://datafl.ws/whatjs`.

JavaScript Visualization Libraries

JavaScript is a general-purpose language mainly used for the Web, but there are visualization libraries you can use so you don't have to start from scratch.

- **D3** (`d3js.org`): Use to makes custom visualizations. It doesn't provide standard chart types and instead makes it more straightforward to bring together and control the elements that comprise a chart.
- **p5.js** (`p5js.org`): It's a JavaScript interpretation of Processing.
- **Vega** (`vega.github.io`): Use to makes charts using a visualization grammar based on the JSON data format. The grammar also integrates with languages other than JavaScript, such as R and Python.
- **Chart.js** (`chartjs.org`): This is a lightweight library for charts on the modern web.
- **Observable Plot** (`observablehq.com/plot/`): This is built on top of D3 with a "grammar of graphics" approach.
- **Laker Cake** (`layercake.graphics`): Svelte is a popular JavaScript web framework, and Layer Cake, which is a framework for Svelte, provides components within the framework.

Find out more about MATLAB at `https:// datafl.ws/matlab`.

MATLAB

MATLAB is a proprietary programming language from MathWorks. Its focus is on computation, but it has some visualization functionality for traditional chart types. I used this during a previous life in electrical engineering but haven't touched it in a long time. If you already use MATLAB, I'd check out what it offers for charts. Otherwise, try the more open options first.

TRADE-OFFS

Learning to program gets you flexibility to visualize data how you want, adapt previous code to new data, and use existing libraries so that you don't have to start every project from scratch. In the long run, it can save time, and you can let your imagination run wilder.

However, you must learn to program first, which takes time, especially if you don't have experience with code yet. This makes point-and-click solutions more inviting, and if all you need is a one-off chart that you will never make or see again, then point-and-click is probably the solution you need.

Installing and setting up your coding environment can also be a pain sometimes, which is one reason I suggest R over other solutions for beginners. Setting up Python can be tricky, and setting up web development environments usually requires multiple steps. Companies and organizations also have their own system requirements and restrictions.

The good news is that you don't have to know how to do all the things all at once to make nice charts. You learn as you go and then take that experience with you for the next project. It's like learning a new language. Basic vocabulary can help you find a toilet in a foreign country. You learn more about the language: more words, how they go together, and grammar. You get more fluent and can converse. With programming, you learn how to use the functions you need, how functions work together, and the logic behind the code. You get more fluent.

MAPPING

From a data design perspective, there is a lot of overlap between geographic mapping and visualization. They both make use of visual perception to show patterns, which means there are similar choices around color, geometry, and space. Charts and maps also often exist in the same context when telling stories with data. It's common to see both in the same project, overlaid on each other, or placed side by side.

However, geographic data is tied to physical places in the world and comes with its own encodings, file formats, and scales. Maps can be used to communicate data like visualization is, but they also exist as an everyday interface for directions and exploring a new space. So, the process of making maps can and should be specialized. That might mean changing your approach with the software you already use or using a map-specific tool.

OPTIONS

I used to research how mobile phones could be used to survey our surroundings. To track location continuously throughout the day, we connected an external GPS device to a phone, and to keep everything powered, we plugged all the things into a laptop in our backpacks. Then, making a dynamic map for the Web that was not a Google map required substantial effort.

Now, location comes standard with most phones. Batteries last a full day. There is no shortage of spatial data that people want to understand, which means there are plenty of tools to make maps. It's also more straightforward to make maps than it was when I wrote the first edition of this book.

In fact, you can make maps with all the tools that I've listed so far, both the point-and-click and programming solutions. The technical requirements of visualization and maps overlap, which means you can stick with the software you know and see how far it takes you. For example, I make most of my maps in R. Sometimes I need JavaScript if I want to make an interactive project. That fits my needs, but if you need more, the following map-specific tools might work better for you.

ArcGIS

ArcGIS, from Esri, is a suite of tools that enables mapping on the desktop (ArcGIS Pro) and online (ArcGIS Online). The names and range of services have changed over the years, but the overall goal to help you make maps stays the same. ArcGIS is a feature-rich tool that lets you make maps, explore spatial data, and process and aggregate data. It is point-and-click, so you don't have to learn to code.

The downside of such a rich feature set is that there are a lot of buttons and menus to go through. Although, like most software, the process grows more intuitive with use. Perhaps the main drawback for most is that ArcGIS requires

FIGURE 2.17 *Google Maps*

Find more on Google Maps at `https://developers .google.com/maps` and more on Bing Maps at `https://datafl .ws/bingmaps`.

integration. When I use Google or Bing Maps for data, it's usually for the application programming interfaces (APIs), which come in handy for data processing and search. Limited usage is free, and heavier usage is available at a varying price, depending on how many queries you need.

TRADE-OFFS

If you analyze spatial data often and need to make a lot of maps, these applications might be worth the added time and cost. A specialized tool means you'll get access to map-specific features that might not be available with more general visualization programs.

On the other hand, if you already use a different visualization tool heavily, learning to make maps with what you know could be a better use of your time. That way, you can stay in your workflow. It's possible your maps might not turn out as well because of software limitations. It's also possible that what you use already provides all that you need.

At the least, it's good to know the tools available so that you have a backup plan when something doesn't work as expected. I don't make enough detailed, cartography-heavy maps to justify paid solutions, but it's been useful to have QGIS available at times when R isn't working for me.

Illustration | 45

ILLUSTRATION

By now, it might seem like you've seen more than enough tools to make great charts. You have! You can do a lot with a combination of code and point-and-click visualization tools, and for the most part, they let you customize graphics to make them more readable. Move some labels here. Adjust a legend there.

However, these small adjustments can be finicky with a lot of applications. They often require a fair amount of trial and error, which is why a lot of charts look like they were made with a certain software. People don't have the time to go through the hassle. But usually, when you make graphics for a presentation, a report, or a publication, you want charts that fit in with the flow. You want to match typography, color scheme, borders, and overall aesthetics so that the charts don't look copied and pasted or out of context. You also want to make the charts readable. You want the charts to look good.

For example, Figure 2.18 shows a set of charts made in R with default settings, which show the age of mothers when their first, second, and third children were born. The age distributions shift to the right as you might expect.

To make the charts easier to read and to explain the differences, I exported a file from R and edited it in illustration software, as shown in Figure 2.19. I changed line widths, edited labels, annotated ranges, and added color to fit within the context of FlowingData.

These are not complex changes. I could make the same edits in R, but I don't know the final layout of a graphic until I've added everything and see how the parts fit together. In R, label placement and custom annotation often require trial and error, whereas illustration software allows you to iterate visually and quickly by clicking and dragging.

OPTIONS

A lot of illustration programs are available, but there are only a few that most people use—and one that almost everyone uses. Cost will likely be your deciding factor. If you just want to dabble at first, I recommend the open-source route, and if your needs expand beyond that, try the other options.

Adobe Illustrator

Adobe Illustrator is the most common illustration software. Most static charts that you see in major news publications are edited in Illustrator. A chart-maker

Note: I use illustration software mostly for a layer of annotation, layout, and small adjustments to color, line widths, and size. Again, R (and other programming languages) let you do this, but the placement of chart components can change slightly when you export an image, and a few pixels is enough to make my brain itchy. Illustration software allows you to interactively adjust, and when you know where you want something to be, you just stop dragging the cursor. I need this level of control, but it's not for everyone.

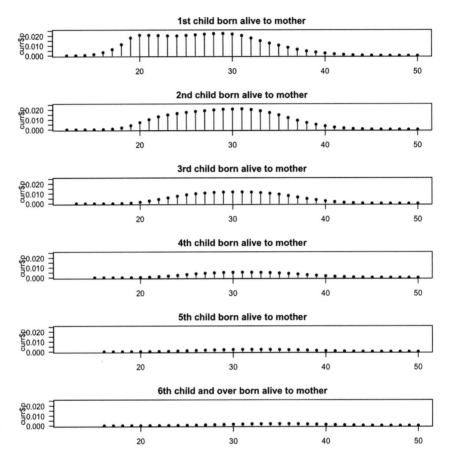

FIGURE 2.18 *Charts made in R to show age of moms*

will produce a vector-based file (which is defined with geometries and can be scaled up without pixelation), such as a PDF or SVG, and import it into Illustrator to finish, as shown in Figure 2.20.

The software was originally designed for font development and later became popular among designers for illustrations such as logos and more art-focused graphics. And that's still what Illustrator is primarily used for.

Illustrator offers some basic graphing functionality via its Graph tool. You can make basic graph types such as bar graphs, pie charts, and line charts. You can paste your data into a small spreadsheet, but that's the extent of the data management capabilities.

Illustration | **47**

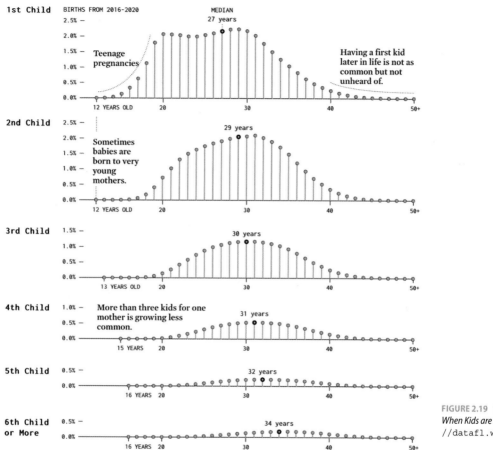

When Mothers Have Their Children in the U.S.

FIGURE 2.19 *"Age of Moms When Kids are Born,"* https://datafl.ws/momage

The best part about using Illustrator, in terms of data graphics, is the flexibility that it provides. However, with that flexibility comes a lot of buttons and menus, which can be confusing at first. In Chapter 4, you'll see some of the basics.

The main downside is that it's expensive when you compare it to doing everything with code, which is free, assuming you already have the computer to install things on. As of this writing, Adobe charges a monthly fee to use the software (and other Adobe products). Illustrator has been ingrained in my workflow for a while now, so the fee is worth it for me, but there are other options.

Check out Adobe Illustrator at https://datafl.ws/7ln.

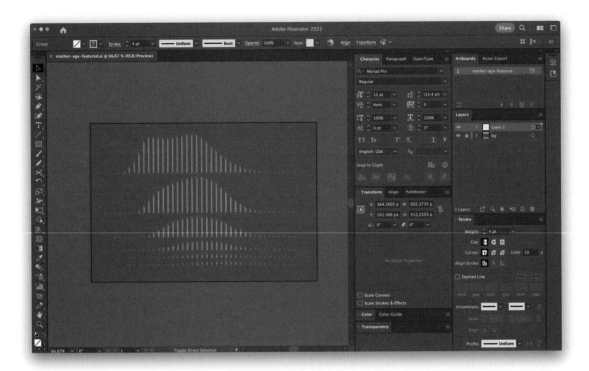

FIGURE 2.20 *Editing a chart in Illustrator*

Affinity Designer

Affinity Designer is newer than Adobe Illustrator and has positioned itself as a worthwhile alternative. Instead of paying a subscription for continued use of the software, you can buy Affinity Designer for a one-time fee.

Get Affinity Designer at `affinity.serif.com`.

Like Illustrator, the software supports major file types and affords you the flexibility to visually edit charts by clicking and dragging.

Inkscape

Get the free design tool Inkscape at `inkscape .org`.

Inkscape is the free and open-source alternative to Adobe Illustrator. If you want to avoid paying for a tool, Inkscape is your best bet. I use Illustrator because when I started to learn the finer points of data graphics on the job, the work required Illustrator. It just made sense. But if I were to start now, I would likely use Inkscape first and Affinity Designer second.

TRADE-OFFS

Illustration software is not made specifically for visualization. It's rooted in graphic design, so chart-makers who use Illustrator, Designer, or Inkscape typically use only a small subset of what is offered. You won't analyze or explore data with these applications. You won't build complex charts from scratch here.

That said, these programs are great if you want to make publication-level graphics. Use them to adjust aesthetics, improve readability, and clean up messy charts.

Visualization is often generalized to analyze a wide array of datasets, and illustration software is one way customize specifically for a single dataset. Manual edits are a way to add a human touch to more mechanical charts. If you use charts only for analysis, then you can probably skip this communication-focused facet of visualization.

SMALL VISUALIZATION TOOLS

So far, you've learned about general tools for visualization that cover a wide range of chart types and methods. This is often enough for the job. However, sometimes there are small, visualization-related tasks that you need to complete in the process. These are small tools to help with these tasks.

OPTIONS

I'm hesitant to include a set of small tools, because they tend not to stick around long. Instead, they come and go with the trends, and if a small task is important enough, the generalized tools eventually implement a new feature.

But small visualization tools can be useful because they are focused on a single task. They're usually easy to use and get the job done quickly. So, while this isn't a comprehensive list of all the small tools available right now, these are the ones I've used and that have been around for a few years.

ColorBrewer

Picking colors for your charts and maps is fun because there are infinite options and combinations. However, color palettes should make sense for your dataset, work for those who are color blind, and, of course, look good. Cynthia Brewer and Mark Harrower designed ColorBrewer, shown in Figure 2.21, in the early

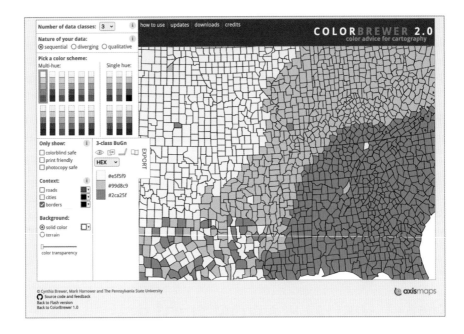

FIGURE 2.21 *ColorBrewer*

Pick your color palettes with ColorBrewer at colorbrewer2.org.

2000s to narrow down the choices. Select from a set of color schemes based on your data, how many shades you want, and limitations with color blindness. The tool was originally intended for thematic maps, but the color themes found their way to visualization more generally.

Chroma.js Color Palette Helper

You might want to make your own color palettes, but still ensure that everyone can see the contrast between different shades and see the differences as you intend. Chroma.js by Gregor Aisch is a JavaScript library that helps with that, and the Color Palette Helper, shown in Figure 2.22, is a point-and-click interface for the library.

Create custom color palettes with Chroma.js at www.vis4.net/palettes.

Pick the two end colors for your scale, and optionally the colors in between, and the small application defines the shades in between. It'll correct for lightness and let you know if the result is colorblind-safe.

Sip

There are many color-related tools. Maybe it's because most color choice is subjective, and the process of picking colors isn't limited to just visualization. Sip, shown in Figure 2.23, is a color-picking app for macOS that lets you select a pixel on the screen to copy its color. There is currently a one-time fee or an

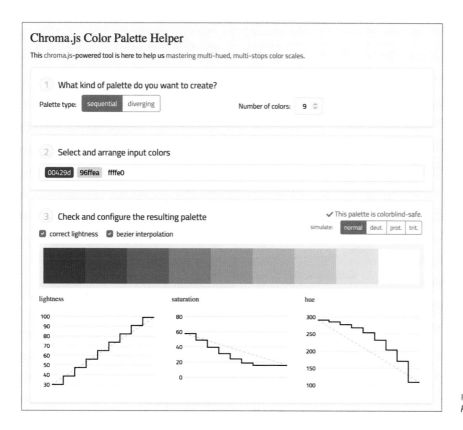

FIGURE 2.22 *Chroma.js Color Palette Helper*

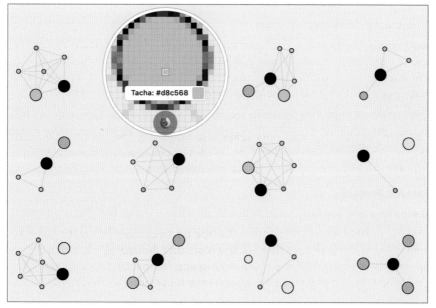

FIGURE 2.23 *Using Sip for color matching*

Grab colors on the screen with Sip at `sipapp.io`.

annual one for updates. Although macOS comes with Digital Color Meter, Sip is design-focused and fits well in the workflow. Windows also has its own Color Picker utility.

Sim Daltonism

Simulate color blindness with Sim Daltonism by visiting `https://datafl.ws/daltonism`.

Sim Daltonism, shown in Figure 2.24, is an open-source color-blindness simulator for macOS and iOS. With the iOS app, you just point a camera, and you'll see from the perspective of a color-blind person. With the macOS app, you drag a window across your screen for similar results.

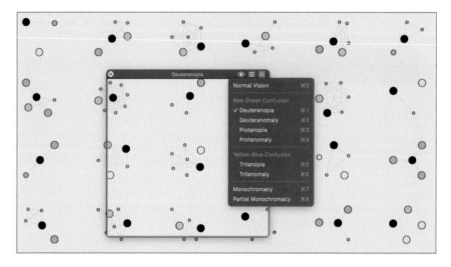

FIGURE 2.24 *Using Sim Daltonism*

TwoTone

Make data-driven music with TwoTone at `twotone.io`.

Sonification of your data, creating sounds based on the numbers, can provide another dimension to your visuals. TwoTone, in Figure 2.25, lets you make music based on a dataset that is uploaded.

Data Viz Project

When there are so many chart types to pick from, it can feel like a bit much. Data Viz Project by Ferdio, shown in Figure 2.26, filters chart types of data structure, purpose, and shape to help you narrow down your choices.

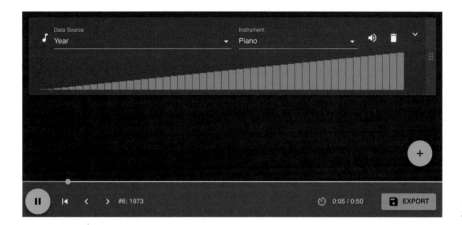

FIGURE 2.25 *TwoTone by Sonify and the Google News Initiative*

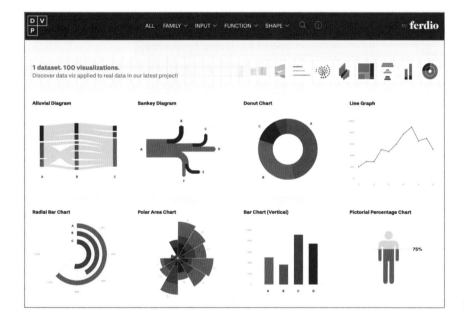

FIGURE 2.26 *Data Viz Project*

It's not going to tell you exactly what to do, but it's a good starting point if you're stuck.

Pick a chart with Data Viz Project at `datavizproject.com`.

FastCharts

Most large newsrooms have an in-house tool to make quick charts. FastCharts, as shown in Figure 2.27, is a public version of *Financial Times'* solution. Copy and paste a comma- or tab-delimited dataset, and it spits out a chart with options.

Make charts fast with FastCharts at `fastcharts.io`.

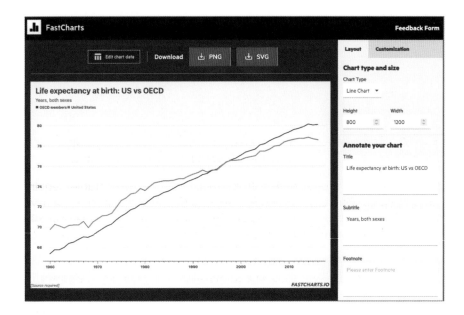

FIGURE 2.27 *FastCharts*

TRADE-OFFS

Except for Sip, these small tools are free to use, and some of them are open source, which is nice, but that also means they might not stick around. The people who create and maintain these tools usually have jobs to tend to.

On the other hand, the tools I've mentioned have been available for a few years, which usually means they'll stay online for at least a bit. Also, these tools are mostly nice-to-haves more than they are core to the workflow. So, give them a try. If they work for you, then great, and if not, you will not have lost that much time or effort.

PENCIL AND PAPER

Finally, I can't leave out the always trusty pencil and paper. I don't finish graphics with them, but almost every nontrivial chart I've made started with a sketch or a scribble. I keep a notepad and pencil within reach.

They're easy access, which helps quickly record ideas and brainstorm new ones. I don't need a computer, and I can think more fluidly. Maybe that's just me, though. Maybe I'm showing my age. But I've always been one to scribble, so it works for me.

TRADE-OFFS

It's pencil and paper. Detailed work might take a while.

SURVEY YOUR OPTIONS

This isn't a comprehensive list of what you can use to visualize data, but it should be enough to get you started. There's a lot to play with here.

Many people start using specific software because their job or studies require it. Some just go with what's available. Use the software that you know or have to know first and focus on the process of visualizing data. The process of asking questions, analyzing data, and deciding what colors and geometries to use translates to other applications.

When your toolset doesn't allow you to make what you want in the time you must make it, then it might be time to switch tools or add new ones. Want to design static data graphics? Maybe try R or Illustrator. Do you want to build an interactive tool for a web project? Try JavaScript. While not always possible, answer questions about how you want to visualize your data and then figure out the tools required.

In a 2021 survey conducted by the Data Visualization Society, people were asked to select among 33 tools they used often to visualize data. Figure 2.28 shows how they answered.

Check out the data from the survey via Data Visualization Society: https://datafl .ws/soti.

Out of the 1,870 people who selected at least one tool, 58% said they used Microsoft Excel, 46% used Tableau, 36% used Microsoft PowerPoint, 33% used R, 28% used Python, and so on. There's another 20% that used "other" tools not covered in this chapter.

So, there are tools that a lot of people use, but there are also a mix of smaller-scale or application-specific tools that come into the picture. Most people use a mix of tools, as shown in Figure 2.29. Only 8% of people used one tool, and only 14% used two tools. Twenty percent used three, and more than half of people used at least four.

Start with what you know or what's available—usually one of the more general applications—and then branch out as you need. People getting started with visualization often get stuck on tool selection, but in many ways, the tool is the least important part of the process. To make great charts, you don't have to learn every aspect of every software application. Focus on the process of visualization and what you want to make, and this guides you toward the features you need.

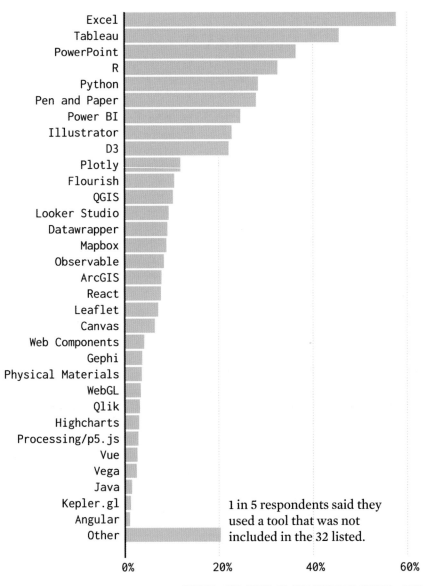

VISUALIZATION TOOLS THAT PRACTITIONERS USE
Percentage of people surveyed who said they used a tool

1 in 5 respondents said they used a tool that was not included in the 32 listed.

FIGURE 2.28 *"Visualization Tools That Practioners Use"*

SOURCE: DVS STATE OF THE INDUSTRY SURVEY, 2021

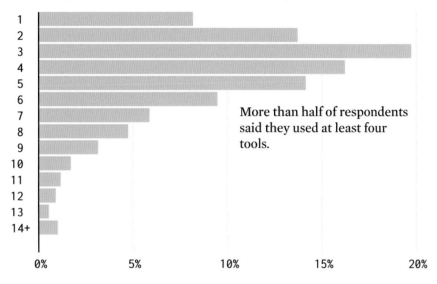

NUMBER OF TOOLS SELECTED
Percentage of people surveyed who said they used a tool

More than half of respondents said they used at least four tools.

SOURCE: DVS STATE OF THE INDUSTRY SURVEY, 2021

FIGURE 2.29 *"Numbers of Tools Selected"*

WRAPPING UP

None of these tools are a cure-all. In the end, the analyses and data design are still up to you. The tools are just that—they're tools. Just because you have a hammer doesn't mean you can build a house. Likewise, you can have great software, but if you don't know how to understand and communicate with data, then the software won't do much good. You decide what questions to ask, what data to use, and what stories to tell. In the following chapters, you'll walk through the process of figuring this out.

In the next chapter, you can try your hand at using some of the tools mentioned. You start at the beginning—the data—because without data there is no visualization.

Handling Data

Before you work on the visual part of any visualization, you need data. Data makes a visualization interesting and worthwhile. Without data, you just have empty charts. That's no fun. Where can you find good data? How can you access it?

Once you have data, you need to format it so that it loads with your software. Maybe you got the data as a comma-delimited text file or an Excel spreadsheet, and you need to convert it to something such as XML, or vice versa. Maybe the data is accessible online spread out over many pages but you want a unified spreadsheet.

Learn where to find data, how to prepare data, and how to process data. Get all your data in order, and the visual part of visualization gets much easier.

DATA PREPARATIONS

Those who are interested in learning more about visualization are often, understandably, focused only on the visual part of the practice. The stuff they see—geometry, color, and patterns—draws them in. However, you need worthwhile data to make worthwhile visualization. Garbage data leads to garbage visualization.

Sometimes, the interesting datasets are given to you, and you get to play right away, but often, the data you need doesn't exist yet or isn't in a format that's useful for your purposes. There's a process behind finding this data and preparing it so that you can more easily visualize it.

I used to work in a restaurant kitchen. My job was to prepare all the ingredients: cleaning, chopping, tenderizing, and marinating. It all went into the walk-in refrigerator where there was a wall of chopped vegetables and meats organized in containers. When an order came in, the chef could quickly grab the prepared ingredients and get to cooking.

This early stage of the visualization process is like kitchen preparations. Sometimes, it can feel tedious, but over time, I have learned to enjoy getting everything ready. It's satisfying to transform a mess of data into a nicely formatted data file. When it's time to make the chart, you can just grab the data and get to visualizing.

FINDING DATA

Data is the foundation of every visualization. If you don't already have the data you need to answer your questions, you have to find it. Fortunately, there are a lot of places to get data, and it's gotten easier to find over the years. You can find data with standard search engines, data-specific applications, data catalogs, governments, researchers, and anywhere else we interact with data, which is just about everywhere these days.

This section covers some of the places to find data. Like most things online, resources tend to fade over time or are replaced by something better (or worse). So, consider these good places to start your search, as of this writing.

SEARCH ENGINES

You can search for data via the common search engines, such as Google or Bing, just like you would search for other bits of information. I use DuckDuckGo. Just enter the topic in the search box with "data" appended to the end of your query, and usually that'll at least point you in the right direction.

GENERAL DATA APPLICATIONS

Some services focus on supplying data or making it searchable, with varying degrees of success. Some applications provide large data files that you can download for free or for a fee. Others are built with developers in mind with data accessible via an application programming interface (API). The following are a few suggested resources:

- **WolframAlpha** (`wolframalpha.com`): This is a "computational search engine" that can be useful for looking up basic statistics.
- **Kaggle** (`kaggle.com`): Known for running data competitions, Kaggle also provides a catalog of public datasets.
- **Wikipedia** (`wikipedia.org`): You might not think of the online encyclopedia as a place for data, but there are many HTML tables within all the articles.
- **GitHub Curated Core Datasets** (`github.com/datasets`): GitHub is a developer platform that hosts a lot of datasets. It keeps a curated list of the more popular ones.
- **Google Dataset Search** (`datasetsearch.research.google.com`): This is a search engine for datasets. It's been out of beta for a while but is more a research project at this point.
- **Data.world** (`data.world/search`): This is a searchable catalog of downloadable datasets.
- **Amazon Data Exchange** (`datafl.ws/71p`): Amazon provides a service for selected groups to provide large publicly available datasets.

- **DataHub (`datahub.io`):** Focused on making it easier for organizations to provide open data, DataHub also provides datasets.
- **The Data and Story Library (`dasl.datadescription.com`):** This is an archive of data files meant to be used for teaching statistics and data science in a classroom setting.

RESEARCHERS

If a data search doesn't provide anything of use, try searching for academics who specialize in the area you're interested in. Sometimes, they post data on their personal sites. If not, scan their papers and studies for possible leads.

You can also try emailing them, but make sure they've done related studies. Otherwise, you'll just be wasting time.

> Running a data site on the Internet has brought me many random emails about data sources. Some people's emails ask for datasets unrelated to anything I've ever done, which confuses me. Make sure your cold queries are relevant to the recipient.

You can also spot sources in graphics published by reputable news outlets. Usually, data sources are included in small print somewhere on the graphic. If it's not in the graphic, it should be mentioned in the related article or in the footnotes or endnotes. This is useful when you see a graphic in the news that uses data you want to explore. Use a search site to find the source, which might lead you to the right person who has the data readily available.

Try Google Scholar to find relevant research at scholar.google.com.

GOVERNMENTS

In efforts to improve transparency, many governments provide data about their municipalities. The data coverage is wide-ranging in topic, format, precision, and regularity of release time. The data availability varies by where you live and who you're getting it from. In some cases, it is written law that certain counts must happen, such as the United States decennial census, which demands a certain level of rigor.

How much you want to dig into government-sourced data depends on your situation. For FlowingData, many of the datasets I use are from the U.S. federal government, which I like for consistency over longer periods of time.

The following are some government-provided places to look for data:

- `Data.gov` (**data.gov**): Catalog for data supplied by U.S. government organizations
- `Data.gov.uk` (**www.data.gov.uk**): Data published by the United Kingdom central government, local authorities, and public bodies
- **Census Bureau Data** (`data.census.gov`): A tool to access data from the U.S. Census Bureau for various geographies, times, and topics
- **General Social Survey** (`gss.norc.org`): An ongoing survey that's been going since 1972 about attitudes and way of life in the United States
- **Integrated Public Use Microdata Series** (`ipums.org`): Collates and unifies individual-level datasets from various government sources

CATALOGS AND LISTS

There are many datasets scattered across the Internet. Some people keep a running list of what they find.

- **Awesome Public Datasets** (`https://datafl.ws/awe`): A community-driven, growing list of public data sources, started in 2014 on GitHub
- **Data Is Plural** (`data-is-plural.com`): Weekly newsletter by Jeremy Singer-Vine for those interested in useful datasets
- **Corpora** (`https://datafl.ws/7lv`): Useful datasets for fun and learning
- **Data Sources on FlowingData** (`https://datafl.ws/datasrc`): A running list of fun and interesting data sources on my blog

TOPICAL REFERENCES

Outside more general data suppliers and applications, there's no shortage of subject-specific sites that provide datasets to download.

The following discussion is a sample of what's available for different topics. I've included only free and open sources, but there are, of course, other services that provide data for a fee.

Geography

Do you have mapping software but no geographic data? You're in luck. Plenty of shapefiles and other geographic file types are at your disposal.

- **Natural Earth** (`www.naturalearthdata.com`): A public domain map dataset available at various scales
- **TIGER/Line Shapefiles** (`datafl.ws/tiger`): From the U.S. Census Bureau, the most extensive detailed data about roads, railroads, rivers, and ZIP codes you can find for the United States
- **OpenStreetMap** (`openstreetmap.org`): One of the best examples of data and community effort
- **U.S. Geological Survey** (`datafl.ws/usgs`): Downloadable topographic maps and geographical data
- **ArcGIS Hub** (`hub.arcgis.com/search`): Catalog with a variety of geographic data files

Sports

People love sports statistics, and you can find decades' worth of consistent sports data. Get it on ESPN or sports league sites, but you can also find more complete datasets on sites dedicated to the data specifically.

Sports Reference (`sports-reference.com`) is the most common place to find comprehensive sports data. They provide data for teams, players, games, and plays for professional basketball, American football, baseball, and hockey. The sites for each sport used to be separate entities but settled under the Reference umbrella over the years.

World

Several international organizations keep data about the world, mainly health and development indicators. Sometimes, it takes some effort to sift through sparse datasets. It's not easy to get standardized data across countries with varied methods, but the following are good places to start your search:

- **World Bank** (`data.worldbank.org`): Data for hundreds of indicators and developer-friendly
- **UNdata** (`data.un.org`): Aggregator of world data from a variety of sources
- **World Health Organization** (`who.int/data`): Again, a variety of health-related datasets such as mortality and life expectancy
- **OECD Statistics** (`stats.oecd.org`): Major source for economic indicators
- **Our World in Data** (`ourworldindata.org`): A view of the world through the lens of data, which you can download

Politics

Politics can be tricky to understand, so organizations have tried to provide clarity through data. Some of the datasets used by these organizations are publicly available.

- **OpenSecrets** (`opensecrets.org`)**:** This provides details on government spending and lobbying.
- **ProPublica Data Store** (`propublica.org/datastore/`)**:** ProPublica makes some of the data that it collates available for free and some for a fee.
- **MIT Election Lab** (`electionlab.mit.edu/data`)**:** Get relevant datasets used to study elections.
- **Pew Research Center** (`datafl.ws/pew`)**:** This runs surveys about American life, often centered around politics.
- **Voting and Registration via Census** (`datafl.ws/voting`)**:** This has data about characteristics of American voters.

COLLECTING DATA

Even with all the sources of data available, maybe you can't find the data you need in a nice, clean format, or what you found doesn't cover the range you're looking for. You can either scrap the project or go with the solution that is more fun and collect the data yourself.

COPY AND PASTE

Data collection sounds fancy, but it doesn't have to be. It might just be copying tables from web pages and pasting to a spreadsheet. For example, Figure 3.1 shows a table of EGOT winners—or entertainers who have won an Emmy, Grammy, Oscar, and Tony—from Wikipedia. Highlight the table and copy. Then paste it in a spreadsheet.

Alternatively, if the tables are on the larger side or you just don't feel like copying and pasting, you can use the `IMPORTHTML` function in Google Sheets (`https://www.google.com/sheets`). As shown in Figure 3.2, it takes a URL, a query that is either a `list` or a `table`, and the index of the list or table. For example, an index of `1` indicates the first table on the page.

Straightforward stuff. We like straightforward.

Note: Be mindful of permissions and credit when you copy and paste from outside sources. Just because something is published online does not make it free to use however you want.

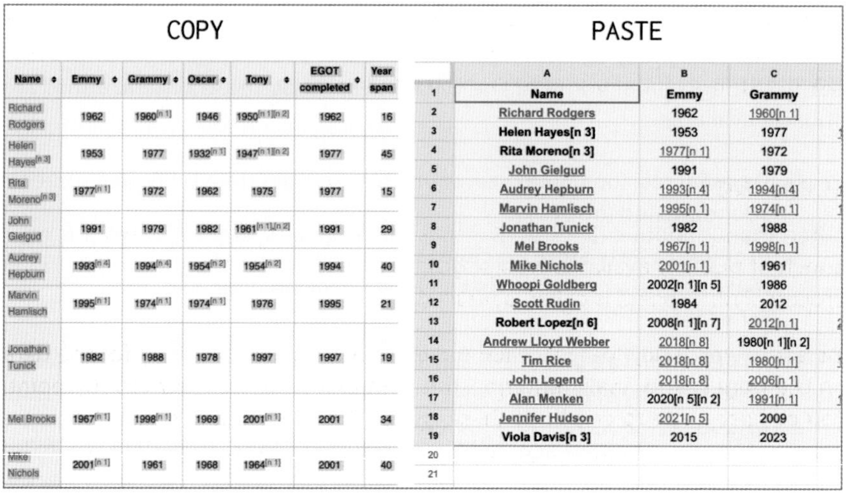

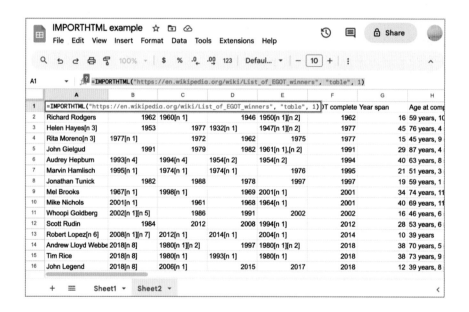

FIGURE 3.1 *Copying and pasting an HTML table to a spreadsheet*

FIGURE 3.2 *Using IMPORTHTML in Google Sheets*

MANUAL COLLECTION

Maybe you know where the data points are, but they are on different sites or pages. You might think that you need (or just want) automation to avoid the tedious tasks of loading pages and entering data in a spreadsheet. Think about scale, though, and how long it might take to write a script to automate the process (and be honest with yourself). If it's not really that much data, try the quick and dirty route. Manual data collection, while sometimes not the most fun, often takes less time and effort than you think it will.

SCRAPING

When manual data collection is not feasible, but the data you want is on a bunch of publicly available web pages, then it might be time to automate the process. This process is called *data scraping*.

Instead of manually loading each page in your browser, looking for the data on the pages, and finally entering the data in a spreadsheet point by point, you can use code to carry out these steps. The assumption is that the pages follow the same structure across a given range, and the data is always in the same place on each page.

For example, Figure 3.3 shows a page from Weather Underground, a site that provides current and historical weather from sensors around the world. The page shows temperature data for August 6, 2020, in Cheektowaga, New York. There's a table that shows the actual, historic average, and record high temperature, low temperature, and so on.

Temperature (°F)	Actual	Historic Avg.	Record	▲
High Temp	78	79.9	94	
Low Temp	58	62.9	47	
Day Average Temp	68.33	71.4	-	
Precipitation (in)	Actual	Historic Avg.	Record	▲
Precipitation (past 24 hours from 04:54:00)	0.00	4.50	-	
Dew Point (°F)	Actual	Historic Avg.	Record	▲
Dew Point	51.21	-	-	
High	54	-	-	
Low	48	-	-	
Average	51.21	-	-	
Wind (mph)	Actual	Historic Avg.	Record	▲
Max Wind Speed	9	-	-	
Visibility	10	-	-	
Sea Level Pressure (in)	Actual	Historic Avg.	Record	▲

FIGURE 3.3 *Weather data from Weather Underground,* `https://datafl.ws/7lx`

If you look at the page for a different date, the structure and placement of the table are the same. The data values are specific to the day.

This is the full URL of the page:

`www.wunderground.com/history/daily/us/ny/cheektowaga/KBUF/date/2020-8-6`

Again, this page is for August 6, 2020, which is specified at the end of the URL with `2020-8-6`. The URL for the next day, August 7, 2020, ends with `2020-8-7`. For exactly one year prior, adjust the date in the URL to `2019-8-7`.

So, if you were to manually collect the high temperature for every day over the past year, you could adjust the date in the URL, load the page in your browser, scroll to the table with the temperature values, copy the high temperature value, and paste to your data file or spreadsheet. Then, just do that 365 times. Or, given the structure of the URL and the structure of the page, you can scrape.

Note: The goals behind the examples in this book are to introduce you to a mix of tools and show that there are different ways to work with data. If the tool used in an example is not for you, take note of the process and logic, which can be used with your preferred tool.

SCRAPING A WEBSITE

Tool used: Python

Try scraping a website with code. In this example, you use Python to scrape tabular data from a simplified website spread out over 20 pages (see Figure 3.4).

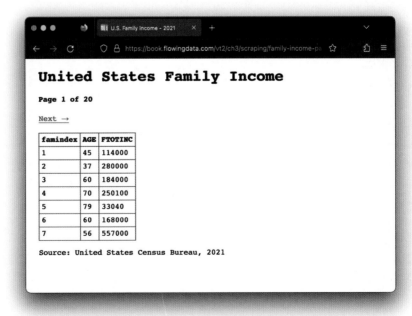

FIGURE 3.4 *Tabular data on a website,* `https://datafl.ws/7m6`

Collectively, the data is a sample of 200 observations from the 2021 American Community Survey. Each row represents a family unit with an index, age of the person who answered the survey, and total family income. You want the data from all 20 pages as a single comma-delimited file.

First, look at the structure of the URL. The full URL of the first page is as follows:

`http://book.flowingdata.com/vt2/ch3/scraping/family-income-page1.html`

The URL for the second page is as follows:

`http://book.flowingdata.com/vt2/ch3/scraping/family-income-page2.html`

The URL for the third page is as follows:

`http://book.flowingdata.com/vt2/ch3/scraping/family-income-page3.html`

For all 20 pages, only the page number changes with each page. Hold on to that thought for later.

Each page is in HTML and follows the same structure, which you can see by viewing the source, as shown in Figure 3.5. There is a header enclosed by `<h1>`, page numbers enclosed by `<h4>`, navigation enclosed by `<div>`, and, finally,

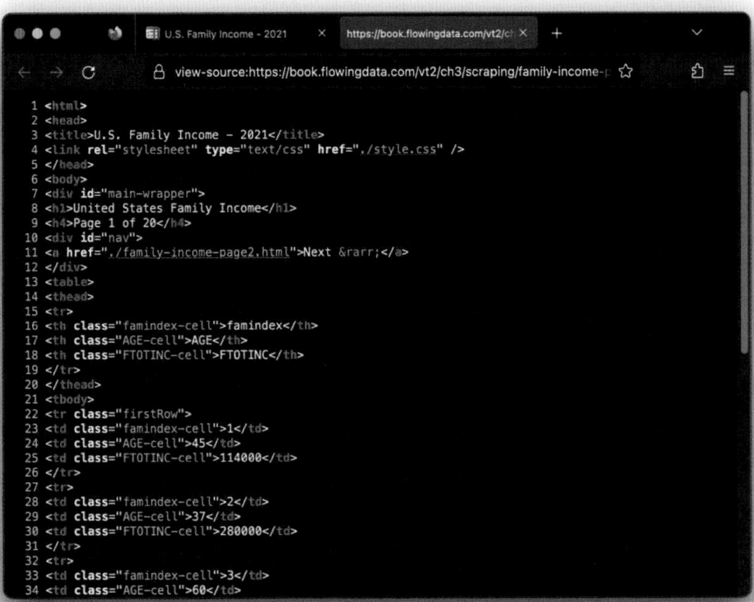

FIGURE 3.5 *Page source with HTML*

To view the HTML source in major browsers, right-click a blank spot of a page and select View Page Source in the pop-up menu. The wording might vary slightly depending on what browser you use. Learn more about HTML at `https://datafl` `.ws/7m4.`

income data enclosed by `<table>`. Each `<tr>` tag indicates a row, and each `<td>` indicates a cell in the table. The first row in the table is the header, enclosed by `<th>`, and the rest of the rows are enclosed by `<tbody>`.

For example, the first row of data in `<tbody>` has 1 in the first cell as an index, 45 for the age of the householder, and 114000 for the family income. The second row has an index of 2, an age of 37, and a family income of 280000.

You know the structure of the URLs and the structure of the pages. You want to write code that does the following:

- Loads each page
- Extracts the data points of interest from each loaded page
- Saves the data as a delimited text file

Visit `Python.org` to download and install Python, which is available on major operating systems. If you're new to programming, check out the "Python for Beginners" guide at `https://datafl.ws/7m2`. Again, if you're not interested in the tool, feel free to read to understand the process.

Assuming you have Python already installed, you will need two libraries. The first is Beautiful Soup, which is a library for parsing HTML and XML. Basically, it breaks up a document into manageable and selectable elements.

Beautiful Soup is a flexible Python library that helps you parse HTML documents. Visit `https://datafl.ws/bsoup` to download it and for installation instructions. You can also find thorough documentation on the site.

With Beautiful Soup installed, start a blank file in your favorite text or code editor, such as Notepad++ for Windows or TextMate for macOS, and save it as `scrape-income.py`. You can also open the finished file in the book source download to follow along.

Import the Beautiful Soup library and the `urllib.request` module, which comes with a fresh Python installation.

```
from bs4 import BeautifulSoup
import urllib.request
```

Start with the first page of data. Assign the URL to page_url.

```
page_url = 'http://book.flowingdata.com/vt2/ch3/scraping/family-
income-page1.html'
```

Create a request.

```
req = urllib.request.Request(page_url)
```

Then open the request.

```
response = urllib.request.urlopen(req)
```

Get the page contents.

```
the_page = response.read()
```

Use Beautiful Soup to parse the contents.

```
soup = BeautifulSoup(the_page, features="html.parser")
```

Using the find_all() method, you can grab all the rows in the table.

```
# Get the table rows
rows = soup.find_all("tr")
```

The first page has seven rows of data with a header on top. To access the header, use index 0 and enter **rows[0]**. To access the first row of data, use index 1 and enter **rows[1]**. To get three cells in the data row, use find_all() again.

```
cells = rows[1].find_all('td')
```

To get the income in the first row, which is the third cell, use the following:

```
inc = cells[2].string
```

That gives you an output of 114000. Checks out.

Use a for loop to get the values from every row on the page. Use the print() function to output each row of values.

```
# Save each row of data
for j in range(1, len(rows)):

    # Get the cells in a row
    cells = rows[j].findAll("td")

    # Comma-delimited row
    print(cells[0].string + "," + cells[1].string + "," +
cells[2].string)
```

This reads as, "For j in 1 to the number of rows, get the cells for the current row, and then output the contents of each row as a string, separated by commas."

> A for-loop is commonly used in programming languages to repeat a section of code multiple times, or *iterate*, over a given condition or range. In this example, you iterate over 1 to the row count to reference the cells for each row, referenced with j. Visit wikipedia.org/wiki/For_loop for more on for loop.

Here is the scraping script in its entirety:

```python
from bs4 import BeautifulSoup
import urllib.request

base_url = 'http://book.flowingdata.com/vt2/ch3/scraping/'

# Header
print("famindex,AGE,FTOTINC")

for i in range(1, 21):

    # Page URL, based on page number
    page_url = base_url + 'family-income-page'+str(i)+'.html'

    # Open the page
    req = urllib.request.Request(page_url)
    with urllib.request.urlopen(req) as response:

        # Save page contents.
        the_page = response.read()

        # Parse.
        soup = BeautifulSoup(the_page, features="html.parser")

        # Get the table rows
        rows = soup.find_all("tr")

        # Save each row of data
        for j in range(1, len(rows)):

            # Get the cells in a row
            cells = rows[j].findAll("td")

            # Comma-delimited row
            print(cells[0].string + "," + cells[1].string + "," +
cells[2].string)
```

The first `for-loop` iterates over a range from 1 to 20 to request the contents of each data page. So, when you run the script, as shown in Figure 3.6, each page is requested, and the data for each row on each page is printed. The output is redirected to a CSV file called `income-scraped.csv`. This shows the script running in the Terminal in macOS. For Windows, you can run the script from the command prompt. You might also use `python` instead of `python3`, depending on your setup.

```
nathany@Nathans-iMac-Pro ch3 % python3 scrape-income.py > income-scraped.csv
```

FIGURE 3.6 *Running Python script to scrape data in macOS Terminal*

The values in the saved file match the values in the HTML tables, and you have a unified rectangular CSV file. This is usually easier to load and analyze in your favorite software.

The web pages that you scrape on other sites are likely more complex than the ones in this example, but the process of loading pages, parsing those pages, and saving the data will be similar. The key is to find the patterns in page structure and the data points on each page.

Tip: Alternatively, you could open and save a file directly in the Python script using the `open()` and `close()` functions.

LOADING DATA

Once you have your data, which is sometimes the hardest part, it's time to load the data files in your software. Usually (and ideally) this is a straightforward process. Most spreadsheet software can easily open its own file format or import competitor's file formats. If you're working with code, most languages let you import data in various formats (discussed in the next section).

Tip: It is a terrible feeling when you think you are nearly done with a visualization project only to realize that you messed up in the beginning and basically have to start over. Check your data early.

Just don't let the ease of loading data trick you into thinking that the software did it correctly. Check for automatically removed rows with missing values, switches from characters to numeric data, truncated large numbers, misinterpretation of foreign languages, missing headers, and anything else that might seem out of sorts. Compare the loaded data and the actual data file to see if the first few rows match and loaded as expected.

The checks you make in the beginning are usually trivial, but can save a lot of time in the end so that you don't make your charts based on error-filled data.

Stay Skeptical

Data, and by extension, visualization, can feel like it provides concreteness to things that are abstract and fuzzy. However, data has its own challenges with bias, errors, and uncertainty because data is generated by and collected by people. On FlowingData, I keep a running list of mistaken data. The following is a sample:

- **When geolocation makes everyone think you stole their phone** (`datafl.ws/7m0`): An exact address was reported when it should've been a range of addresses.

- **Algorithm leads to arrest of the wrong person** (`datafl.ws/7lz`): This was due to faulty facial recognition.

- **Honesty research likely faked data** (`datafl.ws/7ly`): Researchers studied honesty, but the analysis doesn't work if the data is made up.

- **Study retracted after finding a mistaken recoding of the data** (`datafl.ws/7m1`): Researchers found that a hospital program reduced hospitalizations, until they realized the data was not coded as they expected.

When you load a dataset, stay skeptical and always wonder if what you're seeing makes sense.

FORMATTING DATA

Different visualization tools and implementations use different data formats (more on this in the next section). The more flexible you are with the structure of your data, the more possibilities you gain. Make use of data formatting applications, couple that with a little bit of programming know-how, and you can get your data in any format you want to fit your specific needs.

Working with Raw Data

When I first learned statistics in high school, the data was always provided in a nice, rectangular format. All I had to do was plug numbers into an Excel spreadsheet or my handy graphing calculator (which was the best way to look like you were working in class but actually playing Tetris). That's how it was all the way through my undergraduate education. Because I was learning about techniques and theorems for analyses, my teachers didn't spend much time with raw data.

This is understandable, given time constraints, but in graduate school and eventually, in my work, the data never seems to be in the right format. There are missing values, inconsistent labels, typos, and values without any context. Often, the data is spread across several tables when you need everything in one table.

These days, I almost always spend as much time formatting and processing data as I do working on the visual parts of a visualization project. This might seem strange at first, but visualization design comes much easier when your data comes neatly organized, just like it was back in that high school introductory course.

Many of the examples in this book will use data that is at least partially processed so that you get to the visual side of chart-making. When it's time to use your own data, remember that the process might not be so straightforward, which is perfectly normal.

Various data formats, the tools available to deal with these formats, and using code to shift between formats are described next.

DATA FORMATS

People most commonly work with data in Excel. This is fine if you're going to do everything from analysis to visualization in the application, but if you want to step beyond that, you need to familiarize yourself with other data formats. Which data format you use can change by visualization tool and purpose, but the following formats cover most of your bases.

Spreadsheets

You're reading this book. You know the spreadsheet file formats already. The nice thing about this format is that when you open the files in Excel, Sheets, or Numbers, you see the data in a familiar grid layout that you can directly interact with, as shown in Figure 3.7.

FIGURE 3.7 *Basic spreadsheet view with two data points*

Delimited Text

You're probably familiar with delimited text. If you think of a dataset in the context of rows and columns, a delimited text file splits columns by a delimiter. The delimiter is a comma in a comma-delimited file. The delimiter might also be a tab. It can be spaces, semicolons, colons, slashes, or whatever you want, although a comma and tab are the most common.

Delimited text is widely used and can be read into most spreadsheet programs such as Excel or Google Sheets. You can also export spreadsheets as delimited text. If multiple sheets are in your workbook, you usually have multiple delimited files, unless you specify otherwise.

This format is also good for sharing data with others because it doesn't depend on any program.

Here's what the small spreadsheet example with two data points looks like as comma-delimited text:

```
id,val
1,100
2,110
```

Fixed-Width Text

Whereas delimited text separates columns of data by a delimiter, fixed-width text specifies columns by the position of each number or character. For example, a row of fixed-width data might be ten characters long. The first column might be defined as characters one to four. The second column might be five to six, and a third column might be seven to ten.

This file format tends to be less common. It seems to come up when the data provider wants to reduce file size or a rectangular, delimited file format does not work for the given data.

A fixed-width version of the previous two data points might look like the following:

```
0001100
0002110
```

Characters one through four represent the id with leading zeros, and characters five through seven represent val.

JSON

JavaScript Object Notation (JSON) is a common format for the Web. It's designed to be both machine- and human-readable; however, if you have a lot of it in front of you, it'll probably make you cross-eyed if you stare at it too long. It's based on JavaScript notation, but it's not dependent on the language. While there are a lot of specifications for JSON, you can usually get by with just the basics. It uses brackets and key-value pairs.

```
[
    { "id": 1, "val": 100 },
    { "id": 2, "val": 110 }
]
```

Visit json.org for the full specification of JSON. You don't need to know every detail of the format, but it can be handy at times when you don't understand a JSON data source.

XML

Extensible Markup Language (XML) is a common format on the Web. There are lots of types and specifications for XML, but at the most basic level, it is a text document with *content* enclosed by *markup* that starts with < and ends with >. There is a start tag, like <data>, and an end tag, like </data> (with the forward slash). Data points are usually in between the start tag and end tags. Here is how our two data points could be formatted as XML:

```
<data>
    <row>
        <id>1</id>
        <val>100</val>
    </row>
```

```
<row>
    <id>2</id>
    <val>110</val>
</row>
</data>
```

Shapefile

See www.w3.org/XML for XML details and specifications.

The shapefile format is specifically for geographic data. It was developed by and is maintained by Esri, the company behind the mapping tool ArcGIS. It's an open specification and has become the de facto format for sharing spatial data beyond just points with latitude and longitude.

The file format encodes points, lines, and polygons. While an actual shapefile is a single file, the usable format is a directory of files that specifies both geographic geometries and data that is connected to the geometries. The directory and the files in the directory share the same name, just with different extensions.

For example, as shown in Figure 3.8, a shapefile for state boundaries provided by the U.S. Census Bureau contains seven files with the same name `tl_rd22_us_state`. The files with extensions `.dbf`, `.shp`, and `.shx` specify data for each shape, geometry, and shape ordering, respectively, and are included with every shapefile. The other files, not required by the specifications, include metadata about the geometries.

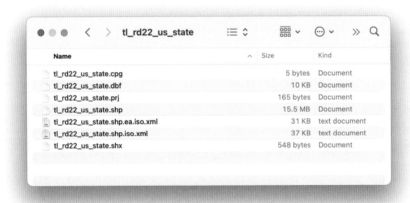

FIGURE 3.8 *Shapefile that specifies boundaries in the United States*

FORMATTING TOOLS

Check out the documentation for shapefiles from Esri at https://datafl.ws/7m5.

You can format data by writing quick, one-off scripts that land in the trash or disappear into the file archives after you're done. After you've written a few scripts, you recognize patterns in the logic, so it's not super hard to write new scripts for specific datasets, but it does take time. Enter the tools to handle the boilerplate routines, which can save time.

Spreadsheet Applications

If all you need is simple sorting, or you just need to make small changes to individual data points, your favorite spreadsheet software is always available. Take this route if you're OK with manually editing data. Otherwise, try the tools that follow, or go with a custom coding solution (especially if you have a large, complex dataset that could get messed up in a spreadsheet).

OpenRefine

OpenRefine, previously called Google Refine, which itself was the evolution of Freebase Gridworks, is an open-source tool to clean and format your data. On the surface, the tool looks like spreadsheet software when you load a dataset, but the focus is on making your data more usable. You can find inconsistencies in your data, consolidate multiple datasets in a relatively easy way, and search the data more flexibly than with spreadsheets.

For example, say you have an inventory list for your kitchen. You can load the data in Refine and quickly find inconsistencies such as typos or differing classifications. Maybe "fork" was misspelled as "frk," or you want to reclassify all the forks, spoons, and knives as utensils. You can easily find these things with OpenRefine and make changes. If you don't like the changes, you can revert to the old dataset with a simple undo.

If anything, OpenRefine is a good tool to keep in your back pocket. It's free to download and runs locally on your computer.

Download the open-source OpenRefine and view tutorials on how to make the most out of the tool at `openrefine.org`.

Tabula

PDF files are good for sharing documents that are meant to be read or used as a reference. The PDF format is not ideal for sharing tables of data that you want to load in visualization software. Sometimes, that's just how the data comes, though, so you can either avoid using it, manually translating data from a document to a spreadsheet, or use Tabula to pull data more automatically. Tabula, shown in Figure 3.9, is probably the less headache-inducing solution.

Open a PDF with Tabula, select the pages with tables, and the software lets you export data files. The process is not fully automated, and sometimes the software gets stuck because tables in PDF files are not standardized, but it usually takes care of the tedious parts.

Download Tabula at tabula. technology. The project is also available on GitHub at `https://github.com /tabulapdf/tabula.`

FIGURE 3.9 *Tabula helps you extract data from PDF files.*

Mr. Data Converter

Often, you might get all your data in Excel or as a comma-delimited file, but then need to convert it to another format to fit your needs. This is almost always the case when you create visualization for the Web. Mr. Data Converter, shown in Figure 3.10, is a free and simple tool that lets you copy and paste data and quickly convert it to various formats, such as JSON or XML. Shan Carter made it when he was a graphics editor for the *New York Times*.

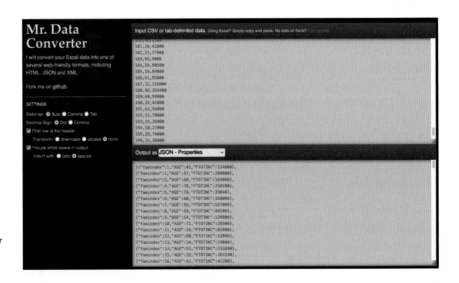

FIGURE 3.10 *Mr. Data Converter makes switching between data formats easy.*

Either you can run it from the site or download the code to run it locally on your computer. You can also extend the application for your own data formats.

FORMATTING WITH CODE

Although point-and-click software can be useful, sometimes, the applications don't quite do what you want. Some software doesn't handle large data files well; they get slow, or they crash.

What do you do at this point? You can throw your hands in the air and give up; however, that wouldn't be productive. Instead, you can write some code to get the job done. With code you gain flexibility, and you can tailor your scripts specifically for your data.

Now, jump right into an example on how to switch between data formats with a quick script.

SWITCHING BETWEEN DATA FORMATS

Tool Used: Python

Go back to the scraped comma-delimited file `income-scraped.csv`. Each row represents a family income and the age of the householder who answered the survey. The first rows look like this:

```
famindex,AGE,FTOTINC
1,45,114000
2,37,280000
3,60,184000
4,70,250100
5,79,33040
6,60,168000
7,56,557000
8,69,84500
9,54,128800
10,72,28500
```

Say you want the data as XML in the following format:

```
<?xml version="1.0" encoding="UTF-8"?>
<rows>
    <row>
        <famindex>1</famindex>
        <AGE>45</AGE>
        <FTOTINC>114000</FTOTINC>
    </row>
```

Try Mr. Data Converter at https://shancarter .github.io/mr-data-converter or download the source on GitHub at https://github.com/ shancarter/Mr-Data-Converter to convert your Excel spreadsheets to a web-friendly format.

Note: This example uses Python, but like the scraping example, the logic translates to other languages. So, if Python is not for you, think about how you might apply the logic with a different tool.

```
    <row>
        <famindex>2</famindex>
        <AGE>37</AGE>
        <FTOTINC>280000</FTOTINC>
    </row>
    <row>
        <famindex>3</famindex>
        <AGE>60</AGE>
        <FTOTINC>184000</FTOTINC>
    </row>
    <row>
        <famindex>4</famindex>
        <AGE>70</AGE>
        <FTOTINC>250100</FTOTINC>
    </row>

    ...
</rows>
```

Each family unit is enclosed in `<row>` tags with a `<famindex>`, `<AGE>`, and `<FTOTINC>`, which match the fields in the CSV file.

To convert the CSV into the preceding XML format, you can use the following code snippet:

```python
import csv

fields = None
with open('income-scraped.csv') as csvfile:

    reader = csv.reader(csvfile, delimiter=",")
    for row in reader:

        # Save header variables
        if fields == None:
            fields = row
            print('<?xml version="1.0" encoding="UTF-8"?>')
            print("<rows>")
        else:
            # Add family unit
            famunit = '<row>'
            famunit += '<' + fields[0] + '>' + row[0] + '</' +
fields[0] + '>'  # famindex
            famunit += '<' + fields[1] + '>' + row[1] + '</' +
fields[1] + '>'  # AGE
            famunit += '<' + fields[2] + '>' + row[2] + '</' +
fields[2] + '>'  # FTOTINC
```

```
            famunit += '</row>'

            # Print family unit
            print(famunit)

    print("</rows>")
```

As before, you import the necessary modules. You only need the csv module in this case to read in `income-scraped.csv`.

```
import csv
```

The second line of code opens `income-scraped.csv` to read using the `open()` function and then reads it with the `csv.reader()` method.

```
with open('income-scraped.csv') as csvfile:
    reader = csv.reader(csvfile, delimiter=",")
```

Notice the delimiter is specified as a comma. If the file were a tab-delimited file, you could specify the delimiter as `'\t'`.

Then you can print the opening lines of the XML file in line 3.

```
print('<?xml version="1.0" encoding="UTF-8"?>')
print("<rows>")
```

In the main chunk of the code, you can use a `for` loop through each row of data and print in the format that you need the XML to be in. In this example, each row in the CSV header is equivalent to each observation in the XML.

```
for row in reader:

        # Save header variables
        if fields == None:
            fields = row
            print('<?xml version="1.0" encoding="UTF-8"?>')
            print("<rows>")
        else:

            # Add family unit
            famunit = '<row>'
            famunit += '<' + fields[0] + '>' + row[0] + '</' +
fields[0] + '>'  # famindex
            famunit += '<' + fields[1] + '>' + row[1] + '</' +
fields[1] + '>'  # AGE
            famunit += '<' + fields[2] + '>' + row[2] + '</' +
fields[2] + '>'  # FTOTINC
```

```
            famunit += '</row>'

            # Print family unit
            print(famunit)
```

Each row has three values: the index, householder age, and family income.

End the XML conversion with its closing tag:

```
print("</rows>")
```

There are two main steps here:

1. Read the data in.
2. Iterate over the data, changing the row in some way.

It's the same logic if you go the other direction and convert the resulting XML back to CSV. As shown in the following snippet, the difference is that you use a different library to parse the XML file:

```
from bs4 import BeautifulSoup

fields = None
with open('income-scraped-to-xml.xml') as xmlfile:

    xmlread = xmlfile.read()

    soup = BeautifulSoup(xmlread, features='xml')

    # Start file
    f = open('xml-back-to-csv.csv', 'w')

    # Write rows to file
    f.write(",".join(['famindex', 'AGE', 'FTOTINC'])+'\n')
    rows = soup.findAll('row')
    for row in rows:
        f.write(','.join([row.famindex.string, row.AGE.string,
row.FTOTINC.string])+'\n')

    # Close file
    f.close()
```

Instead of importing the csv module, you import the BeautifulSoup module. Remember, you used BeautifulSoup to parse the HTML from the sample web pages. However, this time you pass 'xml' to BeautifulSoup().

You can open the XML file for reading with open() and then assign the contents to the xmlread variable. At this point, the contents are stored as a string.

To parse, pass the `xmlread` string to `BeautifulSoup` to iterate through each `<row>` in the XML file. Use `findAll()` to fetch all the rows, and finally, like you did with the CSV to XML conversion, iterate through each row, printing the values in your desired format.

The previous has one small wrinkle in how the file is saved. In the previous snippets, you use `print()`. In this snippet, you open a new file, `xml-back-to-csv.csv`, and then write to the file with `write()` instead of printing, and at the end, you close the file with `close()`.

This takes you back to where you began. The following is the first 10 rows of the output file, which should look familiar:

```
famindex,AGE,FTOTINC
1,45,114000
2,37,280000
3,60,184000
4,70,250100
5,79,33040
6,60,168000
7,56,557000
8,69,84500
9,54,128800
10,72,28500
```

To drive the point home, here's the code to convert the CSV to JSON format:

```
import csv

fields = None
with open('income-scraped.csv') as csvfile:

    reader = csv.reader(csvfile, delimiter=",")
    for row in reader:

        # Save header variables
        if fields == None:
            fields = row

        else:

            # Start JSON string
            if row[0] == "1":
                famunit = '['
            else:
                famunit = ''

            # Add family unit
```

```
            famunit += '{'
            famunit += '"' + fields[0] + '":' + row[0] + ','   #
famindex
            famunit += '"' + fields[1] + '":' + row[1] + ','   #
AGE
            famunit += '"' + fields[2] + '":' + row[2]         #
FTOTINC
            famunit += '}'

            # Close set if at end
            if (row[0] == "200"):
                famunit += ']'
            else:
                famunit += ','

            # Print family unit
            print(famunit)
```

Go through the lines to figure out what's going on, but again, it's the same logic with different output. Here's what the JSON looks like if you run the preceding code:

```
[
    {"famindex":1,"AGE":45,"FTOTINC":114000},
    {"famindex":2,"AGE":37,"FTOTINC":280000},
    {"famindex":3,"AGE":60,"FTOTINC":184000},
    {"famindex":4,"AGE":70,"FTOTINC":250100},
    {"famindex":5,"AGE":79,"FTOTINC":33040},
    {"famindex":6,"AGE":60,"FTOTINC":168000},
    {"famindex":7,"AGE":56,"FTOTINC":557000},
    {"famindex":8,"AGE":69,"FTOTINC":84500},
    {"famindex":9,"AGE":54,"FTOTINC":128800},
    {"famindex":10,"AGE":72,"FTOTINC":28500},
...
]
```

This is the same data, with index, age, and income, but in a different format. Computers just love variety.

PROCESSING DATA

Finding, loading, and formatting data are mostly moving data around between files and locations. These steps are important so that you can work with data using the tools available. As you start to explore and analyze your data, you'll need to process it—aggregate, filter, and calculate—to find patterns.

This is essentially the early stages of an analysis, which should be considered an exploratory phase more than a set of fixed steps to follow. But there are operations that tend to come up more often.

For example, you might be interested in only a subset of the data, in which case, you need to filter. The sampled income data in this chapter comes from a larger representative sample of the United States. I narrowed it down to people who were employed and reported an income, and for the sake of simplicity, I showed only 200 observations instead of 2 million.

Maybe you're interested in comparing groups, but the data represents individuals within each group. You could aggregate for each group and calculate means and medians. If the dataset is big, it might be worth sampling for a more manageable size. If you have probabilities, it might be worth running simulations to produce samples or run tests.

This is part of the fun of working with data because you finally have something to look at and analyze, and if you have interesting data, there are interesting stories to find. However, you must be extra careful because it's not just moving around data. You're mushing data together and pulling things apart. Be careful with the math and the interpretations to avoid miscommunication and becoming someone who accidentally publishes a misleading chart.

FILTERING AND AGGREGATING SAMPLED DATA

Tool used: Python

In this example, you come back to Python for basic data processing. You will need the library NumPy, which makes it easier to work with data in Python. You also need the pandas library, which provides analysis and data manipulation functions. Remember that Python is a general-purpose programming language, but you can use libraries for a focus on data.

Note: My own preference is to switch to R (if I'm not using it already) when I enter the data processing stage, because the stage is tightly coupled with the analysis process. But that's what works for me. There are many paths tool-wise that can lead to the same results.

> NumPy is a helpful Python library for working with data. Download it at `numpy.org` and follow the installation instructions. The pandas library makes it easier to analyze and manipulate data. Download and install at `pandas.pydata.org`.

Instead of writing a script, start the Python interpreter in your terminal or console by entering **python** (or `python3`, depending on your setup). This lets you enter code line by line and get immediate output. When you start the interpreter, you get a prompt that starts with >>> where you can enter code.

Import numpy and pandas.

```
import numpy as np
import pandas as pd
```

Load the data with `read_csv()` from the pandas library.

```
people = pd.read_csv('income-scraped.csv')
```

To see the first few rows of the data to make sure it loaded correctly, use the `head()` method.

```
people.head()
```

This is what you get:

```
   famindex  AGE   FTOTINC
0         1   45    114000
1         2   37    280000
2         3   60    184000
3         4   70    250100
4         5   79     33040
```

With data loaded, it's straightforward to subset. The following uses bracket notation to subset family units with a householder who is older than 40:

```
over40 = people[people.AGE > 40]
```

Using the `head()` method, you can see the first rows, and you can see that only family units with householders older than 40 are shown:

```
   famindex  AGE   FTOTINC
0         1   45    114000
2         3   60    184000
3         4   70    250100
4         5   79     33040
5         6   60    168000
```

Instead of subsetting, you can mark each row as a family unit with a householder who is older than 40. The following creates a new column called `isover40`:

```
people['isover40'] = people['AGE'] > 40
```

Then you can calculate the median family income by group.

```
people.groupby(['isover40'])['FTOTINC'].median()
```

You can also calculate the overall median income.

```
people['FTOTINC'].median()
```

Maybe you want more granular age groups, such as a group for every 10 years of age. You can calculate it as follows, which creates an `agegrp` column:

```
people['agegrp'] = (people['AGE'] / 10).apply(np.floor) * 10
```

Then you can use `groupby()` like before but with the `agegrp` column.

```
people.groupby(['agegrp'])['FTOTINC'].median()
```

You get medians for each 10-year age group, where 20 indicates 20 to 29, 30 indicates 30 to 39, and so on.

```
agegrp
20.0    42000.0
30.0    88000.0
40.0    59000.0
50.0    94400.0
60.0    84500.0
70.0    43210.0
80.0    31400.0
90.0    16900.0
```

These calculations are based on a small sample, so don't put too much weight on the interpretations. Ideally, this gives you a good idea of how filtering and aggregating can work. Most data-centric languages provide useful subsetting and aggregation functions. If not, I'd look for something else since the basic functions are used frequently throughout the analysis.

WRAPPING UP

This chapter covered where you can find the data you need and how to manage it after you have it. This is an important step in the visualization process. A visualization is only as interesting as its underlying data. You can dress up a graphic all you want, but the data (or the results from your analysis of the data) is still the substance, and now that you know where and how to get your data, you're already a step ahead of the pack.

You also got your first taste of programming. You scraped data from a website and then formatted and rearranged that data, which will be useful in later chapters. The main takeaway is the logic in the code. You used Python, but you could have used a different language. The logic is similar. When you learn one programming language (and if you're a programmer, you can attest to this), it's much easier to learn other languages.

You don't always have to use code of course. Sometimes, there are point-and-click applications that make your job a lot easier, and you should take advantage of that when you can. In the end, the more tools you have in your toolbox, the less likely you're going to get stuck somewhere in the process.

OK, you handled data. Now, it's time to get visual. In the next several chapters, you will ask questions about the data, make visualizations to answer the questions, and use charts to communicate insights to an audience.

Visualizing Time

Businesses grow, public opinion changes, populations shift, communities evolve, user counts stagnate, and weight fluctuates. Time passes. With time series data, you can see how things change and by how much. This chapter covers different types of time-series datasets and the charts you can use, depending on what you're looking for. You look at time every day. It's on your computer, your phone, and your watch. It's in your car. It's on your calendar. Even without a clock, you feel time as you wake up and go to sleep. The sun rises, and it sets. Time moves forward, and sometimes it feels like it's standing still. If we're lucky, we get older. So, it's only natural to look at data over time.

Time-series data lets you see how things change through trends, events, and cycles.

Trends represent a shift, such as an increase or a decrease, over a range of time or specific points in time when something significant happens. When the trends and *events* seem to happen again and again, you start to see repeating patterns or *cycles*.

Some charts show these patterns better than others. You'll learn about the options in the following sections. You also get your hands dirty with R and Adobe Illustrator—two programs that go great together.

TRENDS

Are things getting better, worse, or staying the same? Is there growth or decline? Trends in data represent patterns in a certain direction. To see these patterns, you need more than a single data point. Instead, you must visualize data over a range of time to make comparisons between points and to see the data overall.

For example, Figure 4.1 shows the rise of married couple households with dual income and no kids (DINKs) between 1980 and 2022. There is an overall trend upwards with a small dip in the early 2000s. The lines highlight increases and decreases by connecting points in time. The surrounding charts show the trends for other household types, such as a decrease for households with two earners and one kid.

The timespan between 1980 through 2022 is the same for each chart, but the y-axis scales are different. The chart for DINKs uses a scale from 34% to 42% of married couple households, whereas the chart for two earners and one kid spans only 10% to 12%. This was to highlight the trends over the absolute changes.

MORE DUAL INCOME, NO KIDS

People are waiting longer to have kids or not having kids at all, which leads to more dual income households with no kids.

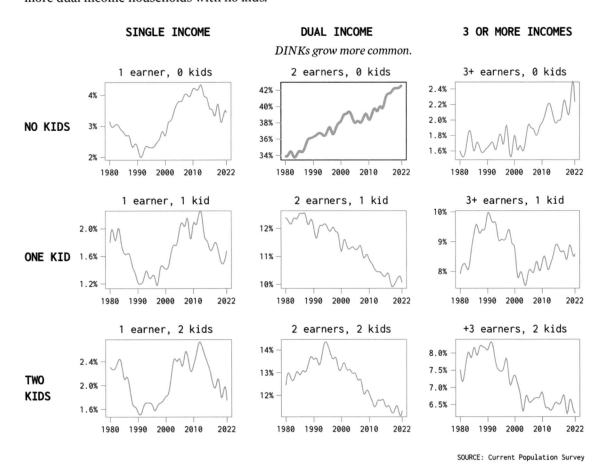

FIGURE 4.1 *"More Dual Income, No Kids,"* https://datafl.ws/dink

Had the question behind the graphic been more about the distribution of household types instead of the rise of dual income and no kids, it might have been better to use the same y-scale for every chart.

Either way, you would be able to compare percentages in 2022 against other years. If you used, say, a pie chart, the comparisons would be less straightforward, because the chart type focuses on parts of a whole rather than how something changes over time.

Tip: Select scales based on what you want to show and the question you're trying to answer. Choose truthfully.

Pick chart types that highlight your insights instead of forcing readers to make connections.

BAR CHART FOR TIME

The bar chart is one of the most common chart types. It is steady. It is universal. You've probably made some. The bar chart can be used to visualize various types of data, but now look at how it can be used in the context of time.

Figure 4.2 shows a basic framework. The horizontal axis, also known as the *x-axis*, represents time. It defines where to place points from left to right. In this case, the range of time is from January to June in a given year, and each increment is a month. The axis could also be by year, by day, by hour, or by some other unit of time. Bar width and bar spacing do not represent values in this example.

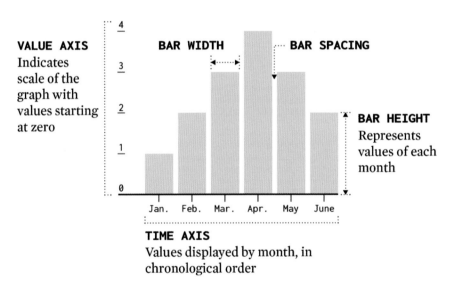

FIGURE 4.2 *Bar chart framework*

The vertical axis, also known as the *y-axis*, represents the scale for the values for a given point in time. Figure 4.2 shows a linear scale where units are evenly spaced across the range of the axis. The scale of the y-axis defines the height of each bar. The first bar, for example, goes up to one unit, whereas the highest bar goes up to four units.

This is important. All charts use *visual encodings*, which are the sizes, shapes, positions, angles, lengths, directions, and colors that represent your data. For bar charts, height is the visual encoding. The lower the value is, the shorter the bar will be. The greater a value is, the taller a bar will be. The heights of all the bars should be proportional to the values, so that when one value is twice that of the other, the bar for the greater value should be twice the height of the other. So, you can see that the height of the four-unit bar in April is twice as tall as the two-unit bar in February.

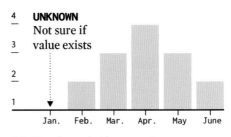

FIGURE 4.3 *Bar graph with nonzero axis*

Many programs, by default, set the lowest value of the y-axis to the minimum of the dataset, as shown in Figure 4.3. In this case, the baseline is set at 1. The April bar is not twice the height of the February bar anymore. The bar for February is one-third that of April. The bar for January is nonexistent. The point: Always start the value axis of a bar chart at zero. Otherwise, the chart provides incorrect comparisons.

MAKING A BAR CHART

Tool used: R

Dataset: Winners from Nathan's Hot Dog Eating Contest, `book.flowingdata .com/vt2/ch4/data/hot-dog-contest-winners.csv`

It's time to make your first chart using real data, and it's an important part of history, vital to our existence as humans. These are the results of Nathan's Hot Dog Eating Contest for the past three decades. Oh, yes.

In case you're unfamiliar with the competitive eating circuit, Nathan's Hot Dog Eating Contest is an annual event that happens every July 4. That's Independence Day in the United States. Competitors celebrate freedom by eating as many hot dogs as they can in 10 minutes.

Throughout the late 1990s, the winners ate 10 to 20 hot dogs and buns (HDBs) in about 15 minutes. However, in 2001, Takeru Kobayashi, a professional eater from Japan, obliterated the competition by eating 50 HDBs. That was more than twice the amount anyone in the world had eaten before him. American eater Joey Chestnut arrived in 2007 to break the world record with 66 HDBs. Chestnut's legend began. Except for 2015, when Matt Stonie won the competition, Chestnut has won every year since.

How much has the HDB count increased over the years?

In R, load data for contest winners from 1980 to 2023 with the `read.csv()` function, as shown here. Remember that the file location is relative to your current working directory.

```
# Load data
winners <- read.csv("data/hot-dog-contest-winners.csv")
```

Research shows that people perceive some visual encodings more efficiently than others. Some interpret such results as a cue to avoid certain encodings, but practitioners tend to be less judgmental. Find more information on encodings at `https://datafl .ws/percep`.

Note: Always start the value axis of a bar chart at zero when you're dealing with all positive values. Anything else is visually misleading, because the height of the bars must be proportional to the values they represent.

Alternatively, you can pass a URL to `read.csv()` for the same result.

```
winners <- read.csv("https://book.flowingdata.com/vt2/ch4/data
/hot-dog-contest-winners.csv")
```

Use `head()` to see the first few rows of the loaded data. Make sure it loaded as expected.

```
# First rows in dataset
head(winners)
```

You should see the following data. There are five columns for the year, the winner(s) during that year, the number of HDBs eaten, the competitor's country, and whether or not the winner set a record.

```
> head(winners)
  year                        winner hotdogs       country record
1 1980 Paul Siederman & Joe Baldini    9.75 United States      0
2 1981                Thomas DeBerry   11.00 United States      1
3 1982                 Steven Abrams   11.10 United States      1
4 1983                   Emil Gomez    10.50        Mexico      0
5 1984                 Birgit Felden    9.50       Germany      0
6 1985               Oscar Rodriguez   11.75 United States      1
```

The data is stored as a *data frame* in R, and you can access each column with the dollar sign ($) *operator*. For example, to access the values in the `hotdogs` column of the `winners` data frame, enter the following:

```
# Using dollar sign operator
winners$hotdogs
```

This returns the values in the column, starting with 9.75, 11.00, and so on. Try using the dollar sign with other columns to see what you get.

Use the `barplot()` function to make a bar chart that shows the `hotdogs` values:

```
# Default bar chart
barplot(winners$hotdogs)
```

Figure 4.4 shows the default bar chart. It shows a series of bars with an upward trend.

The default chart has no labels on the x-axis. In this example, you want to show the years from the `year` column. Pass the values to the `names.arg` argument in `barplot()`.

```
# Year labels
barplot(winners$hotdogs, names.arg=winners$year)
```

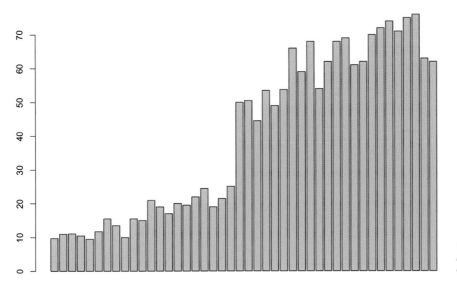

FIGURE 4.4 *Default chart of number of hot dogs and buns eaten, using* barplot() *in R*

Year labels appear on the x-axis of the bar chart, space permitting, as shown in Figure 4.5.

Use the question mark operator, ?, to see documentation for what else you can do with barplot().

```
# Help docs for barplot()
?barplot
```

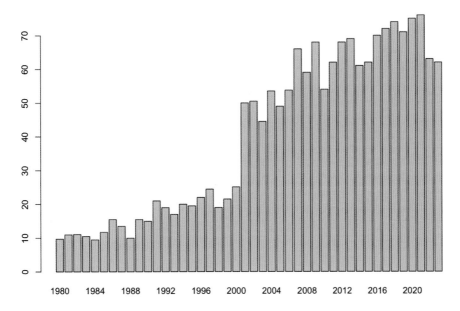

FIGURE 4.5 *Bar chart with labels for years*

To remove the borders around the bars, set the `border` argument to `NA`; to change the space in between bars, set `space` to a proportion of bar width between 0 and 1; to add x-axis and y-axis titles, use `xlab` and `ylab`, respectively; to add a title on top, use `main`.

```
# Axis labels
barplot(winners$hotdogs,
        names.arg=winners$year,
        border=NA,
        space=.1,
        xlab="Year",
        ylab="Hot dogs and buns (HDB) eaten",
        main="Contest Winners")
```

Figure 4.6 shows a bar chart with titles and different bar spacing from the default.

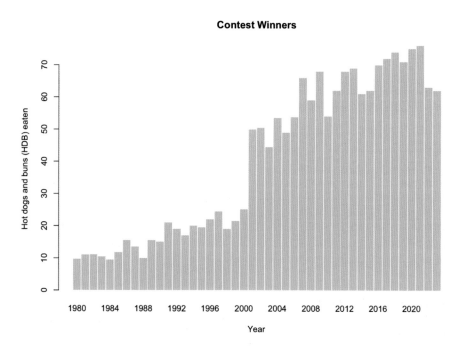

FIGURE 4.6 *Bar chart with titles*

We'll come back to this example. For now, note how R has functions that you can pass data to. You can change the values you pass to function arguments for labeling and aesthetics, and you can always see what you can change and how you can do it through documentation.

LINE CHART

You're probably familiar with this one. As the name suggests, the line chart uses a line to connect points ordered chronologically. The x-axis typically represents time, and the y-axis represents values, so a single coordinate represents a value at a given point in time. Figure 4.7 shows the geometry.

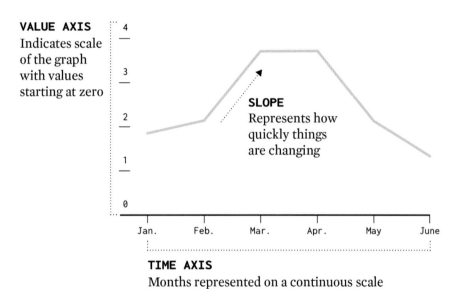

VALUE AXIS
Indicates scale of the graph with values starting at zero

SLOPE
Represents how quickly things are changing

TIME AXIS
Months represented on a continuous scale

FIGURE 4.7 *Line chart framework*

The slope of the line represents the change. The line goes up when there is an increase in value, the line goes down when there is a decrease in value, and the line remains flat when there is no change.

Unlike the bar chart, which must have a baseline of zero, the line chart does not because it uses slope for a visual encoding. You compare one position against another to see how much something changed.

However, this also means you must be careful with how much or how little you stretch the scales. As shown in Figure 4.8, a stretched scale on the y-axis can make a shift appear more dramatic, and a squished scale can make changes less obvious.

Some suggest maintaining a 45-degree angle at the maximum shift, but this is not a hard rule. Choose based on context. If a change is significant in the data's context, then a steeper slope might be better, but if a small shift is just that, then adjust the scale to match the level of importance.

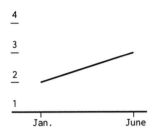 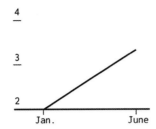  

FIGURE 4.8 *Different scales over the same range*

Note: Sometimes visualization design can seem like a checklist of rules, but a lot of the choices you make should be based on the dataset you're showing. Use design to highlight noteworthy patterns in context.

MAKING A LINE CHART

Tool used: R

Dataset: Winners from Nathan's Hot Dog Eating Contest, `book.flowingdata` `.com/vt2/ch4/data/hot-dog-contest-winners.csv`

Making a line chart in R is similar to how you made a bar chart, except instead of the `barplot()` function, you use `plot()`. If you're starting with a fresh R session, load the hot dog data again with `read.csv()` and assign the data frame to `winners`.

```
# Load data
winners <- read.csv("data/hot-dog-contest-winners.csv")
```

Before you make the line chart, use `par()` to set the graphical parameter `las` to 1. This tells R to set axis labels horizontally. Notice that the previous R charts have y-axis labels that are rotated 90 degrees.

```
# Graphical parameter to make axis labels horizontal
par(las=1)
```

You can use `par()` to set other graphical parameters, such as background color, margins, fonts, and axis types, but keep it simple for now. Enter `?par` for documentation.

Use `plot()` by providing the *year* on the x-axis and *hotdogs* on the y-axis; set the type to l, which stands for "line"; and set axis titles and the main title with `xlab`, `ylab`, and `main`.

```
# Line chart with plot()
plot(winners$year, winners$hotdogs,
    type="l",
    xlab="",
    ylab="Hot dogs and buns (HDB) eaten",
    main="Nathan's Hot Dog Eating Contest, Winning Results,
1980-2023")
```

You get the line chart shown in Figure 4.9, which shows the same trend as the bar chart from Figure 4.6.

Nathan's Hot Dog Eating Contest, Winning Results, 1980-2023

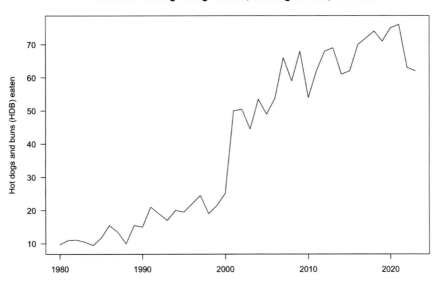

FIGURE 4.9 *Line chart that shows an upward trend*

Just for fun, check out the other types you can pass to `type` in `plot()` for other chart types, as shown in Figure 4.10.

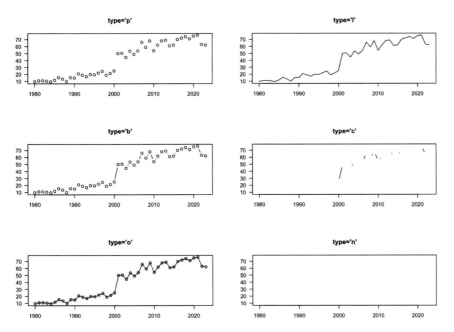

FIGURE 4.10 *Other chart types with* `plot()`

Go back to the line chart. It could use some annotation to point out important bits, such as the sudden spike by Kobayashi in 2001. The `text()` function lets you add words to your charts. The following places a label at the x-y-coordinate (2001, 50) for the year 2000 and 50 hot dogs. The `pos` argument specifies text alignment. In this case, it is set to 2 so that the text appears to the left of the coordinate.

```
# Text
text(2001, 50,
     "In 2001, Takeru Kobayashi nearly doubled the previous
record with 50 HDBs.",
     pos=2)
```

The text appears at the spike, shown in Figure 4.11.

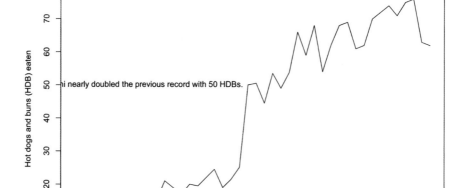

Nathan's Hot Dog Eating Contest, Winning Results, 1980-2023

FIGURE 4.11 *Annotating a line chart*

The text is too long to fit on one line, though, so the words run off the chart on the left. Draw the line chart again with `plot()` and then put line breaks where you want to with `text()`.

```
# Line chart with plot()
plot(winners$year, winners$hotdogs,
     type="l",
     xlab="",
     ylab="Hot dogs and buns (HDB) eaten",
     main="Nathan's Hot Dog Eating Contest, Winning Results,
1980-2023")
```

```
# Text with line breaks
text(2001, 48,
     "In 2001, Takeru Kobayashi
     nearly doubled the previous
     record with 50 HDBs.",
     pos=2)
```

This puts the full text in the body of the chart, as shown in Figure 4.12. Note that the y-coordinate this time is 48 instead of 50. The `text()` function places words by the corner (which corner depends on `pos`). Decreasing the y-coordinate moves the words down on the chart so that the middle of the text body lines up with the 2001 spike.

As usual, find out more about the `text()` function via the documentation.

```
# Find documentation
?text
```

If you're placing annotation at many points on a chart, you probably don't want to manually add line breaks like you did earlier. The `strwrap()` function can come in handy here, as shown next. It breaks up words by number of characters into a *vector*, which is a common data structure in R that contains values that are of the same type, such as numeric or characters. Use `paste()` to put the words back together with a line break character, `\n`. In this example, the following snippet yields the same results as earlier:

Note: One of the best things about R is that you can always easily access documentation in the console. Enter a question mark, ?, followed by the function name, and you get a help page. The documentation includes a description of the function, usage and defaults, details about usage, and examples that you can run. This is great for learning new functions in R and getting unstuck when you run into errors.

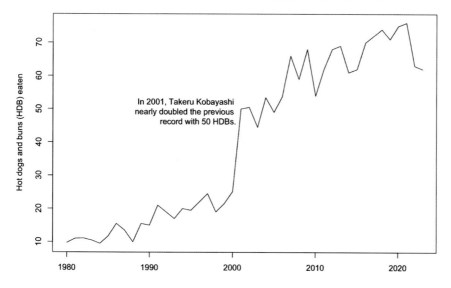

Nathan's Hot Dog Eating Contest, Winning Results, 1980-2023

FIGURE 4.12 *Annotation with line breaks*

```
# Wrapped text
anno <- "In 2001, Takeru Kobayashi nearly doubled the previous
record with 50 HDBs."
text(2001, 48,
     paste(strwrap(anno, 30), collapse="\n"),
     pos=2)
```

While `barplot()` and `plot()` make different types of charts, the approach is similar. You pass data to the functions and set labels through the arguments, which you can look up in the documentation. Use `par()` to set overall graphical parameters, and use `text()`to layer words over your charts.

STEP CHART

A standard line chart uses a straight line to connect one point to another. It implies a steady change between the points, which makes sense for something that is continuously shifting, such as world population. You visually estimate change by the slope of the line between two points in time.

But some things stay at a value for periods of time, and then the data immediately jumps up or falls. Interest rates, for example, can stay the same for months and then increase or decrease right after an announcement. Use a step chart, as shown in Figure 4.13, for this type of data.

VALUE AXIS
Indicates scale of the graph with values starting at zero

FLAT EDGE
Flate line indicates no change during time period

JUMP
No trend, just instant step up to next value

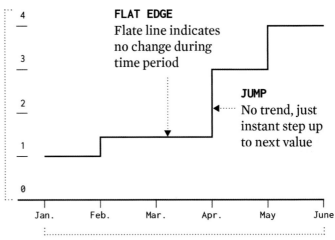

TIME AXIS
Months represented on a continuous scale

FIGURE 4.13 *Step chart basic framework*

Instead of connecting points directly, the line stays at the same value until there is a change, at which point it jumps up or falls to the next value with a vertical segment. You end up with a bunch of steps. Get it? Steps.

MAKING A STEP CHART

Tool used: R

Dataset: Postage prices in the United States, book.flowingdata.com/vt2 /ch4/data/us-postage.csv

While it still amazes me that we can stick a letter in the mailbox and somehow it gets to its destination, the cost to mail a letter in the United States has risen over the years. If you still use physical mail, you've probably noticed the upticks. How much did prices increase and when?

Load the data in R with `read.csv()`. Like in the previous example, you can also pass the function a URL if you don't have the data saved on your computer.

```
# Load data
postage <- read.csv("data/us-postage.csv")
```

Check out the first few rows with `head()` to make sure the data loaded and looks like what you expect.

```
# First few rows
head(postage)
```

You should get the following, where each row represents a price change. There are two columns: `Year` and `Price` to mail the first ounce of mail.

```
> head(postage)
  Year Price
1 1863  0.06
2 1883  0.04
3 1885  0.02
4 1917  0.03
5 1919  0.02
6 1932  0.03
```

The `summary()` function lets you check the ranges, mean, and median of each column. Pass the `postage` data frame to the function.

```
# Summary
summary(postage)
```

You get summary statistics for each column. The Year minimum is 1863, the maximum is 2023, and the median is 1995. The Price minimum is 2 cents, and the maximum is 66 cents. This is useful to get a rough idea of what the data looks like and to make sure the data loaded as expected.

```
> summary(postage)
      Year             Price
 Min.   :1863    Min.    :0.0200
 1st Qu.:1970    1st Qu.:0.0700
 Median :1995    Median :0.3200
 Mean   :1981    Mean    :0.2869
 3rd Qu.:2012    3rd Qu.:0.4550
 Max.   :2023    Max.    :0.6600
```

From the previous example, you already know how to make a line chart with `plot()`. Give it a try with this `postage` data.

```
# Plot as regular time series
par(las=1)
plot(postage$Year, postage$Price, type="l",
     xlab="Year", ylab="Postage Rate (Dollars)",
     main="US Postage Rates for Letters, First Ounce, 1863-2023")
```

Check out Figure 4.14. The price to mail the first ounce didn't change that much during the earlier decades. Prices decreased in the beginning of this data. Then they started to rise relatively quickly in the 1970s.

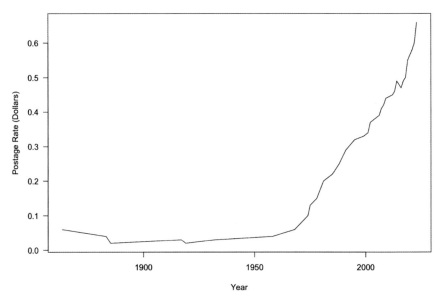

FIGURE 4.14 *Line chart showing postage rates over time*

However, the line chart suggests a steady increase in between years. Price should stay the same for a while and then get an instant bump on an increase. Just set `type` to `s` (for step) instead of `l` (for line) in the call to `plot()`.

```
# Step chart with labels
par(las=1)
plot(postage$Year, postage$Price, type="s",
     xlab="Year", ylab="Postage Rate (Dollars)",
     main="US Postage Rates for Letters, First Ounce, 1863-2023")
```

Figure 4.15 shows a more accurate presentation of the rising postage prices.

Maybe you want to focus on a narrower time range, such as 1991 and on. Subset the data using R's bracket notation, as shown here:

```
# Change limits ("zoom")
postagesub <- postage[postage$Year >= 1991,]
```

Rows that represent prices from 1991 and on are assigned to `postagesub`. Use `head()` to look at the first few rows. The first `Year` observation is for 1991.

```
> head(postagesub)
   Year Price
17 1991  0.29
18 1995  0.32
19 1999  0.33
20 2001  0.34
21 2002  0.37
22 2006  0.39
```

Note: The data frame is two-dimensional, and with the bracket notation, you indicate rows and columns. For example, if you enter `postage[1,1]`, you will get the value in the first row and column of the `postage` data frame. By passing a vector of `TRUE` and `FALSE` values, also known as *Booleans*, to the first part of the bracket, you subset to only the rows that are `TRUE`.

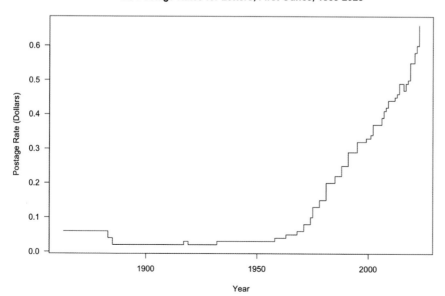

US Postage Rates for Letters, First Ounce, 1863-2023

FIGURE 4.15 *Step chart of postage prices*

Pass `postagesub` to `plot()` for a zoomed-in view of the time series.

```
Par(las=1)
plot(postagesub$Year, postagesub$Price, type="s",
     xlab="Year", ylab="Postage Rate (Dollars)",
     main="US Postage Rates for Letters, First Ounce, 1991-2023")
```

Zooming in lets you show more detail in the selected range, as shown in Figure 4.16.

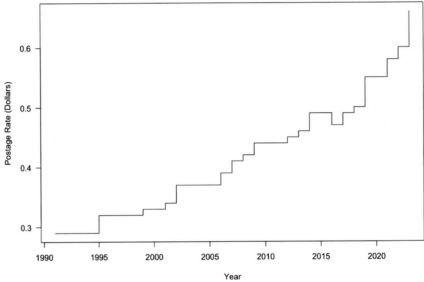

FIGURE 4.16 *Narrower range on the step chart*

The smaller, more frequent steps mean quicker changes to the price, whereas longer, horizontal lines indicate periods with no change. Sometimes these steps are more interesting, and other times the trends you see in a continuous line are more interesting. Your choice should be specific to the context of your data.

SMOOTHING

Sometimes your data might be too noisy with a lot of spikes and dips, even though there's a pattern to show. It might be worth smoothing your data, which can highlight trends over the noise.

There are various ways to do this, which depend on the format of your data. You could try bigger bins, such as aggregating over months instead of days or hours instead of minutes. You could try a *moving average*, which takes the average over set intervals of time. If your data is unevenly spaced over time, you could try *local regression*, which is like fitting many lines to a dataset that connect to make a continuous curve. If you already have a line and just want to smooth out the edges, you could try a *spline*, which fits functions along the range of data points. Covering each of these methods would stretch beyond the scope of this book, but a quick search will yield useful explanations, and there are packages in R that make using the methods straightforward. In the example that follows, you learn how to apply a spline.

USING A SPLINE

Tool used: R

Dataset: Baby names, book.flowingdata.com/vt2/ch4/data/nathan-beatrice.tsv

The Social Security Administration releases baby name data each year. It's a fun time series dataset to play with because there are almost 100,000 names that date back to 1880.

I've used the baby name dataset a bunch of times with FlowingData projects. It never seems to get old.

- The Most Trendy Names in US History, https://datafl.ws/7m8
- The Most Unisex Names in US History, https://datafl.ws/7m9
- Guessing Names Based on What They Start With, https://datafl.ws/7ma

My curiosity started when Hilary Parker went looking for the most poisoned name in U.S. history, which was her own: https://datafl.ws/7mb.

You can download the baby names data directly from the Social Security Administration website (https://datafl.ws/7mc), but the years are split into individual files. To make it easier, load the data via the babynames package in R. Either install through the package manager or use install.packages() in the console.

```
# Install package
install.packages("babynames")
```

Once installed, use `library()` to load the package.

```
# Load package
Library(babynames)
```

Each row of data shows the `year`, `sex`, `name`, number of babies who were given the name (`n`), and the proportion (`prop`) in that year.

```
    year sex    name           n    prop
1   1880 F      Mary        7065 0.0724
2   1880 F      Anna        2604 0.0267
3   1880 F      Emma        2003 0.0205
4   1880 F      Elizabeth   1939 0.0199
5   1880 F      Minnie      1746 0.0179
6   1880 F      Margaret    1578 0.0162
7   1880 F      Ida         1472 0.0151
8   1880 F      Alice       1414 0.0145
9   1880 F      Bertha      1320 0.0135
10  1880 F      Sarah       1288 0.0132
```

Pull out two totally random names from the dataset.

```
nathan <- babynames [babynames$name == "Nathan"
& babynames$sex == "M", ]
beatrice <- babynames [babynames$name == "Beatrice"
& babynames$sex == "F",]
```

Draw a line chart that shows the time series for each name.

```
# Line chart, no smoothing
par(las=1, mar=c(4,5,3,2))
plot(nathan$year, nathan$prop,
     type="l",
     xlab="", ylab="Proportion")
lines(beatrice$year, beatrice$prop,
      lwd=2)
```

Figure 4.17 shows the chart. Beatrice is the line with the peak in the early 1900s, and Nathan is the other line.

There are spiky parts in both lines that might benefit from smoothing with a spline. Use the `spline()` function with coordinates from `nathan` and `beatrice`.

```
natcoords <- spline(nathan$year, nathan$prop)
beacoords <- spline(beatrice$year, beatrice$prop)
```

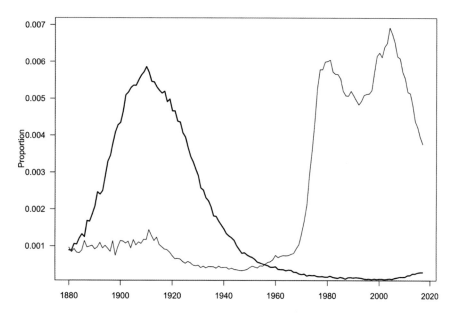

FIGURE 4.17 *Line chart for two names*

Pass the new coordinates to `plot()` and `lines()` like you did earlier. In Figure 4.18, you can see the smoother lines. Use the `col` argument to add some color while you're at it.

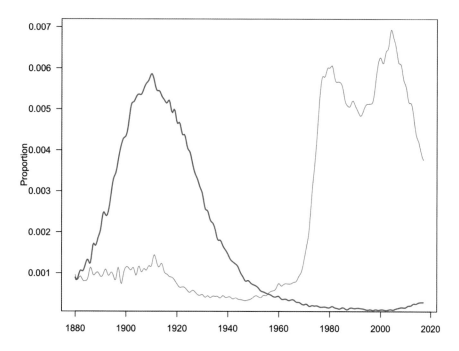

FIGURE 4.18 *Line chart with splines*

```
par(las=1, mar=c(4,5,3,2))
plot(natcoords,
     col="#ac5c5a",
     type="l",
     xlab="", ylab="Proportion")
lines(beacoords, lwd=2, col="#176572")
```

Note: Try changing the value passed to n in spline() to see how the resulting line becomes more or less broad.

You won't want to smooth your time series data all the time, but it can help place more emphasis on a trend or pattern and less on noise and small fluctuations. In this case, the smoother lines are more aesthetically pleasing, so it's worth the trade-off for me. Make the call with your own data. The good news is that it takes only one function call to check it out.

EVENTS

You won't always look for trends with time series data. Instead of highlighting what's increasing and decreasing, the individual events might be the point of focus. When was the last time something happened? How often does something occur? Are the events rare, or do they occur more often than previously thought?

On March 10, 2023, Silicon Valley Bank was unable to fulfill its responsibilities, so the Federal Deposit Insurance Corporation (FDIC) took over. Figure 4.19 shows the bank plotted with previous bank failures.

The focus is on individual events rather than highlighting a trend of bank failures. Charts that show separation between geometries is good for pulling focus to each point.

TIMELINE

The timeline is all about when things happen. As shown in Figure 4.20, in its simplest form, there is just one axis for time, and you place symbols along the axis. More events mean more symbols, and fewer events mean fewer symbols.

With the focus on individual points, the chart can get crowded if you have a lot of events to show. You can either stretch out the timeline for more space or go with a different view.

BANK FAILURES IN THE UNITED STATES, SINCE 2008

Silicon Valley Bank was unable to fulfill its responsibilities, so the Federal Deposit Insurance Corporation took over.

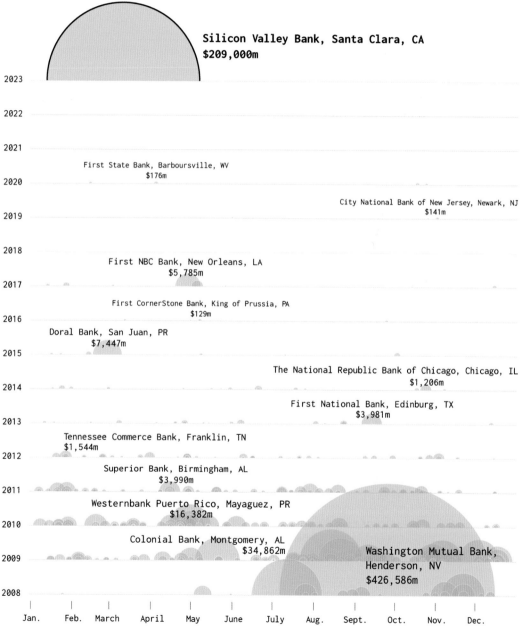

Silicon Valley Bank, Santa Clara, CA
$209,000m

First State Bank, Barboursville, WV
$176m

City National Bank of New Jersey, Newark, NJ
$141m

First NBC Bank, New Orleans, LA
$5,785m

First CornerStone Bank, King of Prussia, PA
$129m

Doral Bank, San Juan, PR
$7,447m

The National Republic Bank of Chicago, Chicago, IL
$1,206m

First National Bank, Edinburg, TX
$3,981m

Tennessee Commerce Bank, Franklin, TN
$1,544m

Superior Bank, Birmingham, AL
$3,990m

Westernbank Puerto Rico, Mayaguez, PR
$16,382m

Colonial Bank, Montgomery, AL
$34,862m

Washington Mutual Bank, Henderson, NV
$426,586m

2023
2022
2021
2020
2019
2018
2017
2016
2015
2014
2013
2012
2011
2010
2009
2008

Jan. Feb. March April May June July Aug. Sept. Oct. Nov. Dec.

SOURCE: Federal Deposit Insurance Corporation

FIGURE 4.19 *"Bank Failures in the United States, Since 2008,"* https://datafl.ws/banks

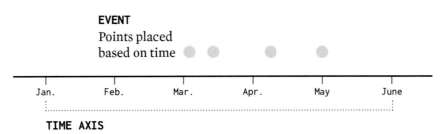

FIGURE 4.20 *Timeline framework*

MAKING A TIMELINE

Tool used: R

Dataset: EGOT winners, book.flowingdata.com/vt2/ch4/data
/EGOT-winners.csv

EGOT is an acronym for Emmy, Grammy, Oscar, and Tony awards. The awards
are given to those with exceptional performances in television, music, movies,
and theatre, respectively. An EGOT winner is someone who has won an award
from each category. How many people have earned EGOT status? When did
they do it?

Load the EGOT dataset with `read.csv()`. You can either load the file locally
or load it with the URL mentioned earlier. The following assumes a local file
in a data folder. Remember to set your working directory in R to where you
downloaded the data.

```
# Load data
egots <- read.csv("data/EGOT-winners.csv")
```

Each row in the dataset represents a winner, when they won awards, and
what they won awards for. Check the dimensions of the `egots` data frame
with `dim()`.

```
# Column names
dim(egots)
```

This returns two values, where the first one is the number of rows and the
second one is the number of columns:

```
[1] 18 15
```

So, there are 18 rows and 15 columns, which means that as of this writing there
have been 18 EGOT winners.

To see the column names, you can check the first few rows with `head()` like in previous examples. You can also use `colnames()` to just see the column names.

```
# Column names
colnames(egots)
```

This returns the column names in the order they appear in the data frame. The first column name is each person's name; the `emmy_year` is when the person won an Emmy; the `emmy_title` is the category they won the award in; the `emmy_desc` is the show they won for. There are similar columns for the other awards. The last two columns, `completion_year` and `category`, are when they achieved the EGOT and what role they play in the industry, such as actor, composer, or director.

```
 [1] "name"            "emmy_year"       "emmy_title"
"emmy_desc"
 [5] "grammy_year"     "grammy_title"    "grammy_desc"
"oscar_year"
 [9] "oscar_title"     "oscar_desc"      "tony_year"
"tony_title"
[13] "tony_desc"       "completion_year" "category"
```

In this example, you are mostly interested in `completion_year`. Check the range of the column with `range()` and the dollar operator to indicate the column.

```
# Range of completion years
range(egots$completion_year)
```

You get two values: the minimum and maximum. That's 1962 and 2023.

```
[1] 1962 2023
```

In the previous R examples, you made charts with built-in chart types, but you can also visualize data piecewise, which provides flexibility in what you want to make. Start with a blank plot with `plot()` and set the type to `n`, which stands for "no plotting." Also, set `yaxt` and `bty` to `n` so that there is no y-axis or bordering box.

```
# Blank plot
plot(NA,
     xlim=range(egots$completion_year), ylim=c(0,2),
     xlab="Completion Year", ylab="",
     yaxt="n", bty="n", type="n")
```

Shown in Figure 4.21, you get a blank plot with an x-axis that goes from 1962 to 2023 and an axis label. The y-axis ranges from 0 to 2. It's not much to look at now, but this is how I start many of my custom plots.

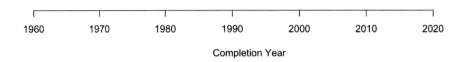

FIGURE 4.21 *Blank plot with x-axis*

Draw a horizontal line at y-coordinate 1 with `abline()`.

```
# Baseline
abline(h=1)
```

Then use `points()` to draw, well, points at the EGOT completion year on the x-axis, all at 1 on the y-axis. The `rep()` function creates a vector of repeating first values that is the length specified by the second value. The following creates a vector of eighteen 1s passed to `points()`:

```
# Points
points(egots$completion_year,
       rep(1, dim(egots)[1]))
```

The chart has points and a line across now, as shown in Figure 4.22.

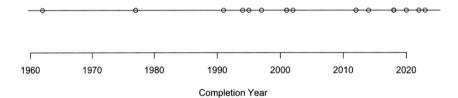

FIGURE 4.22 *A horizontal line added with* `abline()` *and points added with* `points()`

There's an issue. Some years, there are multiple people who achieved EGOT status, but multiple points just look like one on the timeline. For example, look at the data points for 2001:

```
egots[egots$completion_year == 2001, c("completion_year", "name")]
```

Mel Brooks and Mike Nichols earned the status that year:

```
   completion_year          name
10            2001   Mel Brooks
11            2001 Mike Nichols
```

Note: When points are plotted in the same area, the overlap can obscure patterns and make the data unreadable. This is called *overplotting*.

One quick solution is to use `jitter()`, which adds a small amount of noise to the data so that the points are not in the same spot. The following uses `jitter()` with both the x- and y-coordinates. While you're making edits, use `pch` to change the point symbol, `bg` to change the fill color, and `cex` to increase the size of each point.

```
# Jitter
points(jitter(egots$completion_year),
       jitter(rep(1, dim(egots)[1]), factor=2),
       pch=21, bg="#efe2aa", cex=2)
```

The years with multiple winners show more clearly, as shown in Figure 4.23.

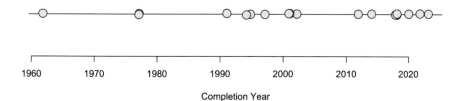

Completion Year

FIGURE 4.23 *Points with jitter*

The timeline could use annotation. Make a note for the first EGOT winner Richard Rodgers. To find his information, use `tail()` to see the last few rows in the `egots` data frame.

```
# Last rows of data frame
tail(egots)
```

Put together the annotation with `paste0()`, which is like `paste()`, but it assumes no space in between the text fragments. Then use `text()` to place the annotation for Rodgers.

```
# Annotation
anntext <- paste0(egots$name[18], "\ncompletes first \nEGOT in ",
                  egots$completion_year[18])
text(egots$completion_year[18]-1,
     1.5,
     anntext,
     pos=4)
```

Text placement is relative to text size and chart size, so the actual spot that text appears can be finicky. So, you might need to adjust the coordinates some to get the text where you want. In the previous code, the x-coordinate is on the year minus 1, and the y-coordinate is set at 1.5. Figure 4.24 shows the chart with the note.

You could make this timeline with a call to `plot()` with `type` set to `p` (for points), but this should give you an idea of how you can add components separately. This gives you the flexibility to make a chart how you want instead of settling for defaults.

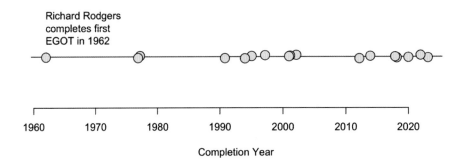

FIGURE 4.24 *Timeline with annotation*

DOT PLOT

Like a bar chart, the dot plot is a general chart type that can be used for various types of data. In the context of time, one axis represents time, and the other represents values, as shown in Figure 4.25.

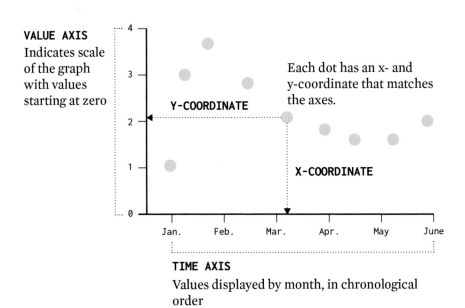

FIGURE 4.25 *Dot plot framework*

If you use each dot to represent an event, the geometry is similar to that of a timeline but with multiple categories or groups.

MAKING A DOT PLOT

Tools used: R, Illustrator

Dataset: EGOT winners, book.flowingdata.com/vt2/ch4/data
/EGOT-winners.csv

Instead of just looking at when individuals completed their EGOT status, it might
be more informative to look at when each person won their awards. What is
the path each person took to get to EGOT? Load the dataset with `read.csv()`
if you haven't done that yet.

```
# Load data
egots <- read.csv("data/EGOT-winners.csv")
```

Your goal is to make a dot plot where each row is a winner's timeline. There
will be a point for each award won, and each award gets its own color dot.
Make a vector of the columns that indicate when each person won their award
and indicate the colors for each award type. The following uses hexadecimal
format to represent colors, which is commonly used in web development.
Most of the color tools from Chapter 2, "Choosing Tools to Visualize Data," will
automatically convert colors to hexadecimal format for you.

```
# Awards and colors
year_cols <- c("emmy_year", "grammy_year", "oscar_year", "tony_
year")
award_colors <- c("#3F78E7", "#cb84cc",  "#BDB63B", "#83c4b3")
```

Make a blank plot with labels set to blank and `type` set to n.

```
# Blank plot
par(las=1)
plot(NA, xlim=c(1930, 2023),
     ylim=c(0, dim(egots)[1]),
     type="n", xlab="", ylab="")
```

Again, it's not much to look at now (Figure 4.26), but think of it as your
blank canvas.

Use a `for` loop to add points for each award type specified in `year _ cols`.
As a reminder, the code inside the brackets, {}, runs multiple times through
the range provided. In this example, you iterate through `year _ cols` and `i`
increases to the length of the vector.

```
# Points
for (i in 1:length(year_cols)) {
    points(egots[,year_cols[i]], 1:dim(egots)[1], pch=19)
}
```

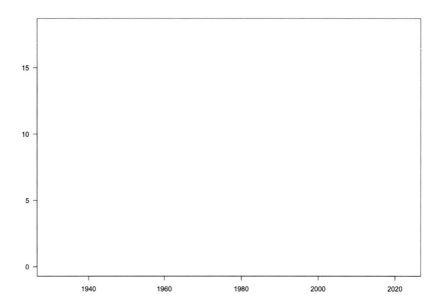

FIGURE 4.26 *Blank plot for multiple timelines*

This gives you a point for each award and winner, as shown in Figure 4.27.

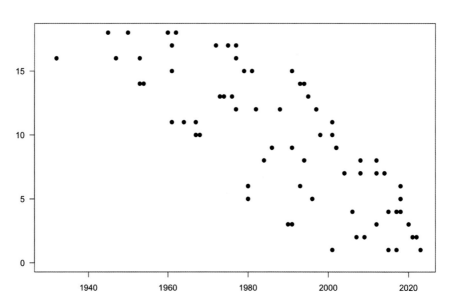

FIGURE 4.27 *Dots for all the awards*

Color would be good. Apply the colors from award _ colors in the for loop:

```
# With color
plot(NA, xlim=c(1930, 2023),
     ylim=c(0, dim(egots)[1]),
```

```
      type="n", xlab="", ylab="")
for (i in 1:length(year_cols)) {
    points(egots[,year_cols[i]], 1:dim(egots)[1],
           pch=21, cex=1.5,
           col="black",
           bg=award_colors[i])
}
```

Each dot is colored accordingly with a black border, as shown in Figure 4.28.

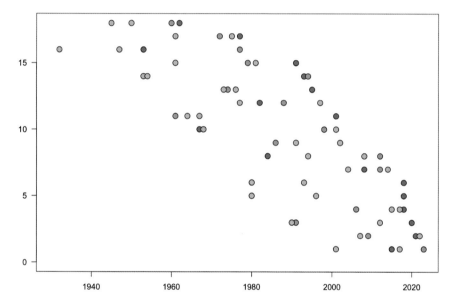

FIGURE 4.28 *Color applied to points*

To add connecting lines, create another `for-loop` before the calls to `points()` so that the lines are under the points. R runs code in the order that you provide, so you can imagine stacking layers on top of a chart with each snippet, like you might use brush strokes to add layers in a painting.

```
# Connect
plot(NA, xlim=c(1930, 2023),
     ylim=c(0, dim(egots)[1]),
     type="n", xlab="", ylab="")
for (j in 1:dim(egots)[1]) {
    endyrs <- range(egots[j, year_cols])
    lines(endyrs, c(j, j))
}
```

```
for (i in 1:length(year_cols)) {
    points(egots[,year_cols[i]], 1:dim(egots)[1],
            pch=21, cex=1.5,
            col="black",
            bg=award_colors[i])
}
```

In Figure 4.29, the lines make it clear that the points are connected on each horizontal.

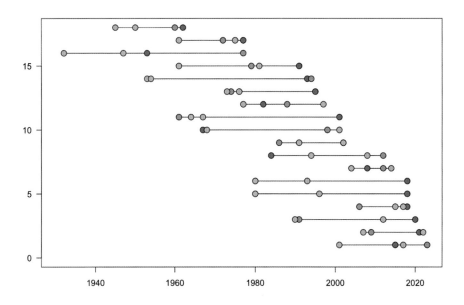

FIGURE 4.29 *Connecting the points with lines*

The y-axis is kind of useless right now, though. It's just numbers by default. It'd be useful to have the entertainers' names. Make a blank plot again, using the mar argument in `par()` to set a wider left margin. Set the y-axis type (`yaxt`) in `plot()` to n.

```
# Blank plot, margin
par(las=1, mar=c(4,12,2,2))
plot(NA, xlim=c(1930, 2023),
     ylim=c(0, dim(egots)[1]),
     yaxt="n", bty="n",
     type="n", xlab="", ylab="")
```

Use `axis()` to add the y-axis manually with labels set to the name column. Also add vertical grid lines.

```
# Axis and grid
axis(side=2, at=1:dim(egots)[1], labels = egots$name,
     tick=FALSE)
grid(NULL, 0, lty=1, lwd=.5)
```

This gives you a blank plot with names on the left side, shown in Figure 4.30.
If you did not set the wider margin on the left with `par()`, the names would
run off the screen.

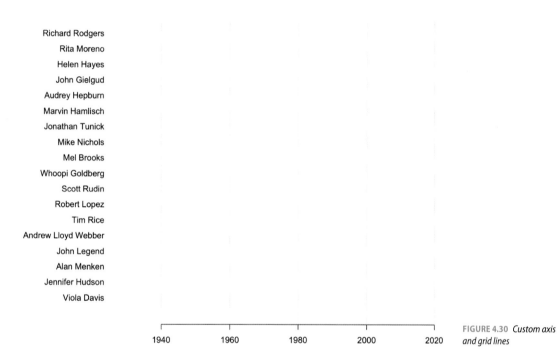

FIGURE 4.30 *Custom axis and grid lines*

Add the lines and points like before:

```
# Lines and points
for (j in 1:dim(egots)[1]) {
    endyrs <- range(egots[j, year_cols])
    lines(endyrs, c(j, j))
}
for (i in 1:length(year_cols)) {
    points(egots[,year_cols[i]], 1:dim(egots)[1],
           pch=21, cex=1.5,
           col="black",
           bg=award_colors[i])
}
```

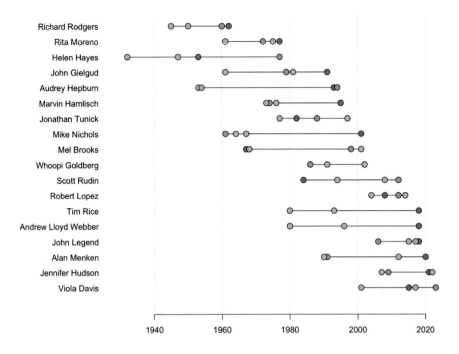

FIGURE 4.31 *Points and lines added*

Figure 4.31 shows a chart with a timeline for each entertainer.

Remember that if any of the functions seem foreign to you, enter a ? followed by the function name in the R console to check out the documentation.

Save the chart as a PDF file. With the R GUI, you can select the menu File ➤ Save As and in RStudio select Export ➤ Save As PDF. Alternatively, you can use pdf() to export, but I prefer to use the menus so that I can quickly test dimensions.

If you've never used Adobe Illustrator, check out the quick-start guide for the basics at https://datafl.ws/7o2.

Edit the Chart   It's time to try Adobe Illustrator for small edits. Nothing too crazy. You'll add notes to indicate what each color represents, change fonts, and align text.

Open the saved PDF file. You can also use egot-winners-raw-dots.pdf found in this chapter's source download if you didn't export from R. You should see a view like Figure 4.32.

Save the PDF as an Illustrator file (with a .ai extension) so that you don't lose edits.

From the tools menu, pick the Direct Selection tool. Click and drag over the outer edge of the chart, as shown in Figure 4.33. This is a rectangle-shaped

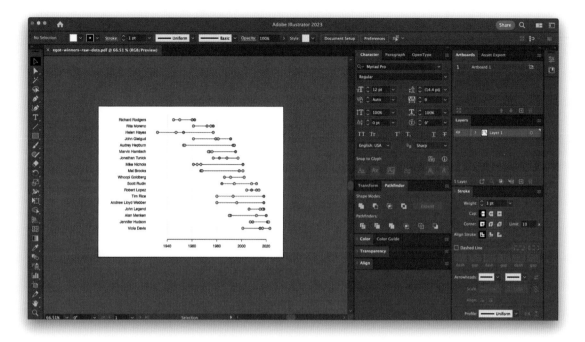

FIGURE 4.32 *PDF opened in Illustrator*

clipping mask, which encapsulates the objects in its area and hides objects that are beyond the mask border. Press Delete or Backspace to remove it. In this example, nothing is hidden by the mask, but deleting the mask makes it easier to select objects in the chart.

Still using the Direct Selection tool , select the names on the left. In Figure 4.34, you can see the blue dots on the left side of each name label. These are the *anchors* and indicate that the text is left-aligned. The labels look right-aligned now, but if you change the size or the font of the text, that will change.

Figure 4.35 shows alignment options. With the name labels still selected, click the icon that has lines that are aligned right. The blue dots should be on the right of the labels now.

To align the labels based on the new anchors, click the icon in Figure 4.36 that shows bars on the left and a vertical line on the right. This aligns objects to the right.

Change the font through the menu shown in Figure 4.37. Your options will vary depending on what fonts you have installed on your computer.

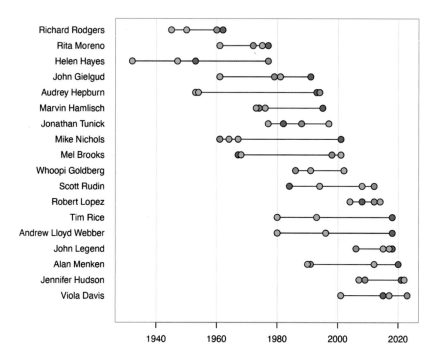

FIGURE 4.33 *Clipping mask selected for deletion*

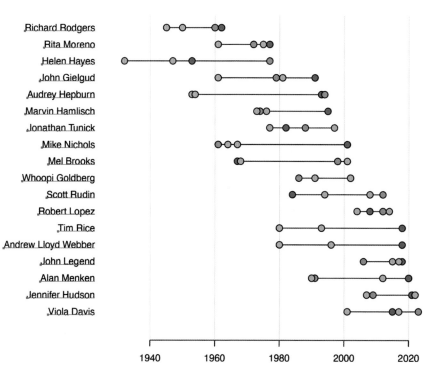

FIGURE 4.34 *Anchors on the left*

FIGURE 4.35 *Text alignment options*

FIGURE 4.36 *Object alignment options*

Figure 4.38 shows labels in Inconsolata.

Figure 4.39 shows options for changing stroke weight, among other things. Figure 4.40 shows color options.

The general theme for editing charts is that you can select objects and change their properties—stroke, color, size, alignment, and other things—by clicking options. You can remove objects. You can add objects. You immediately see what the changes look like so that you can adjust as needed.

Figure 4.41 shows a few more simple edits to the dot plot, mainly direct labels to specify what each color means and a source on the bottom. Try using the Type tool to add the annotation to your chart. With the Type tool selected, you can click the artboard and add your text, or you can click and drag to add a text box with word wrapping.

If you're new to this kind of illustration software, all the buttons can seem like a lot. It takes some getting used to, but you don't have to learn how to use every single tool available. The ones mentioned will get you far with chart editing, and with practice, you figure out what options you need most of the time. So, don't worry if it seems like a bit much. You'll see more in upcoming examples.

FIGURE 4.37 *Font options*

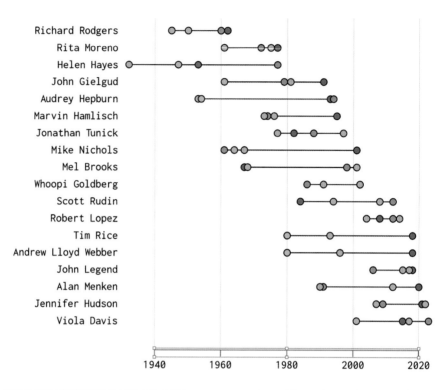

FIGURE 4.38 *Changed font and alignment*

FIGURE 4.39 *Stroke options*

FIGURE 4.40 *Color options*

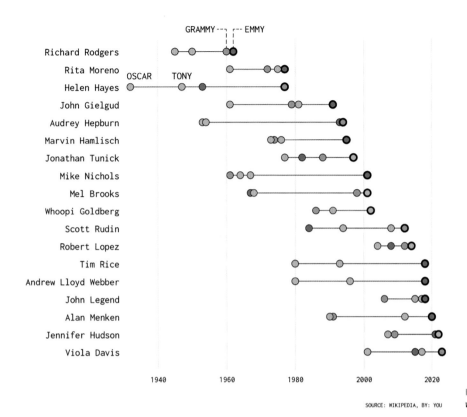

SOURCE: WIKIPEDIA, BY: YOU

FIGURE 4.41 *Added labels with Type tool*

Visual Hierarchy

For visualization, software tends to default to flat charts where each element is given equal visual weight. The axes stand out just as much as the data itself, and background data elements look the same as the points you want to draw focus to.

For example, Figure 4.42 shows a line chart that represents the number of Social Security cards distributed each year between 1880 to 2018, for boys and girls. All the elements—data lines, grids, axes, and labels—are visually on the same level.

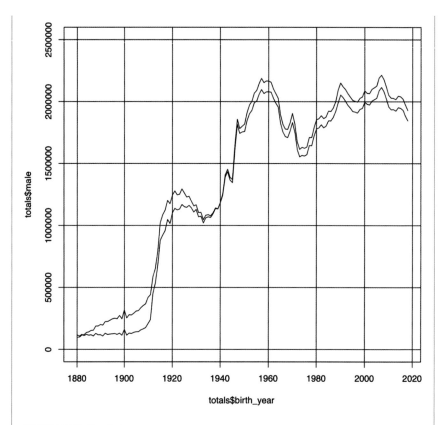

FIGURE 4.42 *Flat line chart*

To make the data stand out more from the chart's supporting elements, design with a *visual hierarchy* in mind. Make the elements that are more important *look* more important. This directs the reader where to look and how to interpret your chart.

The updated chart in Figure 4.43 highlights the data better with trend lines that are different colors from the rest of the chart. Labels are smaller. Grid lines are more subtle. Lines are labeled.

Match visual weight to the insight you want to communicate.

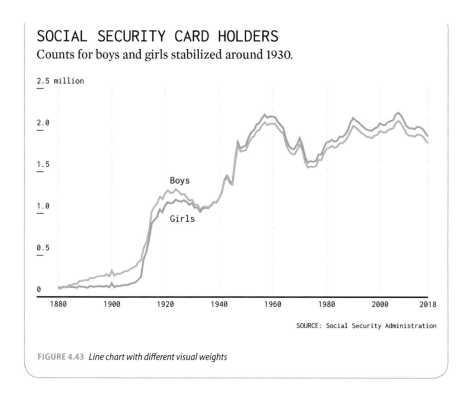

FIGURE 4.43 *Line chart with different visual weights*

CYCLES

Weeks repeat with five weekdays and a weekend. Years repeat every twelve months. The four seasons repeat every year. Are there patterns tied to these repetitions? If there are, are the overall patterns changing, or is it the same thing every cycle?

Figure 4.44 shows the percentage of people in different age groups who are alone over a 24-hour period. There is a recurring pattern of spikes in the morning and dips in the afternoon. The overall percentage rises by age.

When visualizing cycles, you often use similar geometries that you've used so far but cut the data in a way that focuses on repetition. Then place the slices in a way that encourages comparisons.

MORE TIME SPENT ALONE AS WE GET OLDER

Out of women who reported being awake

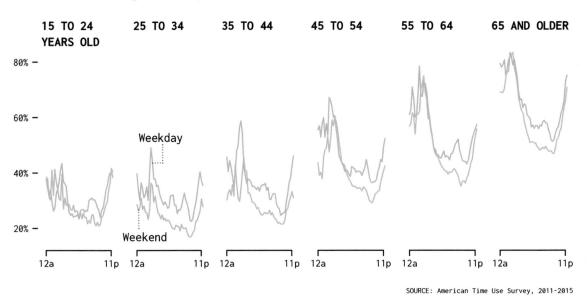

FIGURE 4.44 *"Alone Time,"* `https://datafl.ws/alone`

MULTI-LINE CHART

The geometry of a multi-line chart is the same as a standard line chart with only one line. The former just has more lines on the same scale. Each line might represent a category, a group, or, like in the following example, a timeframe.

The tricky part is when you have a lot of lines to draw. The chart can quickly get too busy and start to look like spaghetti. The key is to differentiate the lines so that you can tell which line represents what. If that doesn't work, you might consider splitting up the data into multiple charts.

MAKING A MULTI-LINE CHART

Tools used: R, Adobe Illustrator

Dataset: Marital status by age, `https://book.flowingdata.com/vt2/ch4/data/mar_w_age_all.tsv`

People are getting married later in life. In the 1940s, people typically married in their early 20s, whereas these days, people typically marry in their late 20s and early 30s. That's just for people who get married. There are many beyond their 30s who are not married. How common is it for someone to be married, and how does that change with age? How much has the commonness of marriage shifted over the years?

Load a dataset of marital status by age, from 1900 to 2021, with `read.csv()`.

```
# Load data
marstat <- read.csv("data/mar_w_age_all.tsv", sep="\t")
```

Use `head()` to see the first rows of the data and to make sure it loaded correctly. You should get a row for each year, age, and marital status. The `n` column is the number of people, and `prop` is the proportion of the population with a given `AGE` who recorded a given marital status, `MARST`, that year.

```
  YEAR AGE MARST       n prop
1 1900   0     6 1916975    1
2 1900   1     6 1750946    1
3 1900   2     6 1825203    1
4 1900   3     6 1825021    1
5 1900   4     6 1826842    1
6 1900   5     6 1804255    1
```

Marital status is encoded as numbers in this dataset, which comes from the decennial Census in the United States. Use `unique()` on the `MARST` column to see the values.

```
unique(marstat$MARST)
```

You get a vector of values 1 through 6.

```
[1]  6  1  2  4  5  3
```

A `MARST` of `1` represents married and the spouse is present, which is the only status you need for this example. Subset using bracket notation.

```
# Subset married
married <- marstat[marstat$MARST == 1,]
```

For now, you only want the rows for the year 2021, so use the bracket notation again on the `married` subset.

```
married2021 <- married[married$YEAR == 2021,]
```

The `married2021` subset shows the proportions for married people in 2021 at different ages.

```
      YEAR AGE MARST      n         prop
5800 2021   15     1   4514 0.001041716
5805 2021   16     1   5579 0.001283682
5811 2021   17     1   6648 0.001556808
5817 2021   18     1 15756 0.003486387
5823 2021   19     1 40502 0.009453335
5829 2021   20     1 98929 0.022342840
```

Start a blank chart with `plot()` like in previous examples, with the type set to n. Set the y-axis limits from 0 to 100, with `ylim` set to `c(0, 100)`. Also set `xaxt` and `yaxt` to n to add custom axes in the next step.

```
par(las=1)
plot(married2021$AGE, married2021$prop*100,
     ylim=c(0, 100),
     type="n",
     bty="n", xaxt="n", yaxt="n",
     xlab="", ylab="",
     main="Proportion of people married, by age")
```

Add axes with `axis()`: first the x-axis with no ticks and then the y-axis with labels from 0 to 100, in increments of 20.

```
axis(1, tick=FALSE)
axis(2,
     at=seq(0, 100, by=20),
     labels=paste0(seq(0, 100, by=20), "%"),
     tick=FALSE)
```

Then use `grid()` to add a grid with default settings.

```
grid()
```

This gives you a blank chart, shown in Figure 4.45. You've done this a few times now. Basically, you're setting up your canvas to draw some data instead of using `plot()` to draw the full chart.

Use `lines()` to draw a line showing married proportions by age.

```
lines(married2021$AGE, married2021$prop*100,
      lwd=2,
      col="#b31dc2")
```

Now, you have a line chart in Figure 4.46.

To draw a chart with multiple lines, start the same way with a blank chart using `plot()`, `axis()`, and `grid()`.

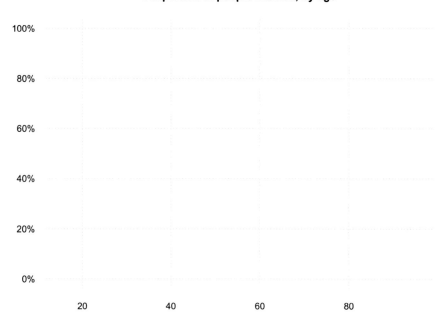

Proportion of people married, by age

Proportion of people married, by age

FIGURE 4.45 *Blank chart with axes and grid*

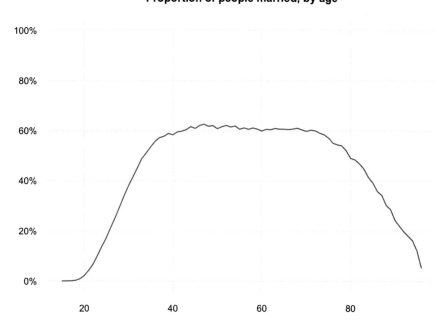

FIGURE 4.46 *Line chart for single year*

```
# All available years
plot(married2021$AGE, married2021$prop*100,
     ylim=c(0, 100),
     type="n",
     bty="n", xaxt="n", yaxt="n",
     xlab="", ylab="")
axis(1, tick=FALSE)
axis(2,
     at=seq(0, 100, by=20),
     labels=paste0(seq(0, 100, by=20), "%"),
     tick=FALSE)
grid()
```

To keep things spicy, use `abline()` to add a baseline at zero.

```
abline(h=0, lwd=2)
```

Instead of using a subset for 2021, you want to draw a line for each available year. Use `unique()` to find each year in the YEAR column of the `married` data frame.

```
years <- unique(married$YEAR)
```

This assigns a vector of values to years, which is a range of decades from 1900 to 2010, ending with 2021.

```
[1] 1900 1910 1920 1930 1940 1950 1960 1970 1980 1990
2000 2010 2021
```

Use a `for` loop to iterate through the `years` values. Subset for the current year on each iteration and draw lines with the subset.

```
for (yr in years) {
    curr <- married[married$YEAR == yr,]
    lines(curr$AGE, curr$prop*100,
          col="#b31dc2")
}
```

A line is added for each year to the chart shown in Figure 4.47. Although each line has the same line width, it's hard to say which line represents the most recent year and which direction the distribution is going.

To give a sense of movement, you can make the lines for more recent decades thicker and the lines for older decades thinner. Make a blank plot like before and then use a `for` loop to draw a line for each year. Except this time, change the line width, `lwd`, when you call `lines()`, based on how far from 2021 it is. The line for 2021 will be the thickest with no more than a width of 3, using the `min()` function to take the minimum between 3 and the calculated width.

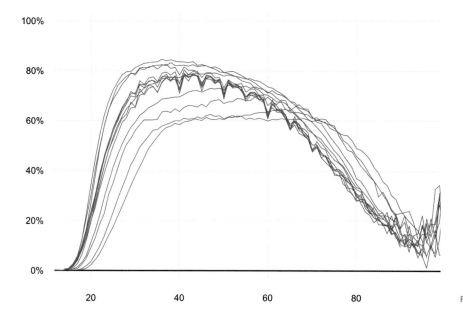

FIGURE 4.47 *Multi-line chart*

I experimented to get to this point, which will be common when you visualize your own data.

```
# Change line width for each year
for (yr in years) {
    curr <- married[married$YEAR == yr,]
    lines(curr$AGE, curr$prop*100,
        lwd=min(c(3, 15*1/(2021-yr+.5))),
        col="#b31dc2")
}
```

In Figure 4.48, you can see the percentages decreasing and the distributions stretching out over time. There's a sense of movement in the lines even though they're static. Some might argue that it'd be better to make a separate line chart for each decade, but it's easier to see the repeated pattern slightly shifted in the multi-line view.

Edit the Chart   From here, you can export the chart with functions like png() or pdf(). If the chart is only for your eyeballs, you might just move on to the next chart to further explore your data. Figure 4.49 shows an example of the previous chart lightly edited and annotated for clarity.

See an animated version of multi-line charts for different marital statuses at https://datafl .ws/7m7.

The spacing, alignment, and font match my taste. Find what works best for you and your applications.

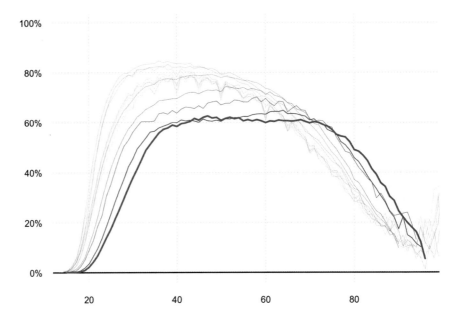

FIGURE 4.48 *Specified line width to show passing time*

PEOPLE MARRYING LATER

Each line represents a decade from 1900 to 2021. Thicker lines are more recent.

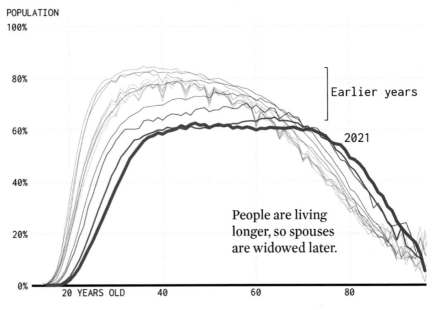

FIGURE 4.49 *Edited multi-line chart*

SOURCE: U.S. CENSUS BUREAU, IPUMS

HEATMAP

The heatmap is a direct translation of a data table. You replace numbers with colors to represent the values, as shown in Figure 4.50.

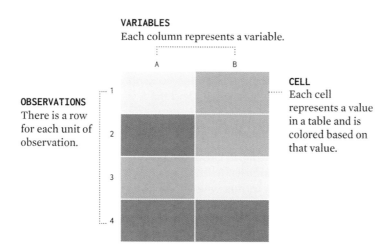

VARIABLES
Each column represents a variable.

OBSERVATIONS
There is a row for each unit of observation.

CELL
Each cell represents a value in a table and is colored based on that value.

FIGURE 4.50
Heatmap framework

You end up with a grid the same size as the original data table, and you find high and low values based on color. Typically, dark or more saturated colors mean greater values, and lighter or less saturated colors represent lower values, but that can easily change based on application.

Note: This is when the color-picking tools listed in Chapter 2 are especially useful. Select colors that are relevant to the data topic, and because heatmaps rely heavily on color, make sure readers can see the differences.

MAKING A HEATMAP

Tools used: Python, R, Adobe Illustrator

Dataset: Fatal motor vehicle crashes involving alcohol, https://book .flowingdata.com/vt2/ch4/data/month_hour_pct_matrix.csv

Image for editing: https://book.flowingdata.com/vt2/ch4 /pmat-heatmap.pdf

In 2015, based on data from the National Highway Traffic Safety Administration, there were 31,917 recorded fatal car crashes that led to 35,092 deaths. Alcohol was involved in many of the crashes, but it varies by time of day. The heatmap from Chapter 2, in Figure 2.12, shows the hourly break-down by month.

You can download the Python and R scripts to make a heatmap at http://datafl.ws/heatmaps.

The chart was made in Python, and like with R, you can export figures as PDF files. This means you can edit the chart in Illustrator. This isn't specific to programming languages either. If you can save a file or export an image as a PDF, you can import it into Illustrator, which is nice if you want to edit by hand.

Edit the Chart   In this example, you'll focus on editing, but you can download the scripts if you want to make a heatmap yourself. The Python version uses the seaborn library to make a heatmap, and the R version uses the `symbols()` function to draw a bunch of squares. If you want to skip to the editing, down-load the PDF version linked at the beginning of this example.

Open the `pmat-heatmap.pdf` file in Illustrator. Through the File ➤ Save As menu, save the PDF as an Illustrator file (with the `.ai` extension). This assures your edits are saved in the right format when you open the file later.

Remove the clipping masks like before by clicking, dragging, and deleting with the Direct Selection tool. Try changing the fonts used by selecting text. Figure 4.51 shows labels with the Inconsolata font, but you can pick what you want.

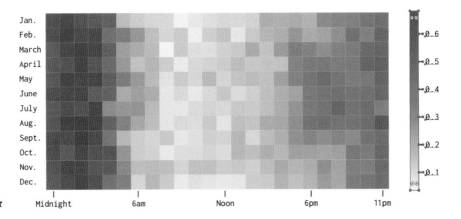

FIGURE 4.51 *Changing label font*

You can select each label with a click, but sometimes it's hard to select text because other objects in the way. One solution is to select a single text object and then use Select ➤ Same to automatically select other matching objects. Figure 4.52 shows the menu options.

Notice the tick marks for time in Figure 4.52? You can use the Pen tool  to draw straight line segments.

Maybe you want to rotate the legend so that it's horizontal instead of vertical. Use a selection tool to click and drag on the legend, and then move your cursor over one of the corners so that a curved arrow appears. Rotate as you like. Hold down the Shift key as you rotate, and it forces rotation in 45-degree increments.

If you selected the full legend with the color scale and numbers and rotated 90 degrees, you would have Figure 4.53. To rotate the labels so that they read horizontally, you could select each one individually and rotate.

There are only six labels, so that would be straightforward. However, you can also select all the labels and via the menu select Object ➤ Transform ➤ Transform Each, and you get the options in Figure 4.54.

FIGURE 4.52 *Menu to select same objects*

Enter **-90°** in the Rotate section to make the labels horizontal. A negative value rotates an object clockwise, and a positive value rotates counterclockwise. From here, you can move elements

FIGURE 4.53 *Rotated labels*

around and organize how you want. Try using the Type tool **T** to add headers or other annotations. Figure 4.55 shows an edited heatmap with a header and a resized legend on the bottom.

WRAPPING UP

It's fun to explore patterns over time. Time is so embedded in our day-to-day lives that many aspects of visualizing time series data are intuitive. You understand things changing and evolving—the hard part is figuring out by how much and learning what to look for in your charts. Start with questions about trends, events, and cycles. Let the answers lead you to more questions and repeat.

FIGURE 4.54 *Transform Each options*

You used R with Illustrator to accomplish this. With R, you built the base, and with Illustrator, you developed a visual hierarchy to direct readers' attention.

In the next chapter on visualizing categories, you use these skills and tools with some others. Even though you'll work with a different type of data, think about how you can apply a similar charting and design process.

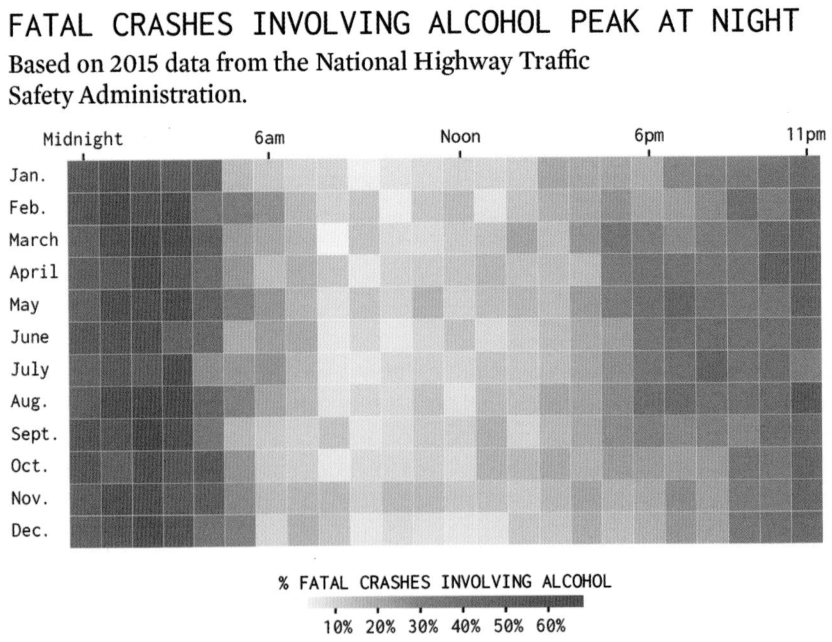

FATAL CRASHES INVOLVING ALCOHOL PEAK AT NIGHT

Based on 2015 data from the National Highway Traffic Safety Administration.

FIGURE 4.55 *Edited heatmap*

Visualizing Categories

What is the best? What is the worst? How does one choice compare to another? How are totals distributed across categories? The stories we tell with categorical data are based on comparisons. This chapter describes the charts that help make such comparisons easier.

When analyzing categorical data, you usually look at *amounts* to figure out scale and magnitude. Together, the categories might form a total, and you'll want to know how the *parts of the whole* are spread out. Then *rank and order* categories in a way that makes sense for your dataset and purpose, which draws focus to the highs and lows.

In a poll, people might be asked if they approve, disapprove, or have no opinion on an issue. Each category represents an answer, and the sum of the parts represent a population. We compare metrics across demographics, such as age, sex, and race. We have food groups. We shop different departments. We watch and listen to various forms of entertainment.

In the sections that follow, you learn to highlight the differences and similarities in categorical data. You use what you learned in the previous chapter and get your first taste of making charts with Python. Then you take a step back from code and try a couple of streamlined point-and-click tools. See how code and point-and-click can be used together.

AMOUNTS

How much? How many? These questions are probably why numbers and data exist in the first place, so there better be ways to visualize the answers. There are, of course. You have the ever-reliable bar chart, which uses the length of rectangles to show data, but you can also generalize this as scaled symbols. Bigger shapes represent greater values, and smaller shapes represent lesser values.

Figure 5.1 shows how common it is for mathematicians and statisticians to marry people with different occupations, on a relative scale, using circles. If you are a mathematician or statistician, you're a lot more likely than the general population to marry another mathematician or statistician.

This is from an interactive graphic that lets you see the matches between hundreds of occupations, based on the American Community Survey. I called it the "Occupation Matchmaker." The size of the circles represent likelihood, so bigger circles mean more likely to marry. Colors represent occupation categories.

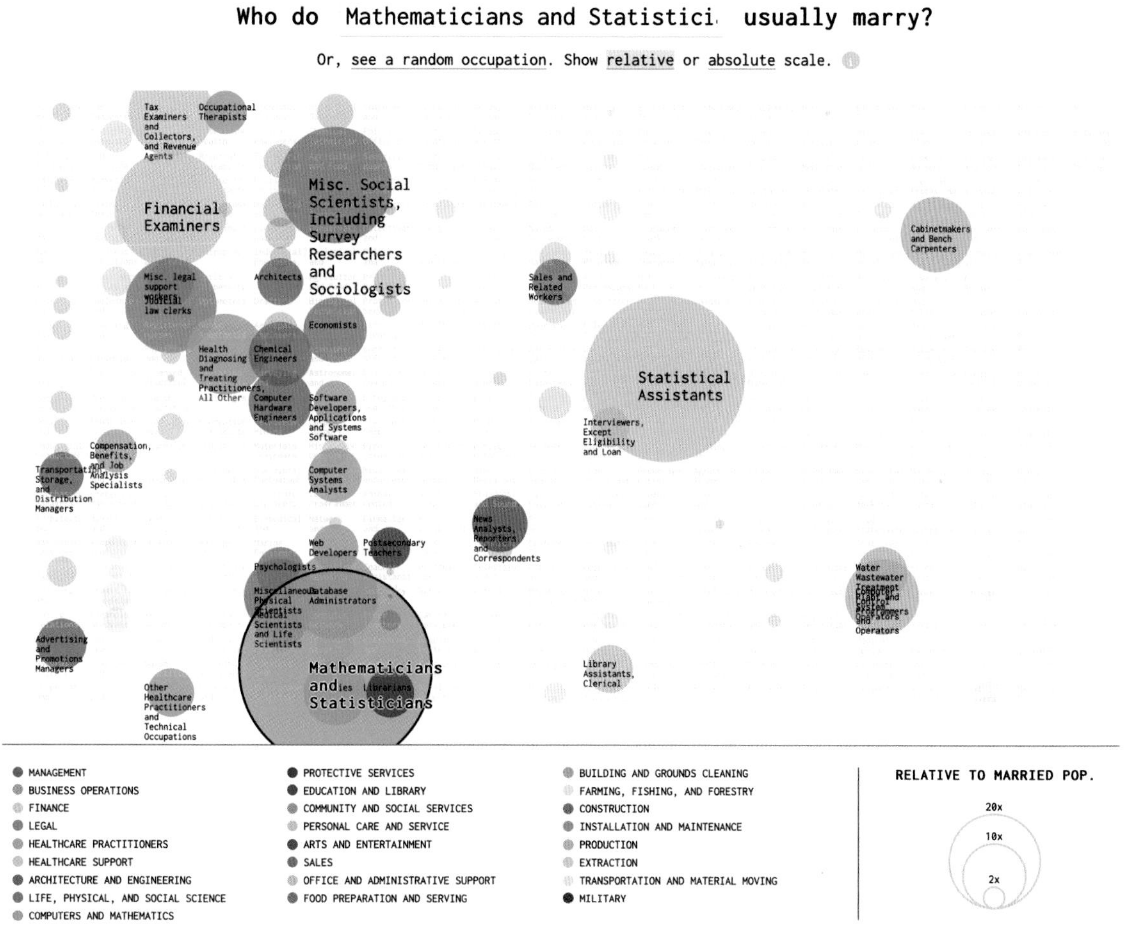

FIGURE 5.1 *"Occupation Matchmaker,"* FlowingData / `https://flowingdata.com/2017/08/28/occupation-matchmaker/` *last accessed 08 February, 2024.*

Overall, it's about how much and how many. Visualization provides a quick way to demonstrate scale, the range of your data from minimum to maximum, and how things are distributed in between.

BAR CHART FOR CATEGORIES

Bar charts for categories use the same visual encoding as the bar charts for time from Chapter 4, "Visualizing Time." The length of a bar represents a value in the data, so a longer bar means a greater value, a shorter bar means a lesser value, and a nonexistent bar means zero (or the data does not exist). The difference is that instead of using an axis to represent time, the axis is used to represent categories, as shown in Figure 5.2.

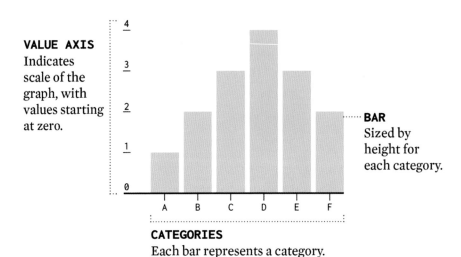

VALUE AXIS
Indicates scale of the graph, with values starting at zero.

BAR
Sized by height for each category.

FIGURE 5.2 *Categorical bar chart framework*

CATEGORIES
Each bar represents a category.

Bar charts for categories, like their time-based counterpart, should always start the value axis at zero. People often try to think of exceptions, but the exceptions require a stretch of the imagination and are always wrong.

MAKING A BAR CHART FOR CATEGORIES

Tools used: Python, Illustrator

Dataset: Occupations Married to Physicians, book.flowingdata.com/vt2/ch5/data/physician-marry.tsv

In the previous chapter, you used R to make a bar chart, and you can apply the same code in this example. It'll be a good exercise. However, it's good to be multilingual in your data explorations, so it's time to make a bar chart in Python.

The American Community Survey, which is run throughout the year by the U.S. Census Bureau, asks people about their occupation. I wondered if people with a given occupation were more likely to marry others with some other occupation. Are software engineers more likely to marry other software engineers? How common is it for a teacher to marry an economist? For a more straightforward view than the graphic from Figure 5.1, I made an interactive bar chart that showed the most common occupations.

Check out the most common occupations that marry at https://datafl.ws/occmar.

The dataset provides a subset. It represents the occupations of spouses who were married to physicians in 2018 and 2019. You'll make a bar chart showing the most common.

There are many ways to make a bar chart in Python. In this example, you use three libraries: Matplotlib, seaborn, and pandas. Matplotlib is a general visualization library, seaborn is built on top of the first to make charting more straightforward, and pandas makes it easier to handle data in Python. Import the libraries, as shown here:

```
import matplotlib.pyplot as plt
import seaborn as sns
import pandas as pd
```

Load the tab-delimited file `physician-marry.tsv` with `read_csv()` from the pandas library. The file path is relative to the directory you are in.

```
# Load data
marjobs = pd.read_csv("data/physician-marry.tsv",
delimiter="\t")
```

This assigns a *DataFrame* to `marjobs`, which is a two-dimensional data structure in Python that is like a data frame in R. This is what it looks like, which should match the TSV file:

```
code                              occname         p      n
 440                        Other managers  0.030421  31477
4850      Sales representatives, wholesale...  0.006934   7175
9130  Driver/sales workers and truck drivers  0.004522   4679
5730      Medical secretaries and administ...  0.000637    659
820               Budget analysts  0.000648    671
 ...                              ...       ...    ...
4530           Baggage porters, bellhops...  0.000184    190
2700                             Actors  0.000468    484
8450                         Upholsterers  0.000156    161
2723      Umpires, referees, and other sp...  0.000080     83
8850      Adhesive bonding machine operato...  0.000262    271
[441 rows x 4 columns]
```

There is one row per occupation. There are four columns that indicate the occupation code (`code`, as defined by the Census Bureau), the name of the occupation (`occname`), the proportion of physician spouses with the given occupation (`p`), and an estimated count (`n`).

Sort the rows by `p` with `sort_values()`.

```
# Sort by most common
marsorted = marjobs.sort_values(by=['p'], ascending=False)
```

With the data ready, you can set the dimensions of the chart, among other parameters.

```
# Set figure size and margin
sns.set(rc={'figure.figsize':(8,8), 'pdf.fonttype': 42 })
```

The previous code snippet uses `set()` from seaborn to set *rcParams*. This is like using `par()` in R to set graphical parameters. The `rc` stands for "run commands," which comes from Unix. The figure will be 8 by 8 inches, and by setting `pdf. fonttype` to 42, the text in the chart will be selectable if you export it as a PDF and edit in Illustrator.

Use `subplots()` to initialize the figure and axes and then `subplots_adjust()` to set a wider left margin:

```
fig, axes = plt.subplots(1, 1)
plt.subplots_adjust(left=.5)
```

The `subplots()` method can also be used to create a grid of charts in a single figure, but in the previous code you create a 1 by 1 grid so that you can set the left margin.

Make a bar chart for the 30 most common occupations that are married to physicians. Use `barplot()`, set the x argument to p, the y argument to `occname`, and the orientation (`orient`) to h for horizontal.

```
P1 = sns.barplot(data=marsorted[0:30],
    x="p", y="occname", orient="h")
```

Get the figure.

```
fig = p1.get_figure()
```

Save the figure as a PDF file.

```
# Save as PDF
fig.savefig("bar-mar.pdf")
```

You get a horizontal bar chart with 30 bars, each one representing an occupation, as shown in Figure 5.3. Physicians most commonly marry other physicians at about 1 in 5.

Like in previous examples, you can take the chart in various directions from here. If it's for analysis, you probably don't need anything more from this chart. The question is answered. For communication, the chart is still rough with cut-off labels and no explanation of what is shown. I'm not a fan of the default color scheme and the gray background. You can work with parameters to move things around and adjust for your needs, or you can click and drag in illustration software.

You can set a lot more parameters, and you can also set them with Matplotlib. See the docs at https://datafl .ws/7mi.

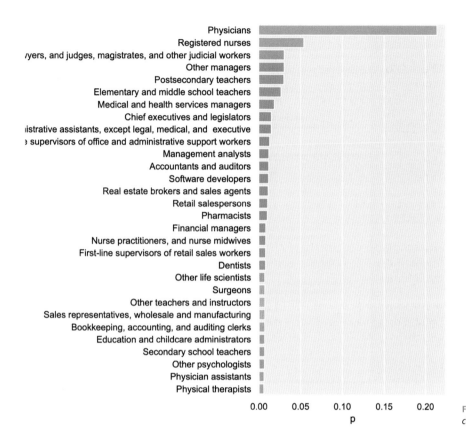

FIGURE 5.3 *Horizontal bar chart of occupations*

EDITING THE CHART

Like in the previous chapter, open the PDF file in Illustrator. If you didn't walk through the Python script, you can open the `bar-mar.pdf` file in the example files linked at the beginning of the book.

Select the outer edge of the chart with the Selection tool, and then right-click to get the menu shown in Figure 5.4. Select Release Clipping Mask.

The clipping mask hides everything outside its boundaries, which is why the labels in the original PDF are clipped. Figure 5.5 shows the chart without the clipping mask, so all the occupation labels and axis labels are visible.

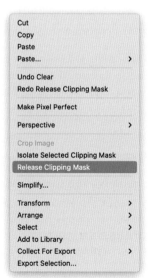

FIGURE 5.4 *Release clipping mask*

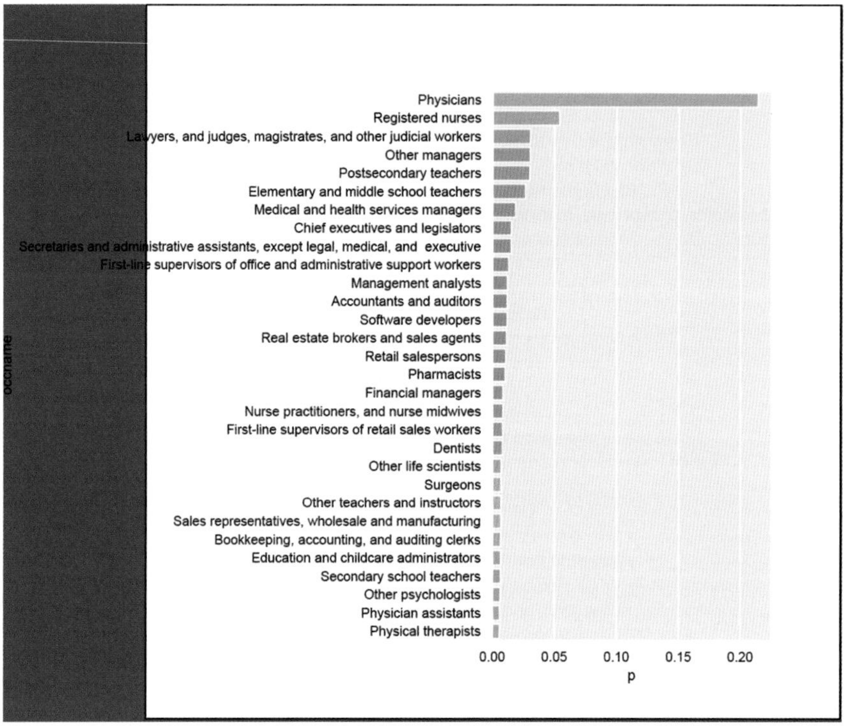

FIGURE 5.5 *Visible labels without a clipping mask*

With everything visible, select objects with the selection tools and edit as you like. Try changing the fonts, experiment with size, edit the colors, and annotate. Figure 5.6 shows an edited version with shortened labels, a different background grid, p changed to percentages, a zero-baseline, and some quick words.

These edits are based on personal taste, which has changed for me over time. I hope that you'll get a chance to develop your own style as you work on more charts. This comes with practice, I promise.

Just make sure you don't accidentally mess up the scales, geometries, or visual encodings as you manually edit. One way around this is to select the objects you don't want to edit and then select Object ➤ Lock ➤ Selection so that they can't be changed when you are editing. When you're done, select Object ➤ Unlock All. You can also lock layers via the Layers window.

Note: Some argue that editing software should be avoided, because it's too easy to mess up a visualization manually, but the same applies for code or point-and-click software.

SCALED SYMBOLS

Bar charts use length to represent values, which is one dimension. Scaled symbols use area, which is two dimensions, as shown in Figure 5.7. Different

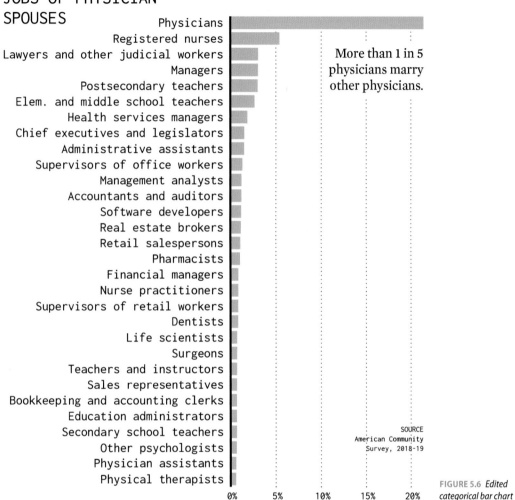

JOBS OF PHYSICIAN SPOUSES

More than 1 in 5 physicians marry other physicians.

SOURCE
American Community
Survey, 2018-19

FIGURE 5.6 *Edited categorical bar chart*

symbols and geometries can be used, such as squares, triangles, or icons, but circles tend to be the most common for now.

In the context of categorical data, each symbol represents a category and is sized based on the category's corresponding value. So in the physician marriage example, the circle for other physicians would be the largest, just like the bar is the longest in the bar chart, as you'll see in the following example.

The main thing to watch out for is that you size the symbols by area. Visualization software often lets you scale symbols, but they vary in how you specify size.

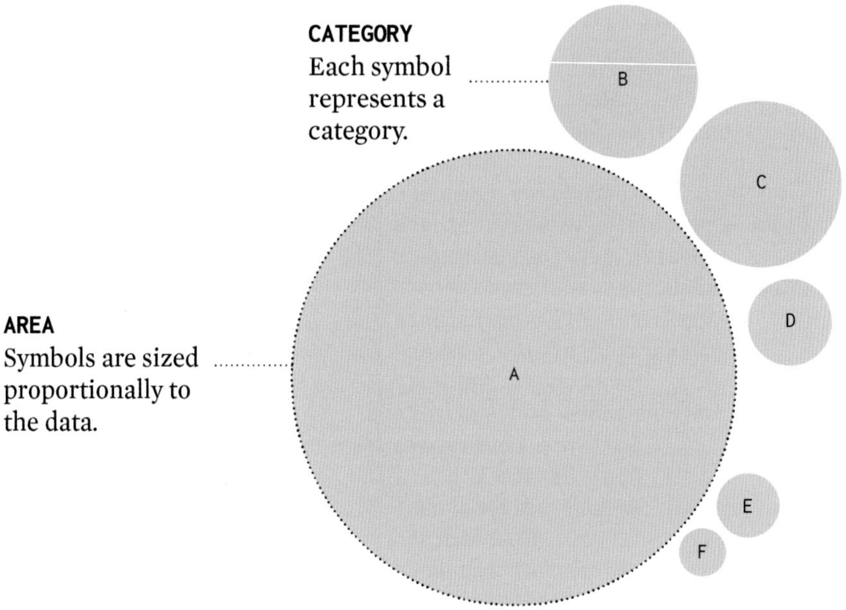

CATEGORY
Each symbol represents a category.

AREA
Symbols are sized proportionally to the data.

FIGURE 5.7 *Scaled symbols framework*

Some take radii as input, whereas some will automatically size by area. As shown in Figure 5.8, if you scale the radius directly by the data, you increase area exponentially, because the area of a circle is pi times the square of the radius. You don't want that. If a value is three times the size of another value, you want the corresponding symbols to be three times the size (by area) as the other.

In more practical terms, compare large and small pizza sizes: https://datafl.ws/pizza. It is a very serious matter.

Scaled symbols can be useful for showing a lot of categories at once because their positioning is not constrained to an x-y-coordinate space like a bar chart is. You can arrange the circles as you like. Although the area-based encoding has a trade-off (like all charts do): It's not as easy to see the differences between categories like with a bar chart. If you want to focus on small differences between categories, you might want to try a different chart type.

USING SCALED SYMBOLS

Tools used: Python, Illustrator

Dataset: Occupations Married to Physicians, book.flowingdata.com/vt2/ch5/data/physician-marry.tsv

We're back with the physician marriage data. This time, you use scaled symbols instead of the bar chart, which you can do with scatter() from

Say you wanted a circle that was three times the size of a base circle. Size by area or by radius?

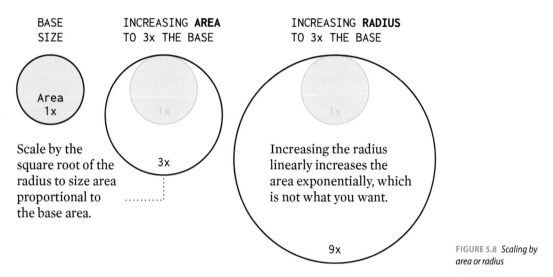

BASE
SIZE

INCREASING **AREA**
TO 3x THE BASE

INCREASING **RADIUS**
TO 3x THE BASE

Area
1x

1x

1x

Scale by the square root of the radius to size area proportional to the base area.

3x

Increasing the radius linearly increases the area exponentially, which is not what you want.

9x

FIGURE 5.8 *Scaling by area or radius*

Matplotlib. Start like before by importing the necessary libraries (no seaborn this time).

```
import matplotlib.pyplot as plt
import pandas as pd
```

Load the data and sort by p, taking just the top 10 for now.

```
# Load data
marjobs = pd.read_csv("data/physician-marry.tsv", delimiter="\t")
marsorted = marjobs.sort_values(by=['p'],
    ascending=False)[0:10] # Top 10.
```

This next part is different. You're going to line up 10 circles vertically from greatest at the top and least at the bottom. Specify the coordinates of each circle in a `DataFrame`:

```
# Prepare data for circles using bubble plot
mardf = pd.DataFrame({
    "x": [1, 1, 1, 1, 1, 1, 1, 1, 1, 1],
    "y": [10, 9, 8, 7, 6, 5, 4, 3, 2, 1],
    "r": list(marsorted.p * 50000)
})
```

This gives you a `DataFrame` with three columns for x, y, and r (for "radius"). The following is what it looks like. The first number in the row is an index.

```
     x   y               r
0    1  10    10705.998328
1    1   9     2692.506560
2    1   8     1526.473729
3    1   7     1521.061559
4    1   6     1503.278712
5    1   5     1330.330867
6    1   4      927.607386
7    1   3      757.510595
8    1   2      750.020537
9    1   1      648.928922
```

Set the `rcParams` for figure size and font size. In the first example, you set parameters with `set()` from the seaborn library, but this time you set the parameters via Matplotlib.

```
# Figure size
plt.rcParams['figure.figsize'] = (7, 10)
plt.rcParams['pdf.fonttype'] = 42
```

Use `scatter()` to make the scaled symbols using the coordinates from the `mardf` DataFrame.

```
# Plot
plt.scatter("x", "y", s="r", data=mardf)
```

Add a label with percentage and occupation name for each circle using `text()`.

```
# Text
for i in range(0, len(marsorted)):
    thelabel = str(round(100*marsorted.iloc[i].p)) + "%, "
    thelabel += marsorted.iloc[i].occname
    plt.text(1, 10-i, thelabel)
```

Save the figure as a PDF file.

```
# Save as PDF
plt.savefig("symbols-chart-mar.pdf")
```

You get 10 circles in a vertical line, as shown in Figure 5.9.

It's not much to look at, but maybe with some editing and limited vertical space, it could be of use. But let's try a wider grid that can accommodate more occupations on the page or screen.

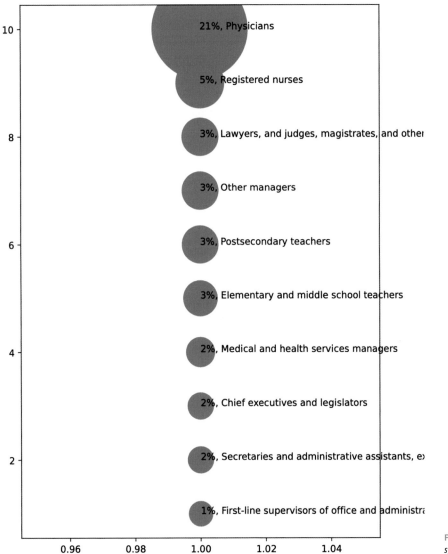

FIGURE 5.9 *Scaled symbols in a line*

Import the libraries.

```
import matplotlib.pyplot as plt
import numpy as np
import pandas as pd
```

This time, you import the numpy library, which provides methods that make handling numbers and doing math easier. Loading the `physician-marry.tsv` file is the same. Sort and get the top 49 occupations.

```
# Load data
marjobs = pd.read_csv("data/physician-marry.tsv", delimiter="\t")
marsorted = marjobs.sort_values(by=['p'], ascending=False)[0:49]
```

Imagine a 7 by 7 grid. Start at the top corner and then move to the right one position. In terms of x- and y-coordinates, the former increases by one, and because you stay on the same row, the y-coordinate stays the same. Move to the right again, and the x-coordinate increases by one again. The y-coordinate stays the same until you to go down to the next row. The x-coordinate goes back to the beginning, and the y-coordinate increments by one. You do this until you get to the last spot in the bottom-right corner. The following snippet calculates these x- and y-coordinates with a `for` loop by row and then with `repeat()`, by column:

```
# Grid coordinates for a 7x7 grid
x = []
for i in range(0, 7):
    x = x + list(range(0, 7))
y = list(reversed(np.repeat(np.arange(0,7), 7)))
```

Store the coordinates, the radius size (based on marriage proportions), the occupation name, and the proportions in a DataFrame.

```
# Prepare data for circles using bubble plot
mardf = pd.DataFrame({
    "x" : x,
    "y" : y,
    "r" : list(marsorted.p * 50000),
    "occname" : list(marsorted.occname),
    "p" : list(marsorted.p * 100)
})
```

This gives you a `DataFrame` with five columns assigned to `mardf`.

Set the `rcParams`. Make it bigger than last time at 13 by 13 inches, and set the PDF font type to 42 for editing text later.

```
# Figure size
plt.rcParams['figure.figsize'] = (13, 13)
plt.rcParams['pdf.fonttype'] = 42
```

Pass the data to `scatter()`.

```
# Plot
plt.scatter("x", "y", s="r", data=mardf)
```

Add text, this time iterating through `mardf` for each occupation.

```
# Text
plt.rcParams['font.size'] = 8
plt.rcParams['pdf.fonttype'] = 42
for i in range(0, len(mardf)):
    thelabel = str(round(mardf.p[i], 2)) + "%\n "
    thelabel += mardf.occname[i]
    plt.text(mardf.x[i], mardf.y[i], thelabel,
        horizontalalignment="center")
```

Save the figure as a PDF.

```
# Save as PDF
plt.savefig("symbols-grid-mar.pdf")
```

Figure 5.10 shows the result. It's a 7 by 7 grid, where each circle represents an occupation. The most common occupation, physician, is in the top left, and the ordering runs left to right and top to bottom.

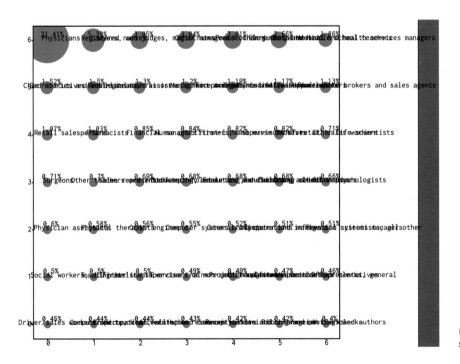

FIGURE 5.10 *Scaled symbols in a grid*

As expected, the grid is not the most readable of charts, but it has the right geometry. You can fix the rest in post.

EDITING THE CHART

Start with the line of top 10 occupations from Figure 5.9. It's `symbols-chart-mar.pdf` in example files. In Illustrator, use the Direct Selection tool 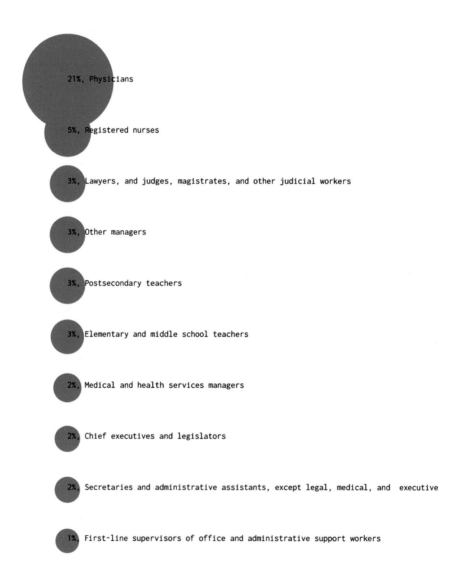 to highlight the clipping mask, outside box, and axes. Press Delete on your keyboard to remove them. Select the labels to change the font and size. Figure 5.11 uses Inconsolata and a smaller font size.

FIGURE 5.11 *No more axes, just scaled circles*

Using the Selection tool  select the circles. Right-click to ungroup the circles, as shown in Figure 5.12. Then with the circles still selected, but ungrouped now, navigate to Object ➤ Transform ➤ Transform Each. Through the menu shown in Figure 5.13, increase the horizontal and vertical size to 120%. This increases the size of each circle by 20% while maintaining their positions. If you transformed without ungrouping, the circles would collectively increase in size, which is not what you want in this case.

Try changing the color of the circles and cleaning up the labels with the Type tool T to match Figure 5.14.

Try similar editing with the grid of charts. The raw output was saved as `symbols-grid-mar.pdf`. Work with the sizes, organize the labels, and remove elements like the axes and border box to start. Figure 5.15 shows a clean version using transparency and no borders for the cir-

FIGURE 5.12 *Ungroup menu*

cles, which puts them more in the background of the labels than with the single line in Figure 5.14.

Edit the charts to how you want them. This can be a challenge because you have so many more possibilities than if you were to always stick with the defaults. It's the burden of choice. To ease the burden, think about what you want first and then design toward that goal instead of surveying all the possibilities and trying to filter. This makes for a more efficient design process.

PARTS OF A WHOLE

Categorical amounts often belong to an overall total. Demographic groups belong to an overall population. Portions of your total income go to taxes, to retirement, and to your checking account. The 24 hours in your day are split up by different activities. Together the parts form a whole.

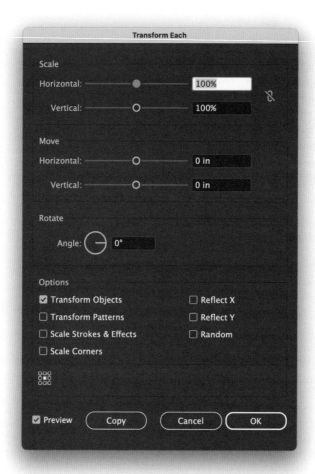

FIGURE 5.13 *Transform menu*

Which part makes up the largest percentage? Which parts are insignificant to the overall count? Which parts of the whole are useful? How is the total distributed across all categories?

Figure 5.16 shows a view from an interactive graphic about the demographics of others. The premise is that there are millions of people like you when you break down the population by broad demographics like sex, age, and race. But even when you look at different groups not like your own, you find areas of common ground.

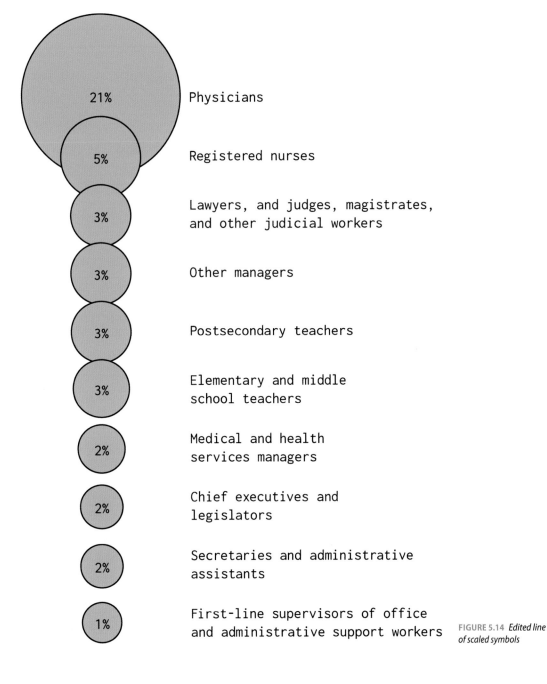

21% Physicians

5% Registered nurses

3% Lawyers, and judges, magistrates, and other judicial workers

3% Other managers

3% Postsecondary teachers

3% Elementary and middle school teachers

2% Medical and health services managers

2% Chief executives and legislators

2% Secretaries and administrative assistants

1% First-line supervisors of office and administrative support workers

FIGURE 5.14 *Edited line of scaled symbols*

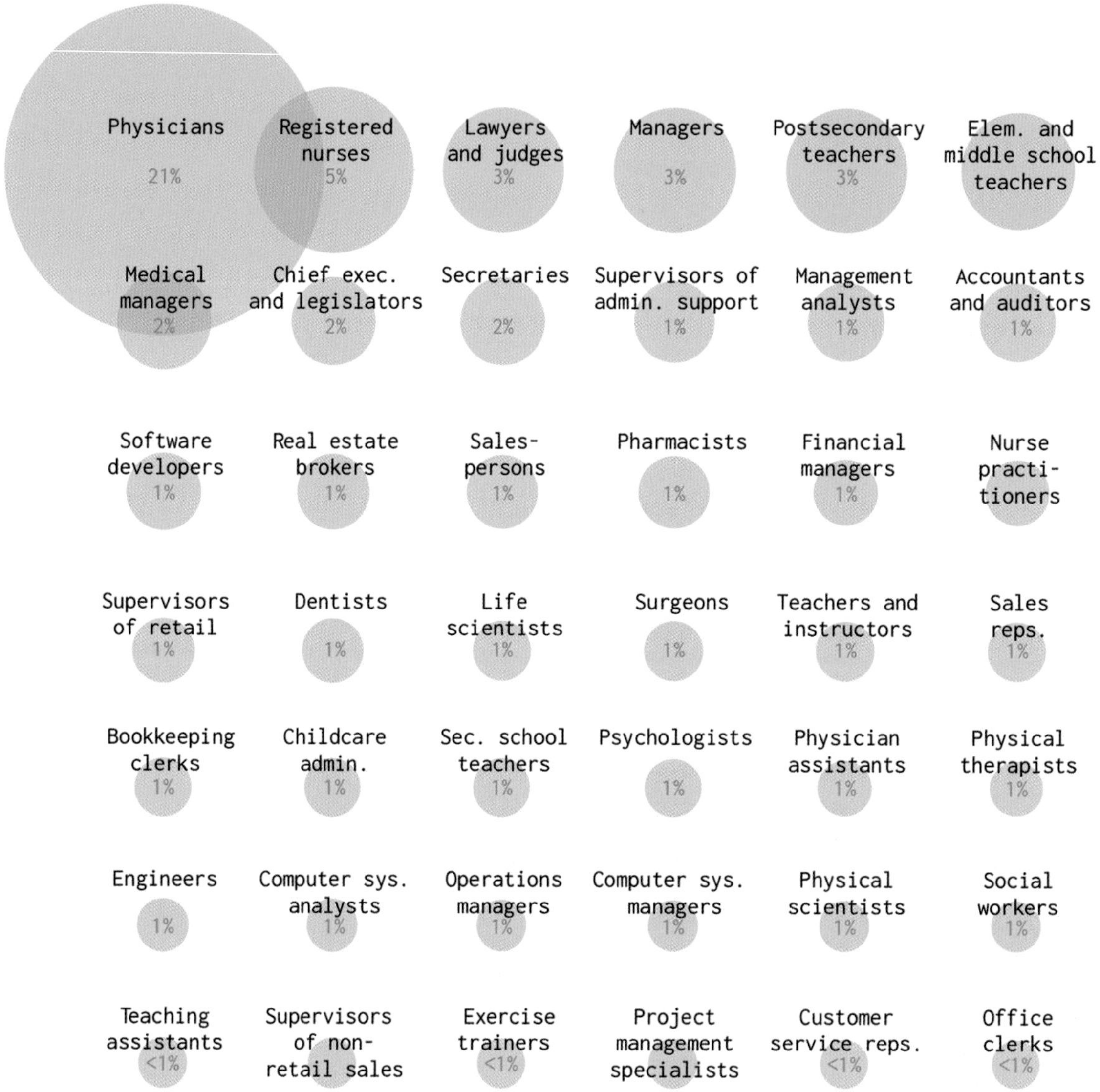

FIGURE 5.15 *Edited grid of scaled symbols*

An overall count along with a set of square pie charts update when you select different demographics. Each grouping of squares represents a whole, or 100%. The highlighted portion represents a portion of the whole.

While you can show percentages separately using the chart types you've seen already, there are views that emphasize how the parts fit together.

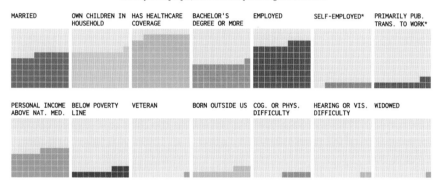

FIGURE 5.16 *"The Demographics of Others,"* FlowingData / https:// flowingdata.com/2018/ 01/23/the-demographics- of-others / *last accessed February 08, 2024.*

PIE CHART

The pie chart was created by William Playfair in the early 19th century, placing a focus on parts of a whole. However, more recently, there was a short period of time when a lot people decided that the food-based data slices weren't for them. Unlike a bar chart, which uses length to represent values, the pie chart uses angles, which are more difficult to read as quickly and accurately. You can read them, but it's harder to figure out the exact value each slice represents.

Even with all the haters, the pie chart persevered, and people seem to have softened their stance that the chart should be avoided at all costs. People still use pie charts. The chart is familiar to many people, and they read the slices with little complaint. That seems enough reason to keep the pies around.

The pie chart has limitations just like every chart. Work within those limitations, and you will be good. Figure 5.17 shows the framework. You start with a circle, which represents a whole, and then cut wedges, like you would a pie. Each wedge represents a part of the whole.

The percentage of all the wedges should add up to 100%. Be careful here, because most software spits out a pie chart whether or not your parts

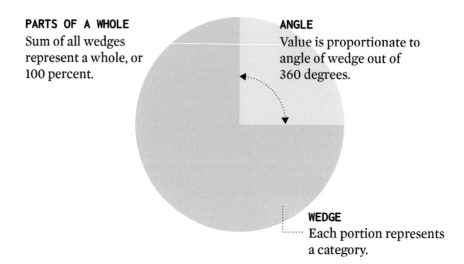

PARTS OF A WHOLE
Sum of all wedges
represent a whole, or
100 percent.

ANGLE
Value is proportionate to
angle of wedge out of
360 degrees.

WEDGE
Each portion represents
a category.

FIGURE 5.17 *Pie chart framework*

sum correctly. The software will just normalize the data as if it were counts. So, if the sum of the parts is anything other than 100%, you have done something wrong.

You also must limit the number of slices that you use in a single pie chart. As shown in Figure 5.18, space is limited to the 360 degrees of a circle. Increase the number of slices, and it gets harder to compare categories, especially for the small values.

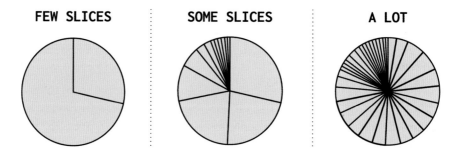

FEW SLICES   **SOME SLICES**   **A LOT**

FIGURE 5.18 *Limiting the slice count*

Try clumping smaller categories into an "other" category or making multiple pie charts that split up categories in a logical way. If that doesn't work, you might need a different chart.

MAKING A PIE CHART

Tool used: Datawrapper, `datawrapper.de`

Dataset: Meeting Online, `book.flowingdata.com/vt2/ch5/data /met-online-2010s.txt`

There are many ways to make a pie chart. Every visualization tool mentioned in Chapter 2, "Choosing Tools to Visualize Data," lets you easily make one. So far, you've made charts in R, Python, and Illustrator, which all have functions to make a pie chart. There are various ways to get the same result.

For this example, you'll check out the web-based tool Datawrapper. It's free to use for individuals and is very good at helping you make charts for the Web that work on all devices. You don't even have to create an account to get started, which is saying something these days.

Since 2009, researchers at Stanford University have been asking American couples how they met through the How Couples Meet and Stay Together (HCMST) survey. They publish the data so that others can also learn from the survey. The data used here is a small, processed subset of the data to answer a simple question: how commonly did people meet online in the 2010s?

The data is just two rows and two columns. The first column (`waymet`) is how people met, and the second column (`p`) is the percentage of people who said they met online or offline.

```
waymet,p
"Met Online",18.9
"Met Offline",81.1
```

Navigate to Datawrapper in your favorite browser. If you don't have an account, click the Start Creating button. If you have an account, go to the dashboard and select Create New ➤ Chart. Either way, you should see a place to copy and paste data, as shown in Figure 5.19.

Copy and paste the two-row data into the text area. Click Proceed. Datawrapper smartly guesses data formats and asks that you make sure it guessed right (Figure 5.20). If it looks right, proceed.

You get a grid of chart types to pick from. Select the pie chart option, and you get the chart shown in Figure 5.21.

About 1 in 5 couples who met in the 2010s met online. Mystery solved.

Tip: People often like to focus on the tools used to visualize data, but from a reader's point of view, a near-zero percentage of people care how we make charts. They just want to see the chart, which is liberating in some ways from a chart-maker point of view.

Find the full HCMST dataset at `https://data .stanford.edu /hcmst2017`.

FIGURE 5.19 *Adding data in Datawrapper*

FIGURE 5.20 *Formatting data*

There is a Refine tab next to Chart Type that lets you adjust the chart for your needs. Through the menus, change the color of the "Met Offline" slice to a light gray to emphasize the "Met Online" slice. Change the number format to show a percent symbol, as shown in Figure 5.22.

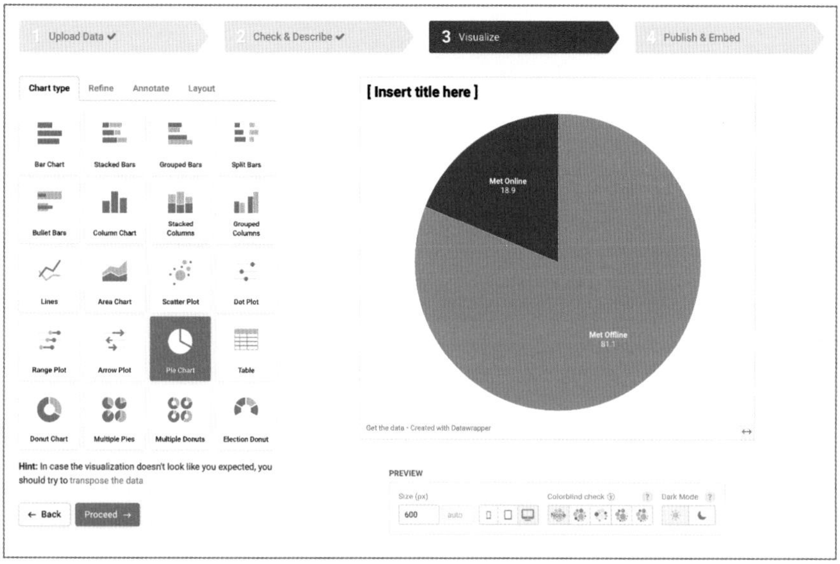

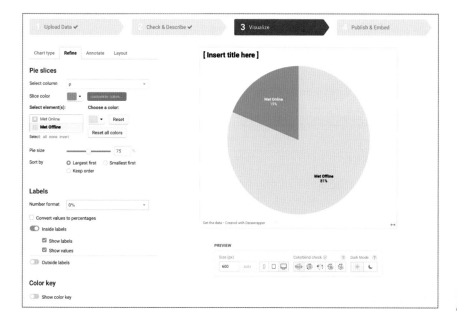

FIGURE 5.21 *Pie chart*

FIGURE 5.22 *Refine the pie chart.*

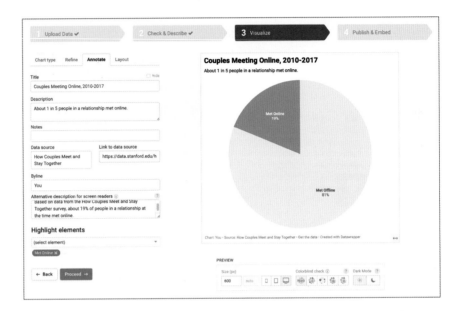

FIGURE 5.23 *Annotate the pie chart.*

Use the next tab over to annotate with a title, description, data source, and other information, as shown in Figure 5.23. Proceed.

At the end of the four-step process, you can either publish or export the chart to put online or prepare for print. That's it. With an account, the chart and data can be saved for later. For more customization options, you must upgrade to a paid plan, but the free plan is still useful.

DONUT CHART

Your good friend the pie chart also has a lesser cousin: the donut chart. It's like a pie chart, but with a hole cut out in the middle so that it looks like a donut, as shown in Figure 5.24.

Because there's a hole in the middle, you don't judge values by angle anymore. Instead, you use arc length. The same challenges with space and number of categories apply.

I tend to avoid the donut chart, and I don't think I've ever used a donut chart to show data in a project. To my eyes, pie charts look better. The hole in the middle pushes the data to the background, and I'm usually trying to move it to the foreground. But I leave the choice up to you.

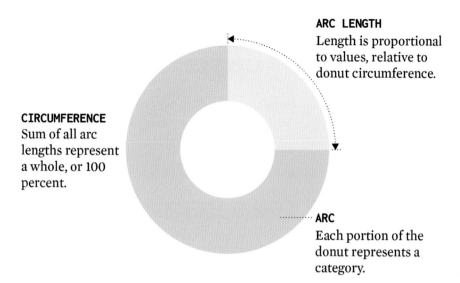

ARC LENGTH
Length is proportional
to values, relative to
donut circumference.

CIRCUMFERENCE
Sum of all arc
lengths represent
a whole, or 100
percent.

ARC
Each portion of the
donut represents a
category.

FIGURE 5.24 *Donut chart framework*

MAKING A DONUT CHART

Tool used: Datawrapper, datawrapper.de

Dataset: Meeting Online, book.flowingdata.com/vt2/ch5/data/met-online-2010s.txt

Sticking with Datawrapper and the HCMST dataset, you can easily switch from a pie chart to a donut chart. As shown in Figure 5.25, go back to step 3 in the process, select the Chart Type tab, and click Donut Chart. The settings from the pie chart stay the same.

Like before, you can refine, annotate, and adjust the layout. Publish or export when you're done.

All the charts that Datawrapper offers follow a similar process of loading data, checking the data, visualizing, and publishing. It's straightforward with an intuitive interface, which explains why so many news organizations use the application.

The trade-off is that you're limited to the chart types that are offered, and unless you have access to the paid offering, which is priced more for organizations, you can't customize as much.

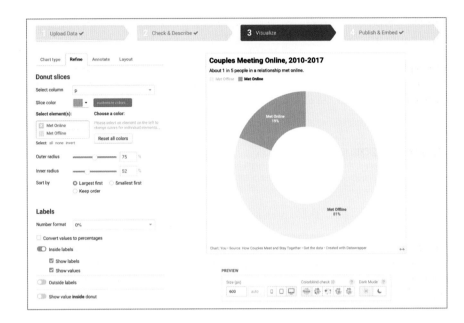

FIGURE 5.25 *Donut chart in Datawrapper*

Note: For FlowingData, I tend to make more ad hoc charts, so Datawrapper is not for me. But if you don't need to customize too much and just need solid charts (and maps) to share on the Web, then Data-wrapper is worth a try.

SQUARE PIE

Not everyone loves pie and donut charts. Sometimes, you just want more visual accuracy but still want to show the distribution of parts of a whole. Enter the square pie chart, also known as a *waffle chart*. Shown in Figure 5.26, it is usually a 10-by-10 grid for a total of 100 squares, and each cell in the grid represents a percentage point.

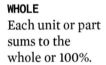
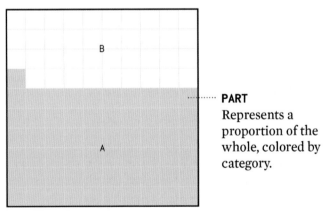

WHOLE
Each unit or part sums to the whole or 100%.

PART
Represents a proportion of the whole, colored by category.

FIGURE 5.26 *Square pie framework*

You see percentage points explicitly, so there are no issues with figuring out what geometry represents what value. You just count.

The square pie is a relatively new chart type, which means it doesn't come standard with a lot of software. But, if you can draw squares and fill in the colors, then you can make a square pie chart.

MAKING A SQUARE PIE CHART

Tool used: Illustrator

Dataset: Meeting Online, book.flowingdata.com/vt2/ch5/data /met-online.tsv

Based on the HCMST data, you can compare couples who met in the 1990s against those who met in the 2010s. As you might have heard, there was this Internet thing that came around that changed how we do a lot of things, including meeting significant others.

In the dataset file, which, again, is a simpler processed version of the full HCMST data, there is a row for each decade that indicates the proportion of couples who met online and offline.

```
"year"   "ponline"       "poffline"
1960     0.0042  0.9958
1970     0.0032  0.9968
1980     0.0002  0.9998
1990     0.0153  0.9847
2000     0.0949  0.9051
2010     0.189   0.811
```

We'll focus on the 1990s and 2010s. In the 1990s, only 1.5% of people reported meeting online, whereas in the 2010s, that figure rose to 18.9%. The square pie requires round percentages, though, so we'll say 2% and 19%, respectively. Meeting online has gotten way more popular (and I'm guessing more so in the 2020s). It's kind of funny to think back to when meeting online seemed strange.

Open a new document in Illustrator. The first step is to make a grid.

Using the Pen tool ✐, create a straight horizontal line. Click and release and then, while holding the Shift key on your keyboard, click and release to where you want the other end of the line. This should give you a single line. Do this 10 more times to make 11 horizontal lines total, one on top of the other, as shown in Figure 5.27. Create 11 vertical lines in the same way.

Select the vertical lines and evenly distribute them horizontally ⬛ via the Align window. Then select the horizontal lines and evenly distribute them vertically ⬛. You should have something like the second step in Figure 5.27.

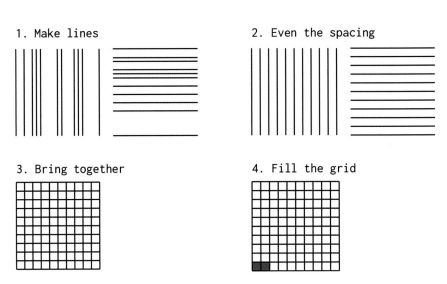

1. Make lines

2. Even the spacing

3. Bring together

4. Fill the grid

FIGURE 5.27 *Making a grid in Illustrator*

Note: You might have to resize the lines to make a square, in which case select and then click and drag so that width and height are equal for both the horizontal and vertical lines. You can also enter width (W) and height (H) in the properties panel, which typically appears at the top of your screen when you select objects.

Select the vertical lines and drag them over the horizontal lines to create a grid.

Click and drag to select the lines. Select the Live Paint Bucket tool ⬛. Choose your border (i.e., stroke) and fill color via the Color window and then hover over the selected grid of lines. Click. The selected square should change color like in the fourth step of Figure 5.27.

This gives you a single square pie that you can use to represent percentage values. Copy and paste to make additional square pies. Figure 5.28 shows a comparison between the 1990s and 2010s.

If you're new to Illustrator, this probably seems like a lot of random clicking and dragging with a sprinkle of various tools. Starting a chart from scratch isn't as straightforward as editing an existing chart, and it admittedly takes some getting used to because of all the buttons and menus.

Just remember that if you can draw a grid of squares, then you can make a square pie chart. You could do this in R, Python, Microsoft Excel, or pen and paper.

MORE PEOPLE MEETING ONLINE

In the 1990s, only about 2% of people in relationships met online. In the 2010s, about 19% did.

1990s

2010s

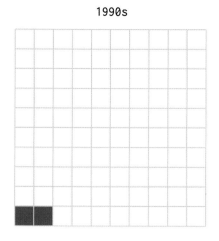
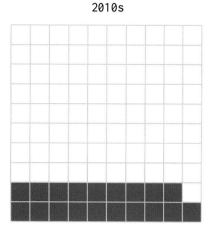

SOURCE: How Couples Meet and Stay Together 2017

FIGURE 5.28 *Square pie comparison*

TREEMAP

In 1990, Ben Shneiderman wanted to visualize what was going on in his always-full hard drive. Given the hierarchical structure of directories and files, he first tried a tree diagram. It got too big too fast to be useful, though. The treemap was his solution.

As shown in Figure 5.29, it's an area-based visualization where the size of each rectangle represents a metric. Outer rectangles represent parent categories, and rectangles within the parents are subcategories.

See `https://datafl .ws/11m` for a full history of treemaps and additional examples described by the creator, Ben Shneiderman.

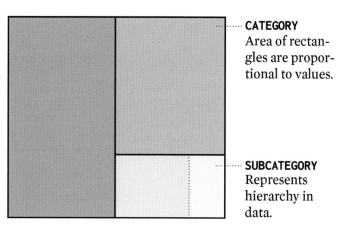

PARTS OF WHOLE
Sum of all rectangle areas represent a whole, or 100 percent.

CATEGORY
Area of rectangles are proportional to values.

SUBCATEGORY
Represents hierarchy in data.

FIGURE 5.29 *Treemap framework*

MAKING A TREEMAP

Tools used: R, Illustrator

Dataset: How People Meet, 2010s `book.flowingdata.com/vt2/ch5/data/how-met-2010s.tsv`

Illustrator doesn't have a treemap tool, but there is an R package. It is aptly named *treemap*. Open R and install the package with `install.packages()`.

```
# Install package if have not yet
install.packages("treemap")
```

Load the package with `library()`.

```
# Load package
library(treemap)
```

Like you did in previous R examples, load the data with `read.csv()`.

```
# Load data.
howmet2010 <- read.csv("data/how-met-2010s.tsv", sep="\t")
```

Check out the dataset to make sure it loaded right.

```
> head(howmet2010)
                           waymet            category year      p
1          Met Through Family Friends and Family 2010 0.0638
2          Met Through Friend Friends and Family 2010 0.1722
3       Met Through Neighbors Friends and Family 2010 0.0304
4        Met Through Coworker               Work 2010 0.0853
5                  Met Online             Online 2010 0.1890
6 Primary or Secondary School             School 2010 0.0461
```

There are four columns: `waymet` is how couples met, there's a `category` for each way of meeting, the `year` (which represents the decade), and the proportion `p` of people who met in each way in the decade.

Call `treemap()` with the `howmet2010` data frame.

```
# Draw treemap
treemap(howmet2010,
        index = c("category", "waymet"),
        vSize = "p",
        algorithm = "squarified",
        title = "How People Met, 2010s")
```

The `index` argument specifies the hierarchy of the data. Start with the highest level and then work your way down. In this case, `category` is the highest level and then `waymet`. The `vSize` argument specifies which variable to use for rectangle size. The `squarified` treemap algorithm is used to organize the rectangles, and `title` specifies the main title at the top of the treemap. Figure 5.30 shows the result.

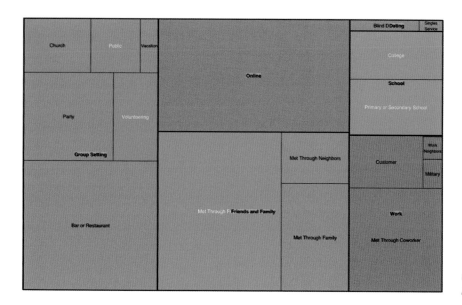

FIGURE 5.30 *Treemap of how people met*

In the 2010s, people mostly met in a group setting or through friends and family. The other categories follow.

EDITING THE CHART

Export the chart as a PDF either through the menus in R or with the `pdf()` function. For the latter, check out the documentation with `?pdf`, but in a nutshell, you can call `pdf()` before `treemap()` and then call `dev.off()` after `treemap()` to close the device. But again, unless you must export a lot of PDF files at once or you have a memory-hungry graphic to make, the menu route will do fine.

I won't go through all the steps in Illustrator since they're the same as in other examples. Use the Selection tool to select objects and the Direct Selection tool to select individual objects. When you select an object, you can change the stroke weight and colors through the Stroke and Color windows, respectively.

In Figure 5.31, I thickened the borders for the categories and changed the color of each category to a single color instead of the variations used by `treemap()`.

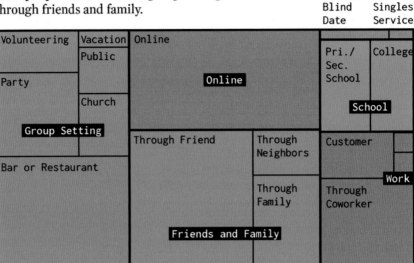

HOW PEOPLE MET, 2010s
Most people either met in a group setting or
through friends and family.

FIGURE 5.31 *Edited treemap*

SOURCE: How Couples Meet and Stay Together 2017

I also moved the labels for ways of meeting to the top-left corner of each
rectangle where I could and emphasized the category labels with a dark background. There's a title, lead-in text, and a source.

The default treemap from R is available in the chapter source download if you
don't want to go through the script. Open the file in Illustrator or related and
think about what you would add, remove, or edit. What changes will you make?
Can you change the focus of the treemap through design? Can you change
the chart to fit within your current reporting framework? You can! Your tastes
for what you like and don't like will evolve with practice.

RANK AND ORDER

Time series data carries a natural progression from oldest to most recent. Ordering by the passage of time is usually the most intuitive route. With categorical
data, ordering is usually based on amounts.

When we compare categories, we want to get a sense of the range. What is
the most? What is the least? How are things distributed across all categories?

Sorting your data with these questions in mind can help make it easier for readers to decipher rank and order in the data.

In the examples so far, the categories are sorted from least to greatest, or vice versa. For example, Figure 5.6 shows the jobs of physician spouses. Start at the top for the most common and work your way down to less common. If the ordering is random, like in Figure 5.32, you can quickly pick out the job that sticks out, but you must examine more closely to figure out the rest.

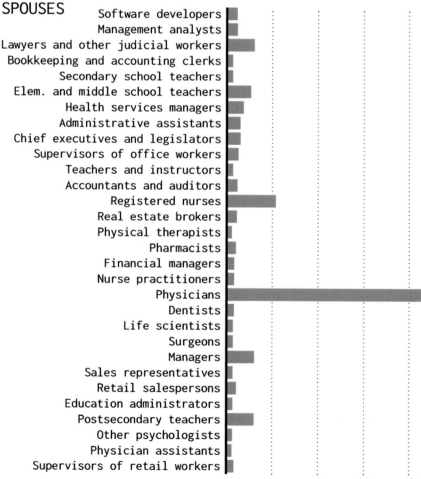

JOBS OF PHYSICIAN SPOUSES

FIGURE 5.32 *Bar chart with random order*

Sorting also makes it easier to see differences between categories because you don't have to skip around visually to decide what's bigger and what's smaller.

Figure 5.33 shows two pie charts. One is unsorted, and the other is sorted. They show the percentage of households in the United States that are of a certain type. (You will look at this dataset closer in the next section.) There is no clear reading direction for the unsorted pie chart. You just kind of look at it. With the sorted pie chart, you can see that single households are most common, and you move your eyes clockwise.

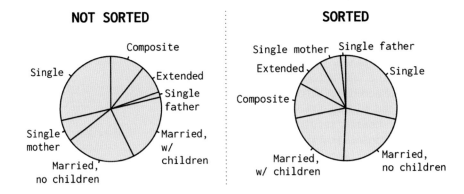

FIGURE 5.33 *Unsorted and sorted pie charts*

For reference, Figure 5.34 shows the same values as unsorted and sorted bar charts. The contrast in readability still applies.

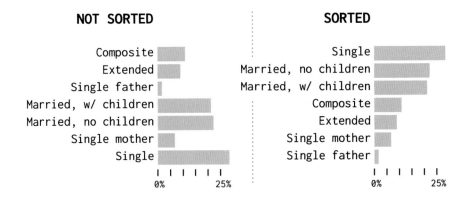

FIGURE 5.34 *Unsorted and sorted bar charts*

These are basic examples with not that many data points, but you can see the difference. Sorting grows more important as you add complexity.

After one of those long days as a parent, I thought about how different life is before and after kids. You must spend your time with different responsibilities, which means time spent on other things decreases. Based on data from the American Time Use Survey, Figure 5.35 shows the activities that show the biggest median drops timewise.

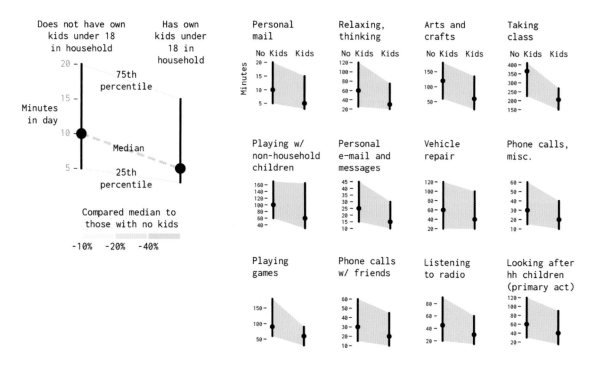

FIGURE 5.35 *"How Much the Everyday Changes When You Have Kids," Adapted from How Much the Everyday Changes When You Have Kids*

This shows just a subset of the available activities. The ATUS uses 605 activity classifications at the time of this writing. Out of the activities that showed a drop, they are sorted from biggest drop to least. Without sorting, the graphic would be a mess, especially if I didn't sort in the analysis phase and included hundreds of activities.

How you sort and what you sort changes with the data that you use and the questions you want to answer. You can sort by maximums, minimums, means, and medians. Sort from least to greatest or greatest to least. If your chart is meant as a lookup reference, you might want to sort alphabetically so that your readers can quickly find the data point they want.

Visualization is usually about finding the order in things. Sort the data so that the order is more obvious.

CATEGORIES AND TIME

You've seen how you can visualize categories. You've seen how you can visualize time. Now, put the two together to see how categories change over time because life is too complex and interesting to keep the two separated.

Figure 5.36 is a representation of a weekday in 2020. It shows how people move into different activities throughout the day, based on data from the American Time Use Survey. More dots mean more people during the 24 hours.

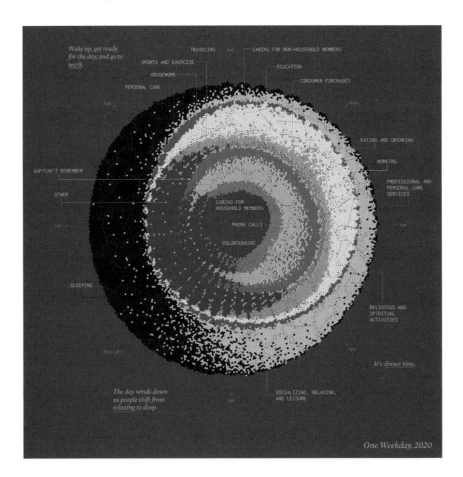

FIGURE 5.36 *"Cycle of Many," a 24-hour snapshot for a day in the life of Americans,* Nathan Yau / 2007-Present FlowingData / `https:// flowingdata.com/ 2021/08/25/cycle-of- many /` *last accessed February 08, 2024*

Each color represents a category. Time moves clockwise. Both aspects of the data could be visualized separately (which I have done plenty), but it wouldn't be as fun.

Did I mention the ATUS is my favorite dataset? Find more at `https://datafl.ws/timeuse`.

STACKED BAR CHART

As shown in Figure 5.37, the geometry of stacked bar charts is like regular bar charts. The difference, of course, is that rectangles are stacked on top of each other to represent subcategories.

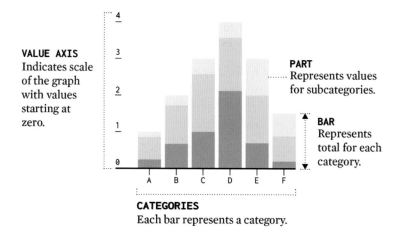

VALUE AXIS Indicates scale of the graph with values starting at zero.

PART Represents values for subcategories.

BAR Represents total for each category.

CATEGORIES Each bar represents a category.

FIGURE 5.37 *Stacked bar chart framework*

Also, like bar charts, you can use them to show data over categories and over time. Use them to show percentages or use them to show counts. It depends on what you want to highlight and the context of your data.

Usually, it's a good idea to limit the number of subcategories because the stacks can get messy if there are a lot of thin, barely visible bars. If you have a lot of subcategories, try grouping the small ones into an "other" subcategory or split the data into separate charts.

MAKING A STACKED BAR CHART

Tool used: R; RAWGraphs, `rawgraphs.io`

Dataset: Household types, 1976–2021, `book.flowingdata.com/vt2/ch5/data/household-types.tsv`

How common is it to live in a household as a married couple with children? What about as a single person? Has the share of household types changed much over the years? The Current Population Survey, run by the U.S. Census Bureau for the Bureau of Labor Statistics, publishes household data that can help answer these questions.

You'll use a stacked bar chart to see how proportions for different household types changed over time. The open-source, web-based RAWGraphs will be the tool of choice in this example, but first, you use R to format and prepare the data.

FORMATTING THE DATA

Oftentimes, the data you want to visualize comes in a different format or structure than you need it be. Depending on your line of work, this might be the case all the time.

Download the household dataset. Open R, set your working directory to where you downloaded the data, and use `read.csv()` to load the tab-delimited file.

```
# Load data
htypes <- read.csv("household-types.tsv", sep="\t")
```

Use `head()` to see the first few rows to make sure it loaded correctly.

```
> head(htypes)
  year                    htype          n           p
1 1976                composite  2628779.6 0.035917149
2 1976                 extended  5395372.8 0.073717252
3 1976           nuclear-father   617377.9 0.008435266
4 1976  nuclear-married-children 27239504.1 0.372174729
5 1976 nuclear-married-nochildren 16911072.9 0.231056848
6 1976           nuclear-mother  5147660.4 0.070332745
```

There are four columns: year (`year`), household type (`htype`), estimated count (`n`), and proportion of households (`p`). Each row represents the share of a given household type in a year. For example, in 1976, households with a married couple with children (`nuclear-married-children`) made up 0.37 of households, or 37%.

To use this data in RAWGraphs, you need to reformat it so that each row represents a year with a column for each household type. Get the unique years and household types with `unique()`.

```
# Unique years and household types
years <- unique(htypes$year)
uhtypes <- unique(htypes$htype)
```

Start a new data frame.

```
# Start data frame
htypes_new <- data.frame(year = years)
```

Add columns to the data frame `htypes_new` for each household type.

```
# Add columns
for (uht in uhtypes) {
    curr <- htypes[htypes$htype == uht,]
    curr_name <- paste0("p_", gsub("-", "_", uht))
    htypes_new[, curr_name] <-
        curr$p[match(htypes_new$year, curr$year)]
}
```

The for-loop iterates through each household type and subsets the data from the original `htypes` data frame, assigning it to `curr`. It sets a column name based on the current household type `uht` by substituting hyphens for underscores, because R doesn't like hyphens in column names. Then the proportions from the `curr` subset are matched to the years in the new data frame to make a new column.

Tip: Be sure to check out the documentation for any function with a question mark (?) followed by the function name if you're not sure how to use them.

Here are the first two rows and first four columns for the new data frame `htypes_new`. In 1976, 3.6% of households were composite, 7% were extended families, and less than 1% were single-father.

```
> htypes_new[1:2,1:4]
  year p_composite p_extended p_nuclear_father
1 1976  0.03591715 0.07371725      0.008435266
2 1977  0.03993042 0.07273152      0.008507778
```

With the data in the format you need, use `write.table()` to save the data frame as a tab-delimited file.

```
# Save formatted data
write.table(htypes_new,
            file="data/htypes_rectangular.tsv",
            sep="\t",
            row.names=FALSE)
```

MAKING THE CHART

Navigate to RAWGraphs in your web browser. Click the Use It Now button. Then follow the steps. Paste the saved data from R, or if you skipped the formatting step, the file is also available in the source download for this chapter. After copying and pasting the data, the tool guesses the formatting, as shown in Figure 5.38. Check to make sure it looks right.

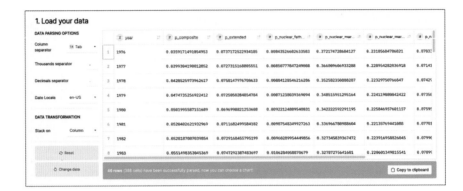

FIGURE 5.38 *Loading data in RAWGraphs*

Scroll down to choose a chart. As shown in Figure 5.39, there are several options (31 of them as of this writing). Select the stacked bar chart option.

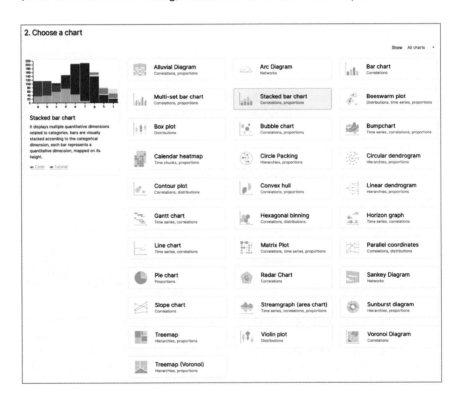

FIGURE 5.39 *Choosing a chart*

Scroll down more to the third step: Mapping. This is where you specify which variable defines the x-axis and the size of the bars in each stack. In this example, year goes on the x-axis, and the household type proportions define bar size. Click and drag the variables (labeled "dimensions" here), as shown in Figure 5.40.

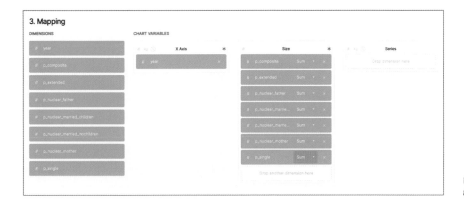

FIGURE 5.40: *Mapping data to geometry*

Scroll down to see the stacked bar chart. Figure 5.41 shows the customization options for padding, sorting, and colors.

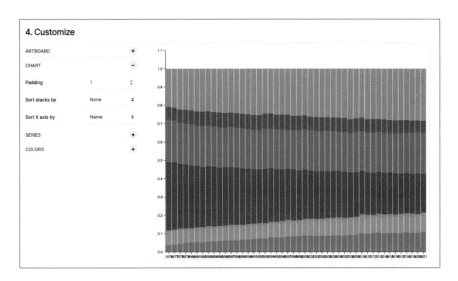

FIGURE 5.41 *Customizing the stacked bar chart*

Scroll to the end, and you can export the chart in SVG, PNG, JPG, or RAWGraphs format to use with the tool later. You can use the graphic as is, but the goal of the tool is to provide a link between chart-making software and graphics editors, so usually, the next step, with the visual encoding part taken care of, is to edit elsewhere.

STACKED AREA CHART

The stacked area chart is the continuous version of a stacked bar chart, as shown in Figure 5.42. Points are connected, as opposed to separated stacks in a bar chart, so the stacked area chart is specific to changing categories over time.

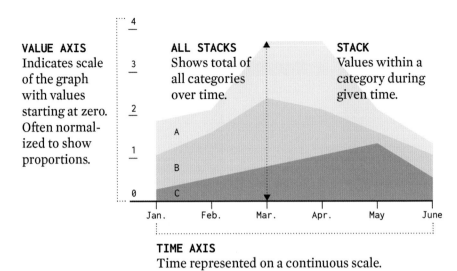

VALUE AXIS
Indicates scale of the graph with values starting at zero. Often normalized to show proportions.

ALL STACKS
Shows total of all categories over time.

STACK
Values within a category during given time.

TIME AXIS
Time represented on a continuous scale.

FIGURE 5.42 *Stacked area chart framework*

Tip: See https:// datafl.ws/area for more examples and variants of area charts.

If you only have one stack, then you have yourself an *area chart*. There is also a chart called a *streamgraph*, which is a variant of a stacked area chart that shifts the baseline to the center and orders stacks from greatest to least from the inside out.

MAKING A STACKED AREA CHART

Tool used: RAWGraphs

Dataset: Household Types, 1976-2021, book.flowingdata.com/vt2/ch5/data/household-types.tsv

Let's stay with RAWGraphs since you just used it and make a stacked area chart for the household type data. You might expect to use the same data format as in the bar chart example, but the stacked area chart is specific to time, so RAWGraphs takes a different format. It's the format of the original file.

Navigate to RAWGraphs if you haven't already. Copy and paste the data. You should see the four columns, for year, household type, count, and proportion. Select the Streamgraph (Area Chart) option in the next step. Then use `year` for the x-axis, `p` for the size, and `htype` for the streams in the Mapping step, as shown in Figure 5.43.

Tip: Some chart types, especially the newer ones, have different names depending on who you ask. RAWGraphs has a streamgraph option, which is a kind of stacked area chart.

This should get you the chart shown in Figure 5.44. You get options that are specific to the chart type you select, so you can specify ordering, curve type (the way that each point is connected), and alignment, among other things.

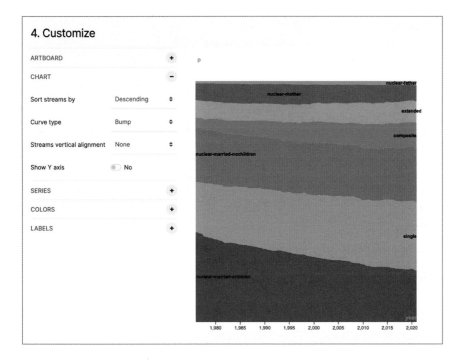

FIGURE 5.43 *Data selection for stacked area chart*

FIGURE 5.44 *Stacked area chart*

Again, you can export the chart in different file formats and edit as you like, but let's save the editing for later.

A challenge with stacked areas and bars is that the geometries' position on top depends on the geometries on the bottom. For example, if there were a spike on the bottom area for married households with children, that spike would ripple through each area. The same vertical offset can also make smaller differences harder to see, which is why I often use the next chart type.

ALLUVIAL DIAGRAM

With stacked area charts, the ordering of the areas or streams stay the same throughout. If an area starts on the bottom, then it will stay on the bottom

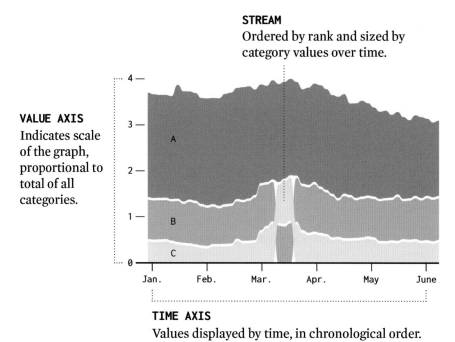

STREAM
Ordered by rank and sized by
category values over time.

VALUE AXIS
Indicates scale
of the graph,
proportional to
total of all
categories.

TIME AXIS
Values displayed by time, in chronological order.

FIGURE 5.45 *Alluvial
diagram framework*

until the end. An alluvial diagram, as shown in Figure 5.45, changes the order of the streams based on the values. The diagram is named after the naturally occurring alluvial fans because of its appearance.

The change in ordering lets you show amounts, parts of a whole, and rank over time. Given the right data, alluvial diagrams are intuitive, informative, and nice to look at. However, they come with a caveat: If there are a lot of ranking switches over time across several categories, overlapping streams can get messy, rendering the chart a useless view of spaghetti. Use your best judgment.

Note: Alluvial diagrams can also be used to look at correlation between variables by showing the flow between one group and another. However, it's difficult to glean useful relationships in this format, so I stick to showing categories over time.

MAKING AN ALLUVIAL DIAGRAM

Tools used: RAWGraphs, Illustrator

Dataset: Household Types, 1976-2021, book.flowingdata.com/vt2/ch5 /data/household-types.tsv

We'll use RAWGraphs one more time to show how household types changed between 1976 through 2021. The nice thing about the newer point-and-click tools, which weren't around during the first edition of this book, is that it's a lot easier to backtrack or pick up where you left off.

The alluvial diagram with RAWGraphs does not assume changes over time. Instead, it assumes changes over categories. However, the *bump chart* option does show changes over time in the layout that you want in this example.

I'd argue that this option produces an alluvial diagram and that a bump chart, outlined in the next section, uses lines to show rankings. But there's overlap between the chart types, so I can see how one might be called the other. Semantics. The point is that you can make the thing.

Copy and paste the same data you used for the stacked area chart. Select the Bumpchart option, and, as shown in Figure 5.46, map `year` to the x-axis, `p` to the size, and `htype` to the streams.

FIGURE 5.46 *Mapping variables for an alluvial diagram in RAWGraphs*

This gives you an alluvial diagram that shows the growth of single households, the climb to the top spot, and the decline of married households with children, as shown in Figure 5.47. Married households with no kids moved up to the number-two spot.

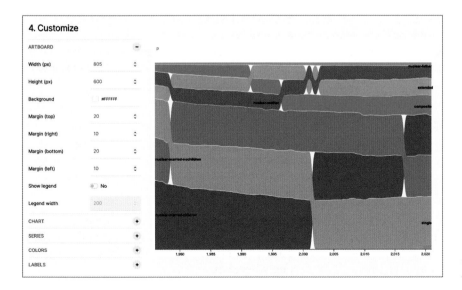

FIGURE 5.47 *Alluvial diagram in RAWGraphs*

As the name suggests, RAWGraphs produces charts that you should consider not quite done. It translates data to visual encodings. You take care of the design to make the output useful for your audience and purpose.

Figure 5.48 shows an edited version of Figure 5.47. The goal was to make the trends in the data obvious to someone who doesn't look at data all the time.

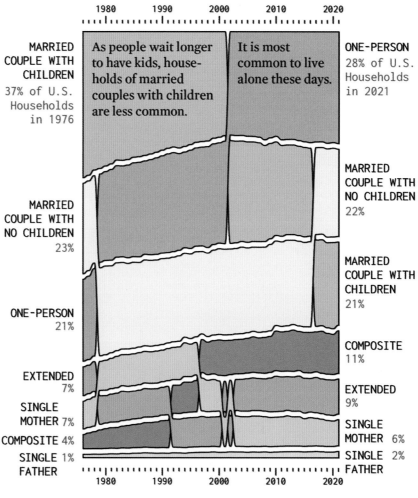

CHANGE IN COMMON HOUSEHOLD TYPES

MARRIED COUPLE WITH CHILDREN
37% of U.S. Households in 1976

As people wait longer to have kids, households of married couples with children are less common.

It is most common to live alone these days.

ONE-PERSON
28% of U.S. Households in 2021

MARRIED COUPLE WITH NO CHILDREN
23%

MARRIED COUPLE WITH NO CHILDREN
22%

ONE-PERSON
21%

MARRIED COUPLE WITH CHILDREN
21%

COMPOSITE
11%

EXTENDED
7%

EXTENDED
9%

SINGLE MOTHER 7%

SINGLE MOTHER 6%

COMPOSITE 4%

SINGLE 1%
FATHER

SINGLE 2%
FATHER

SOURCE: Current Population Survey / IPUMS

FIGURE 5.48 *Edited alluvial diagram for clarity*

I changed the color scheme. I'm in a phase of less saturated colors, so I edited the areas to my taste. The horizontal axis is year-focused instead of using a comma to separate the thousands position. There are also labeled axes on both the top and bottom so that you don't have to look to the bottom and move your eyes up to see the year of a point. The names for each household type are less ambiguous than the made-for-computers classifications. Start and end percentages are also included. A layer of annotation is placed over the areas for more context.

Think about who the chart is for, what it is for, and what you want to show, and let that tell you what you need to edit.

BUMP CHART

Alluvial diagrams to show categories over time are like stacked area charts that reorder as you go. Bump charts are like alluvial diagrams but without the changing sizes. It's just rank over time for each category, as shown in Figure 5.49.

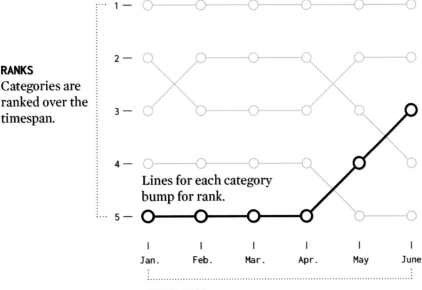

RANKS
Categories are ranked over the timespan.

Lines for each category bump for rank.

TIME AXIS
Values displayed by discrete points in time, in chronological order.

FIGURE 5.49 *"Bump chart framework,"* Nathan Yau / 2007-Present FlowingData / `https://flowingdata .com/2021/08/25/cycle- of-many` / *last accessed February 08, 2024.*

So, if you're interested only in the ordering of things and not so much the amounts, a bump chart might work. However, the lines tend to turn into spaghetti even quicker than the alluvial diagram because all the categories get the same visual weight.

To make a (pseudo-)bump chart in RAWGraphs, follow the steps in the previous alluvial diagram example, but remove p for size in the data-mapping step. Alternatively, you can think of the bump chart as a multi-line chart with ranks, which you made in the previous chapter.

WRAPPING UP

Visualizing categories is about looking at amounts, how those amounts are spread out across a whole, and the range of the data for a sense of scale.

But it's not just that. Categories can go together with time so that you can see how groups change rather than exist as a single snapshot of the way things used to be.

We like to talk about data types separately: categorical data, time series data, spatial data, and so forth. But data types are often intertwined and can represent different things at once. Visualization, a representation of the data, should be able to show such relationships. That's usually where the interesting bits are. Look for the interesting bits.

Hopefully, by now, you can also see how different visualization tools can be used together to make charts more efficiently. You don't always have to use R, Python, or Illustrator. You can use a code-based tool to analyze and process data, you can use a point-and-click tool to handle more complex chart types, and you can use another tool to edit and annotate. It's in your best interest to keep adding to the toolbox, especially as technology and the uses for visualization shift in the field.

In the next chapter, you'll test more tools you might want to add to your collection. You'll use them to look at relationships between multiple variables and datasets and how people, places, and things relate to each other.

Visualizing
Relationships

What are the similarities between groups? Within groups? Within subgroups? How are things connected? Statistically, the relationship that most people are familiar with is correlation. One variable tends to change when another variable changes in an expected way. However, the relationships in your data grow more complex as you consider more factors or find patterns that aren't one-to-one. This chapter discusses how to use visualization to find such relationships and highlight them for storytelling.

So far, you looked at basic relationships in time series data and categories. You learned about trends over time and compared proportions and percentages to see the least and greatest and everything in between. Now you'll look at relationships between variables.

Correlation is how two variables change with each other. This is a common relationship that you look for in data, but it's not the only one. When comparing two things, it's often worth focusing on the *differences*, maybe over time or across categories. You can look for relationships across *multiple variables*, which adds complexity and is sometimes a good thing. Relationships are also about *connections*. How are data points linked to each other?

When you zoom in close to people, places, and things, it can seem like everyone and everything functions independently. However, take a step back and you see that the world is connected in many ways. In this chapter, you focus on these relationships. You try your hand at making charts for the Web using HTML, CSS, and JavaScript. Then you come back to R with a shift toward the data exploration phase of visualization.

CORRELATION

Correlation is probably the first thing you think of when you hear about relationships in data. Maybe you've heard of or calculated a correlation coefficient that expresses the relationship between variables quantitatively. In regular people terms, *correlation* is a way to express how one thing tends to change in an expected way as another thing changes. It can be a strong or a weak relationship. We don't always know why the things change together in predictable ways, but they do.

For example, when you plot occupations in the United States by median salary against divorce rate, the latter appears to decrease as the former increases. As shown in Figure 6.1, there is a negative correlation between the two.

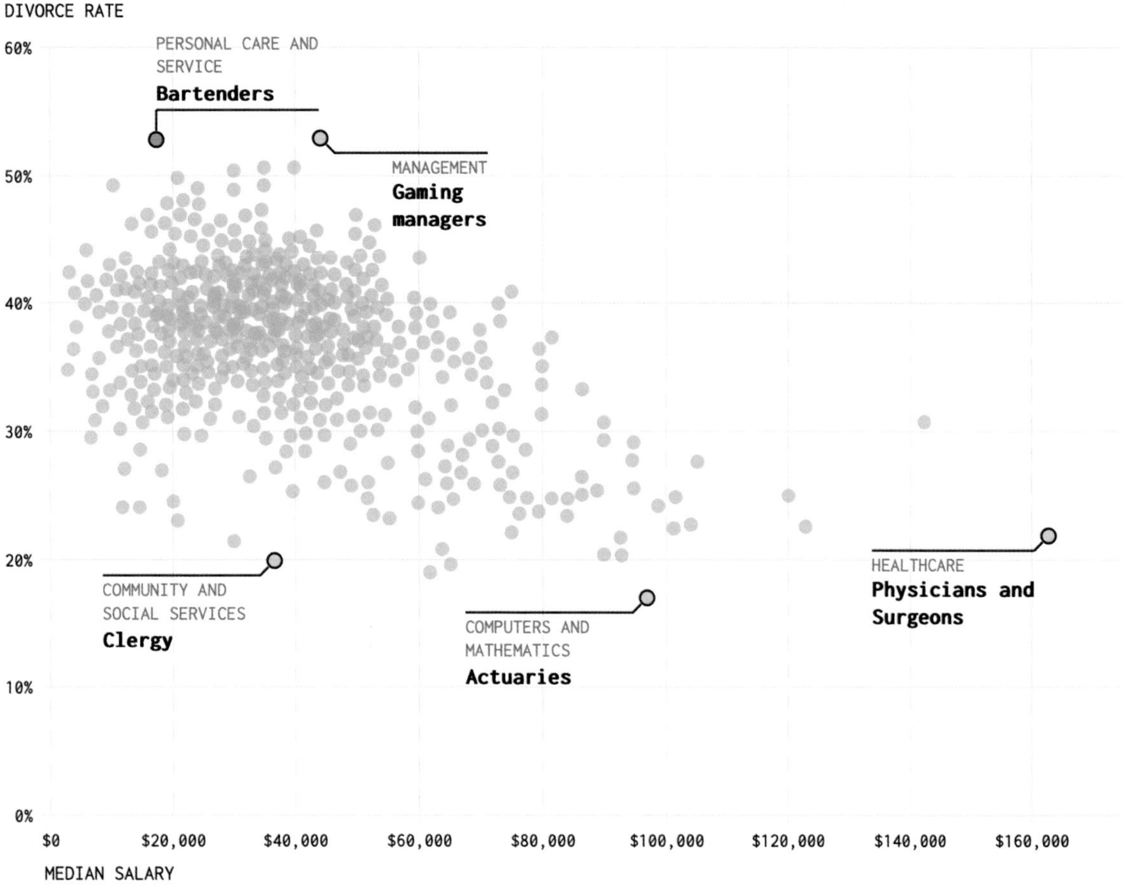
DIVORCE RATE
60%
50%
40%
30%
20%
10%
0%
PERSONAL CARE AND SERVICE
Bartenders
MANAGEMENT
Gaming managers
COMMUNITY AND SOCIAL SERVICES
Clergy
COMPUTERS AND MATHEMATICS
Actuaries
HEALTHCARE
Physicians and Surgeons
$0
$20,000
$40,000
$60,000
$80,000
$100,000
$120,000
$140,000
$160,000
MEDIAN SALARY

FIGURE 6.1 *"Divorce and Occupation,"* Nathan Yau / 2007-Present FlowingData / `https://flowingdata.com/2017/07/25/divorce-and-occupation` / *last accessed February 08, 2024.*

However, does a higher salary *cause* lower divorce rates? If you gave every working person a raise, would divorce rates decline nationally? Are divorce rates lower for people with certain occupations because the jobs say something about temperament or marrying tendencies? If we made everyone stay married, would incomes rise?

It's difficult to account for every outside or *confounding factor*, which makes it challenging to prove causation. However, just because one doesn't always mean the other, correlation can be a good indicator of how things are related and what we might be able to do to change those things if needed. Oftentimes, correlation is all we can do, so we do the best with what we have and consider the evidence surrounding the calculations.

Spurious Correlations by Tyler Vigen pokes fun at the difference between correlation and causation with unrelated variables that are highly correlated: `https://datafl.ws/spurious`.

As the comic xkcd put it, "Correlation doesn't imply causation, but it does waggle its eyebrows suggestively and gesture furtively while mouthing 'look over there.'" See https://xkcd.com/552.

SCATTERPLOT

In Chapter 4, "Visualizing Time," you learned about a *dot plot* to show patterns over time. It's a general chart type that, as the name indicates, uses dots to show data that can be placed using various axes. Dots can be placed on a single timeline, they can be stacked on top of each other, or they can be organized in a grid layout. A *scatterplot* is a specific type of dot plot where both the x- and y-axes represent values, as shown in Figure 6.2.

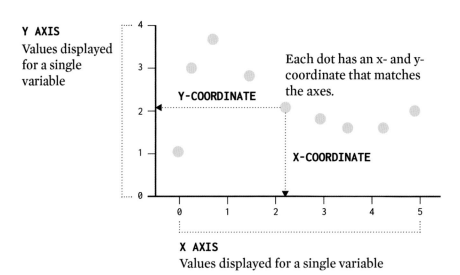

FIGURE 6.2 *Scatterplot framework*

The purpose of the scatterplot is to see how two variables, the one on the x-axis and the one on the y-axis, are related. Usually, the relationship of interest is correlation, shown in Figure 6.3.

Relationships between two variables can be more complex than positive and negative correlation but for communication and storytelling purposes, these cover most of your bases.

MAKING A SCATTERPLOT

Tools used: HTML, CSS, JavaScript, D3.js

Dataset: Meaningfulness and Happiness, book.flowingdata.com/vt2/ch6/data/act_means.tsv

So far, you've visualized data mostly with individual tools. You've made charts completely with Python, R, and point-and-click applications. In some examples,

POSITIVE CORRELATION
Points going up and right

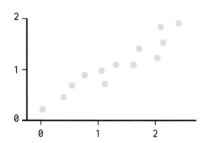

NEGATIVE CORRELATION
Points going down and right

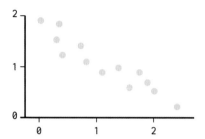

WEAK CORRELATION
Appear loosely related

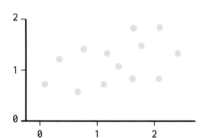

NO CORRELATION
Points do not follow a pattern

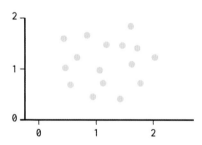

FIGURE 6.3 *Correlations shown in scatterplots*

you used Illustrator to edit, but you could have also stopped before that step or worked within the parameters of the current tool.

Visualization for the Web tends toward more parts that you must fit together, usually HTML, CSS, and JavaScript at the minimum. The process of fitting these parts together can grow more complex depending on your setup. This makes point-and-click tools like Datawrapper useful because they let you make charts quickly, and you can copy and paste a code snippet to your site.

However, there is also fun in making your own charts that are custom fit for the dataset, in exchange for more complexity. It's the little differences between projects and chart-makers, the little bits of charm, that make visualization most interesting and compelling.

The following example uses D3, which is a JavaScript visualization library without functions for specific chart types. Instead, it provides functions for visualization *components*, such as axes, scales, data transformations, and geometries.

You'll learn how to make a scatterplot, among other standard charts in this chapter, but pay special attention to how the components fit together and

See Chapter 2, "Choosing Tools to Visualize Data," for JavaScript libraries that have built-in functions to make standard chart types.

the similarities across various charts. The charts are different, but the building process between the examples repeats itself.

You come back to the well-being module from the 2022 American Time Use Survey. People were asked to score meaningfulness and happiness while engaged in daily activities. How are meaningfulness and happiness related?

Open the `scatterplot` folder in the chapter source to follow along in your favorite code editor, such as Sublime Text, which is available for macOS, Windows, and Linux. There are three main parts that we'll look at separately.

If you are new to D3 or making things for the Web in general, it will help to work through a primer to familiarize yourself with how the library works at `https://datafl.ws /d3intro`. You can also find a beginner tutorial on FlowingData at `https: //datafl.ws/d3start`.

- `index.html`: HTML for structure
- `js/scatterplot.js`: JavaScript for handling data, adding interaction, and dynamically adding elements based on the data
- `style/style.css`: CSS for styling

This needs to run on a web server so that the JavaScript runs when the page loads. So, make sure you have a development environment set up on your system.

For Windows, check out `https://datafl.ws /windev` for setting up a development environment. For macOS, see `https: //datafl.ws/macdev`.

HTML for Structure

There is not much to the HTML file `index.html`. It starts with a header, which defines the page title with the `<title>` tag and loads the `style.css` file with the `<link>` tag. You'll come back to the CSS later.

```
<head>
<meta charset="utf-8">
<title>Activities, Happiness, and Meaning</title>
<link rel="stylesheet" href="style/style.css" type="text/css"
media="screen" />
</head>
```

A couple of `<div>` tags serve as holders for things you'll add with D3.

```
<div id="main-wrapper">
    <h1>Meaningfulness with Happiness</h1>
    <div id="chart"></div>
</div>
```

Load D3 and a JavaScript file named `scatterplot.js` with the `<script>` tags. Alternatively, you can load the hosted version using `https://cdn.jsdelivr .net/npm/d3@7` as the `src`.

```
<script src="js/d3.v7.min.js"></script>
<script src="js/scatterplot.js"></script>
```

That's it for the HTML. If you load the page now, you'll just see a title that reads "Meaningfulness with Happiness" with nothing else.

JavaScript for Construction

This is when you put together the actual chart. You'll use D3 functionality to construct an SVG object that loads on the page. Open `js/scatterplot.js`. Start by setting the dimensions of the chart in terms of margins, width, and height.

```
// Dimensions of chart.
let margin = { top: 20, right: 10, bottom: 50, left: 45 },
    width = 600 - margin.left - margin.right,
    height = 750 - margin.top - margin.bottom;
```

Scalable Vector Graphics (SVG) is an image format based on Extensible Markup Language (XML). See https://datafl .ws/7mr for the full specifications for SVG. The format will allow you to draw lines, shapes, text, and other visual elements.

There will be a top margin of 20 pixels, a right margin of 10 pixels, and so on. The full width of the chart will be 600 pixels wide, and the chart will be a bit taller than it is wide at 750 pixels.

Start the SVG by selecting the `<div>` with an ID set to `chart` in `index.html`. Append an `svg` tag with `append()`.

```
// Start SVG
let svg = d3.select("#chart").append("svg")
    .attr("width", width + margin.left + margin.right)
    .attr("height", height + margin.top + margin.bottom)
  .append("g")
    .attr("transform", "translate(" + margin.left + ","
+ margin.top + ")");
```

If you load the page now, you still just get a title, but right-click the page and select Inspect or Inspect Element in the menu, depending on which browser you use. This brings up a Web Inspector that shows the elements on the page, including the ones added with JavaScript, like Figure 6.4. This is useful for debugging and making sure your code does what you expect.

Define the x-scale for meaningfulness scores with `d3.scaleLinear()`. Set the domain from 3 to 6, which covers the span of average meaningfulness scores in the data. Then define the range from 0 to `width`, which refers to how values between 3 and 6 will translate to the space on the page. For example, a meaningfulness score of 3 maps to a pixel value of 0, and a score of 6 maps to a pixel value equal to `width`.

D3 provides other scales, such as logarithmic and category-based scales. You can find the full list in the documentation at https://d3js.org /d3-scale. We'll keep the scales linear for now, though.

```
// x scale
let x = d3.scaleLinear()
    .domain([3, 6])
    .range([0, width]);
```

FIGURE 6.4 *Web Inspector*

Define the y-scale similarly, but set the domain as 2 to 6 and the range for `height` to 0. Why not the other direction from 0 to `height`? Unlike charts where the *origin* at (0, 0) is typically at the bottom with increasing y-values as you move up, the SVG coordinate system starts (0, 0) in the top-left corner. The x-coordinates increase left to right, which is the same as most charts, but y-coordinates increase top to bottom, so the range is reversed. Sometimes you might want a chart that shows lower values at the top, such as ranks, in which case you would use 0 to `height`.

```
// y scale
let y = d3.scaleLinear()
    .domain([2, 6])
    .range([height, 0]);
```

Now create an x-axis using `d3.axisBottom()` with four ticks that extend the height of the chart plus eight with a padding of five between the tick marks and tick labels.

```
// x-axis
let xAxis = d3.axisBottom(x)
    .ticks(4)
    .tickSize(-height-8)
    .tickPadding(5);
```

Add the x-axis to the SVG with `append()`. Set attributes as shown here:

```
// x-axis element
let xAxisEl = svg.append("g")
    .attr("class", "x axis bottom")
    .attr("transform", "translate(0,"+(height+8)+")");
```

Add a text label to the x-axis element.

```
xAxisEl.append("text")
    .attr("class", "axistitle")
    .attr("text-anchor", "start")
    .attr("x", 0).attr("y", 0)
    .attr("dx", -1).attr("dy", "2.5em")
    .text("Meaningfulness Score Average");
xAxisEl.call(xAxis);
```

Load the page; there's an x-axis with grid lines that extend the height of the chart, as shown in Figure 6.5.

It's likely the JavaScript so far looks like gibberish to you, especially if you've never written a line of JavaScript before. This will grow more intuitive with practice and repetition, but stay with me here. At each step, the main thing you are doing is defining, then adding, and then setting attributes for what you added.

Add a y-axis by defining the axis with `d3.axisLeft()`, adding an element with `append()`, adding the axis label with `append()` again, and then applying the defined `yAxis` to the element with `call()`.

```
// y-axis
let yAxis = d3.axisLeft(y)
    .ticks(5)
    .tickSize(-width-8)
    .tickPadding(5);
let yAxisEl = svg.append("g")
    .attr("class", "y axis left")
    .attr("transform", "translate("+(-8)+",0)");
yAxisEl.append("text")
    .attr("class", "axistitle")
    .attr("x", 0).attr("y", 0)
    .attr("dx", "4px")
```

Meaningfulness with Happiness

FIGURE 6.5 *The x-axis added*

MEANINGFULNESS SCORE AVERAGE

```
        .attr("dy", "-1.5em")
        .style("text-anchor", "end")
        .attr("transform", "rotate(-90)")
        .text("Happiness Score Average");
yAxisEl.call(yAxis);
```

Figure 6.6 shows the chart set up with a grid.

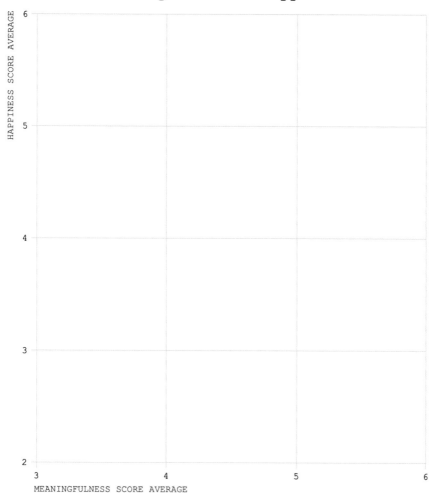

Meaningfulness with Happiness

HAPPINESS SCORE AVERAGE

MEANINGFULNESS SCORE AVERAGE

FIGURE 6.6 *Blank chart with grid*

With the coordinate system and axes defined, you can make the points for the data. Create two variables, or *declare*, `activities` and `circle`. The former is to assign data, and the latter is for each point.

```
let activities;
let circle;
```

Here is a sample from `data/act _ means.tsv`, where each row represents an activity, and there is a column for the average happiness score, `schappy _ mean`, and a column for average meaningfulness score, `meaning _ mean`.

```
"activity"       "schappy_mean"       "meaning_mean"      "descrip"
"010301"         3.65     5.2875    "Health-related self care"
"010399"         0.4441   4.332     "Self care, misc."
"020101"         4.3016   5.0383    "Interior cleaning"
"020102"         4.1979   4.866     "Laundry"
```

Prepare to the load the data, as shown next. This creates a Promise object in JavaScript, which in this case is a way to make sure the data loads before any other code executes. Like with other software, the file path, specified in d3. tsv(), is relative to the location of the main file, in this case index.html.

```
// Load data
const activitiesData = Promise.all([
    d3.tsv("data/act_means.tsv", d3.autoType)
]);
```

Load the data, and when the data is loaded, run initChart() (defined by the Promise object's then() method), which you define in the next step.

Find more details about the Promise object in JavaScript at https: //datafl.ws/promise.

```
activitiesData.then(function(data) {
    activities = data[0];
    // console.log(activities);

    // Initialize chart now that data is loaded.
    initChart();
});
```

The function initChart() adds the circles, one for each activity. The average meaningfulness score is on the x-axis, and the average happiness score is on the y-axis. Using the standard syntax with D3, use selectAll() to select the circle elements (of which there are currently none), bind the data activities, and use join() to join a circle for each observation, with the given attributes for id, the center coordinate of each circle (cx and cy), and a fill color.

```
function initChart() {
    // Circle for each node.
    circle = svg.append("g")
        .selectAll("circle")
        .data(activities)
        .join("circle")
        .attr("id", d => "circle"+d.activity)
        .attr("cx", d => x(d.meaning_mean))
        .attr("cy", d => y(d.schappy_mean))
        .attr("fill", "#5a8171")
        .attr("r", 3);
}
```

As shown in Figure 6.7, you get a scatterplot of meaningfulness versus happiness.

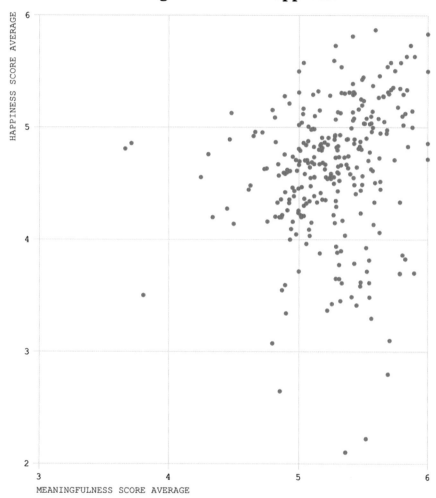

FIGURE 6.7 *Scatterplot in D3*

Again, don't worry if this section has been confusing. D3 has a reputation for having a steep learning curve, and there are a few more examples in this chapter to cover the details more closely. The flexibility gained has proven to be a fine advantage over the years, but if that flexibility is unnecessary in your work, you can always fall back on the previously mentioned JavaScript libraries that provide specific chart types as functions.

Joins in D3 can be confusing at first, but they do seem to grow more intuitive with repetition. Mike Bostock, the creator of D3, provides a guide on thinking with joins at `https://datafl.ws/d3join`.

CSS for Styling

The chart assumes that you already set styles in `style.css` that match the class names you set with `.class()` in the JavaScript. Here you can set positioning on the page (not just the SVG), font styles, colors, line widths. Start with positioning the chart `<div>`.

```
#chart {
    margin: 0 auto;
}
```

This sets the margins on the left and right automatically based on the width so that the `<div>` is centered. Set the font style for the axis text.

```
.axis text {
    font-family: "Courier New", Courier, monospace;
    font-size: .8rem;
}
```

Set separate properties for the axis titles. Set the color of the axis lines to a light gray with a stroke width of one pixel.

```
.axis .axistitle {
    text-transform: uppercase;
    fill: #333;
    font-size: .8rem;
}
.axis path,
.axis line {
    fill: none;
    stroke: #ccc;
    stroke-width: 1px;
    shape-rendering: crispEdges;
}
```

Note: So far, you've seen visualization in terms of named chart types. There is a function or a guided interface to make a bar chart or a line chart. This will cover most of your bases, but for maximum control and flexibility, it pays to think of visualization as components: coordinate systems, scales, visual encodings, and context. Think about this moving forward, and we'll cover this more in Chapter 9, "Designing with Purpose."

You can go on and on here. Try changing values in the file and reloading the page to see what happens. You might have to clear your browser cache so that the stylesheet reloads.

BUBBLE PLOT

A bubble plot shares the same geometries as a scatterplot, using x- and y-coordinates for placement. It shows the relationship between two variables. However, as shown in Figure 6.8, scaled circles, or bubbles, let you show a third variable.

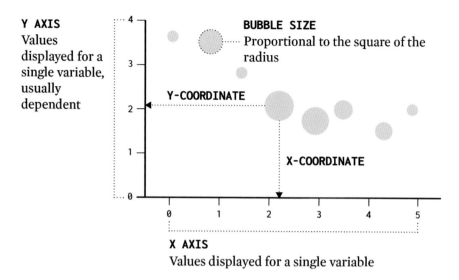

Y AXIS
Values displayed for a single variable, usually dependent

BUBBLE SIZE
Proportional to the square of the radius

Y-COORDINATE

X-COORDINATE

X AXIS
Values displayed for a single variable

FIGURE 6.8 *Bubble plot framework*

Like scaled symbols discussed in Chapter 5, "Visualizing Categories," bubbles are sized by total area. Again, take note of how your software scales the circles so that you do not accidentally exaggerate or diminish differences between categories.

The typical use case for bubble plots is when you have two variables that are normalized, like rate, percentage, or an average, and a third variable that represents an absolute count (usually). The normalized variables define placement, and the absolute count defines size.

For example, in Hans Rosling's famous use of a moving bubble plot (referenced in Chapter 1, "Telling Stories with Data"), fertility rate is on the x-axis, life expectancy is on the y-axis, and each bubble representing a country is sized by population. This gives greater visual attention to places with more people.

Find bubble plot examples at https://datafl.ws /bubble.

The bubble plot gives you a chance to see how three variables might relate. The trade-offs are similar to that of scaled symbols described in Chapter 5. It is more difficult to see differences between areas than with length or positions. Scaled circles also use more space than points on a scatterplot, which can make a mess of a plot quickly if you use larger circles relative to the size of the plot. You decide if the trade-off is worth it. The good news is that if you already made a scatterplot, it's usually straightforward to make a bubble plot to see if it's worthwhile.

MAKING A BUBBLE PLOT

Tools used: HTML, CSS, JavaScript, D3.js

Dataset: Meaningfulness and Happiness, book.flowingdata.com/vt2/ch6 /data/act_means.tsv

Coming back to average meaningfulness and happiness scores from the scatterplot example, you don't have to start from scratch. You can load data, create axes, and place points (which were small circles) in the same way. The difference is in circle size. In the scatterplot, the radius of every circle was set to 3 in initChart(). In bubbleplot.js, which is in the chapter download, define a third scale for radius, r, after the x and y scales.

```
// Radius scale
let r = d3.scaleSqrt()
    .domain([0, 10])
    .range([0, 25]);
```

The act_means.tsv data file has a relwt column, which was calculated based on the number of people who engaged in an activity on their survey day. The variable is on a scale from 0 to 10, where 0 means no one engaged in the activity and 10 means a lot of people did. The radius scale uses d3.scaleSqrt() with a domain from 0 to 10 (the extent of the data) and a range from 0 to 25 (the extent of the pixels on the screen).

Then in initChart(), you append circles and set the r attribute based on relwt instead of 3 with the .attr() method.

```
// Circle for each node.
circle = svg.append("g")
    .selectAll("circle")
    .data(activities)
    .join("circle")
    .attr("id", d => "circle"+d.activity)
    .attr("cx", d => x(d.meaning_mean))
    .attr("cy", d => y(d.schappy_mean))
    .attr("fill", "#5a8171")
    .attr("r", d => r(d.relwt));
```

Notice that .attr() is called several times after the join to set the attributes of the circles. For most of the attributes—the id, the center x-coordinate (cx), the center y-coordinate (cy), and the radius (r)—a function is provided. The functions are applied to each data point for each attribute. However, the fill is set to a hexadecimal value #5a8171, in which case, all the circles' fill attribute is set to the value.

This gives you the bubble plot shown in Figure 6.9, which looks like inkblots.

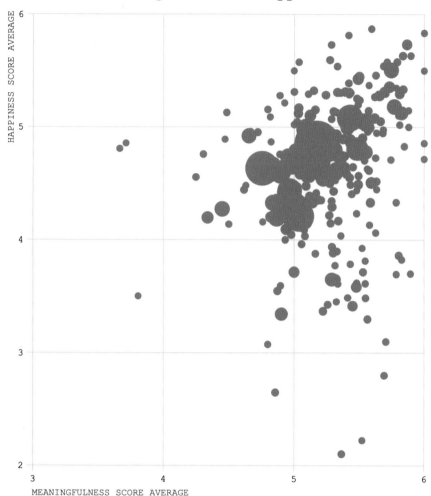

Meaningfulness with Happiness

HAPPINESS SCORE AVERAGE

MEANINGFULNESS SCORE AVERAGE

FIGURE 6.9 *Scaling bubbles from the scatterplot version of the chart*

The chart needs adjustments, but you can see how the change in radius shifts the dynamic of the chart. Whereas the scatterplot focused on the x-y relationship between two variables, the bubble chart highlights the relationship along with how common each activity is. The activities that are less common show less prominently.

To focus on the more common activities, you can adjust the domains for the x and y scales to zoom in on the relevant area. Make the x domain 4 to 6 and the y domain 3 to 6.

```
let x = d3.scaleLinear()
    .domain([4, 6])
    .range([0, width]);
let y = d3.scaleLinear()
    .domain([3, 6])
    .range([height, 0]);
```

For the circles, change the `fill-opacity` attribute to 0.75 so that you can see what's behind each circle, and add a white border to each circle with the `stroke` and `stroke-width` attributes to provide more separation.

```
// Circle for each node.
circle = svg.append("g")
    .selectAll("circle")
    .data(activities)
    .join("circle")
    .attr("id", d => "circle"+d.activity)
    .attr("cx", d => x(d.meaning_mean))
    .attr("cy", d => y(d.schappy_mean))
    .attr("fill", "#5a8171")
    .attr("fill-opacity", .75)
    .attr("r", d => r(d.relwt))
    .attr("stroke", "#fff")
    .attr("stroke-width", ".5px");
```

Changing the height to be the same as the width, you get the chart in Figure 6.10, which is less inkblot-ish and bubblier.

It's more readable than the first version. You can see all the circles. But it would be nice to know what each circle represents so a reader can easily pick out outliers or investigate areas that might be worth looking into. You could just place labels on top of every circle, but that would get messy and illegible quickly unless you had a lot of space for a few circles.

How about a label appears when you hover over or press a circle? D3 lets you define functions to run when these *events* occur. In `setInteraction()` of `bubbleplot.js`, you listen for "mouseover" events to trigger a label to appear for the circle you hover over. The function is called at the end of `initChart()`. You have to call the function for the following to apply to the circles:

```
function setInteraction() {

    // Create label
    labeltext = svg.append("text")
        .attr("text-anchor", "middle");
```

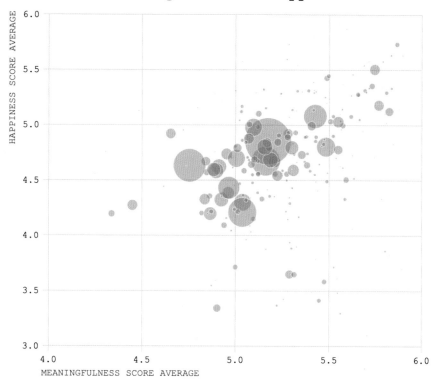

Meaningfulness with Happiness

FIGURE 6.10 *Bubble chart with improved visibility*

```
// Hover events
circle.on("mouseover", function(e,d) {
    d3.selectAll(".current").classed("current", false);
    d3.select(this).classed("current", true);

    let curract = d3.select(this).datum();

    labeltext.text(curract.descrip)
        .attr("x", x(curract.meaning_mean))
        .attr("y", y(curract.schappy_mean)-r(curract.relwt)-5);
})
.on('mouseout', function(d) {
    d3.select(this).classed('current', false);
    labeltext.text('');
}); // @end mouseover

}
```

A blank text element is added to the SVG. Then on a mouseover, the current circle selected is given a CSS class of `current`, and any previous elements that were classed as `current` are set to `false`. The class is defined in `style/style.css` to make the border of the circle black.

The data bound to the circle is assigned to `curract`. This data is used to set the label text and set the x and y attributes to place the text just above the current circle, as shown in Figure 6.11.

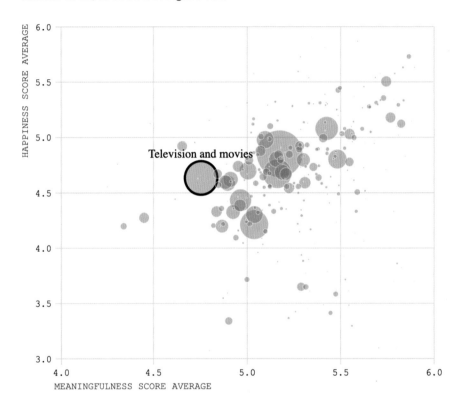

FIGURE 6.11 *Bubble chart with hover text*

On a `mouseout` event, when the cursor moves away from a circle, the CSS class is removed, and the text is set to blank.

DIFFERENCES

How different is one thing from another? Are they the same? Have the differences changed over time? In comparing ourselves and situations to others, we can't help but look for the differences. The unevenness. My young children are

Note: When I first learned JavaScript and how to use D3, I was caught off guard by how much I had to define to make charts interactive. Part of this comes from D3 intended for custom visualization, but it's also partly the nature of making things for the Web.

especially in tune with who got what and what is fair, which I then respond with their differences in age and the need to adjust their expectations.

In the grown-up world, we often highlight the differences between men and women. There are differing expectations, responsibilities, and motivations that diverge and converge over time. For example, Figure 6.12 shows percentages of male and female employees for jobs that were once mostly male but shifted to majority female. A lot of the change comes from women more commonly entering the workforce, and some is from a shift in culture.

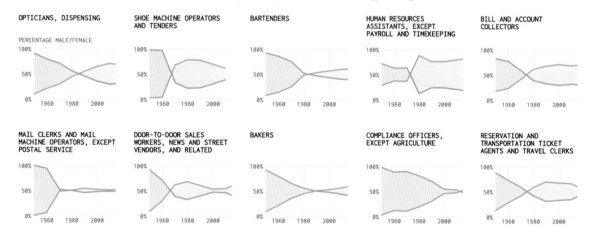

FIGURE 6.12 *"Most Male and Female Occupations Since 1950,"* Nathan Yau / 2007-Present FlowingData / https://flowingdata.com/2017/ 09/11/most-female-and-male-occupations-since-1950 / *last accessed February 08, 2024.*

The example uses difference charts, which you'll see more of in this section, to highlight the space between male and female percentages over time. You could show the same percentages with a two-line line chart or a stacked bar chart, but these focus specifically on which category is greater during a given time. Telling stories with data is about directing attention to the insights of interest.

BARBELL CHART

A barbell chart is like a dot plot that focuses on the difference between two categories across various groups. Visualization folks like to name chart types after things in the physical world, and as shown in Figure 6.13, the comparisons look like barbells. I guess it's catchier than my description.

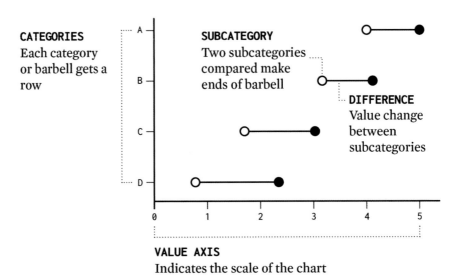

FIGURE 6.13 *Barbell chart framework*

The chart is useful for direct comparisons between two categories, such as demographic groups. Think age groups, sex, or race. The dots let you show where each category is, and the line in between emphasizes the difference. So you often see the chart used to show gaps between the sexes, which is what you'll look at in the following example.

MAKING A BARBELL CHART

Tools used: HTML, CSS, JavaScript, D3.js

Dataset: Taking Care of Kids, Men and Women, book.flowingdata.com/vt2 /ch6/data/hh-activities-withkids.tsv

Sticking with D3, there are again three parts with HTML, CSS, and JavaScript. The HTML and CSS are like the previous examples, which you can look at in the barbell folder of this chapter's source. The main difference is in the JavaScript (js/barbell.js), but there are also parts that you'll recognize.

In this example, you compare the time spent by mothers and fathers on childcare-related activities based on American Time Use Survey responses between 2013 and 2017. Men have shifted toward more responsibilities in taking care of children, but there is still a noticeable difference between men and women, who tend to take on more. How much do they differ, and in what?

As before, set the dimensions and start the SVG in the same way. The left margin is wider than that of the scatterplot and bubble chart to give more space for labels.

```
// Dimensions of chart.
let margin = { top: 20, right: 20, bottom: 50, left: 290 },
    width = 650 - margin.left - margin.right,
    height = 550 - margin.top - margin.bottom;
// Start SVG
let svg = d3.select("#chart").append("svg")
    .attr("width", width + margin.left + margin.right)
    .attr("height", height + margin.top + margin.bottom)
  .append("g")
    .attr("transform", "translate(" + margin.left + ","
+ margin.top + ")");
```

Define the x- and y-scales. Use `d3.scaleBand()` this time for the y-scale, which is useful for showing categories on an axis. The domain will be set after loading the data.

```
// Scales: x and y
let x = d3.scaleLinear()
    .domain([0, 80])
    .range([0, width]);
let y = d3.scaleBand()
    .range([height, 0]);
```

Load the dataset, which is a TSV file. Each row represents an activity, and there are columns for the percentage of women who engaged in the activity, the percentage of men who engaged in the activity, and an activity code with a description. The following snippet sorts the rows by the percentages for women, from least to greatest. A function `initChart()` is called when the data loads.

```
// Load data
const activitiesData = Promise.all([
    d3.tsv("data/hh-activities-withkids.tsv", d3.autoType)
]);
activitiesData.then(function(data) {
    activities = data[0].sort((a, b) => a.pctkidsf - b.pctkidsf);

    // Initialize chart now that data is loaded.
    initChart();
});
```

In `initChart()`, set the domain of the y-scale based on the data that was loaded. The domain, or the range of the data, will be the description of each activity, such as physical care, homework, and attending events. Whereas in the previous examples the y-scale was linear, defined by `.scaleLinear()`, the y-scale here is defined with `.scaleBand()` to indicate a categorical scale that is evenly split across the range (from `height` to 0 in this case).

```
// y-scale domain
y.domain(activities.map(d => d.desc));
```

With axes defined, they are added by `initChart()`. Figure 6.14 shows what the chart looks like so far.

Who Takes Care of the Kids

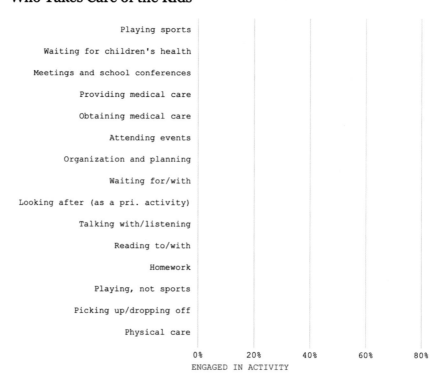

FIGURE 6.14 *Axes added for barbell chart*

For each activity, add an SVG group element, <g>, translated vertically to the corresponding position on the y-scale.

```
// barbells
barbell = svg.selectAll(".barbell")
    .data(activities)
    .join("g")
    .attr("class", "barbell")
```

```
    .attr("transform", d =>
        "translate(0,"+(y(d.desc)+(y.bandwidth()/2))+")")
    .attr("id", d => "act"+d.code);
```

Then for each group element, add a connecting `line` from the percentage for men to the percentage for women on the x-axis.

```
// connecting lines
barbell.append("line")
    .attr("x1", d => x(d.pctkidsm))
    .attr("x2", d => x(d.pctkidsf))
    .attr("y1", 0).attr("y2", 0)
    .attr("stroke", "#000000");
```

Append the circles for the men's percentages. The `cx` attribute sets the x-position of the circle. The `cy` attribute is set to 0, because the group element that the circle is appended to was already translated. Generally speaking, the position of child elements in a <g> element are relative to the parent <g> element. The `r` attribute, for radius, is set to 6.

```
barbell.append("circle")
    .attr("class", "men")
    .attr("cx", d => x(d.pctkidsm))
    .attr("cy", 0)
    .attr("r", 6);
```

except use `pctkidsf`.

```
barbell.append("circle")
    .attr("class", "women")
    .attr("cx", d => x(d.pctkidsf))
    .attr("cy", 0)
    .attr("r", 6);
```

Finally, add labels for the circles as <text> elements so a reader knows what colors represent men and women.

```
// labels
svg.append("text")
    .attr("x", x(activities[14].pctkidsm))
    .attr("y", y(activities[14].desc))
    .attr("text-anchor", "middle")
    .text("MEN");
svg.append("text")
    .attr("x", x(activities[14].pctkidsf))
    .attr("y", y(activities[14].desc))
    .attr("text-anchor", "middle")
    .text("WOMEN");
```

The barbell chart, shown in Figure 6.15, shows a higher percentage of women than men engaged in each activity. The biggest difference is in physical care and pick-up and drop-off.

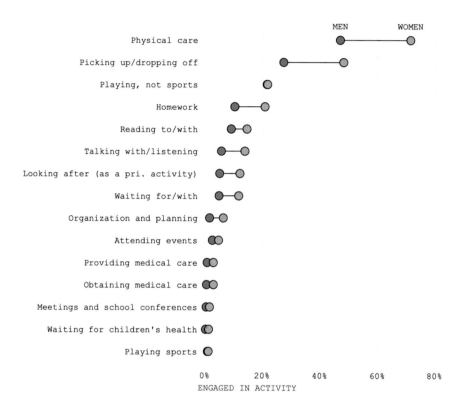

FIGURE 6.15 *Barbell chart comparing categories*

DIFFERENCE CHART

Imagine a line chart with two lines. Each line represents a category, and over time, you want to highlight which category is greater. So, you fill the area between the two lines based on which category is greater. This is a difference chart, as shown in Figure 6.16.

You can still see the trends over time, like with a line chart, but the focus is on the difference between the two represented categories. The gap gets bigger and smaller over time, and color indicates which is greater.

The main trade-off with this chart is that not everyone will understand how to read it right away because it's not as widely used as line charts. However, you can make the patterns more obvious with annotations that guide readers where to look.

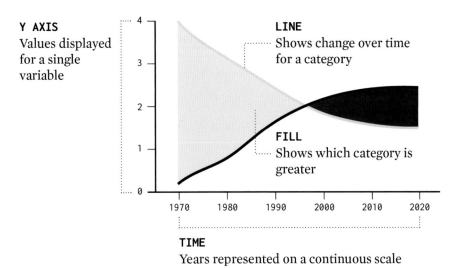

Y AXIS
Values displayed for a single variable

LINE
Shows change over time for a category

FILL
Shows which category is greater

TIME
Years represented on a continuous scale

FIGURE 6.16 *Difference chart framework*

MAKING A DIFFERENCE CHART

Tools used: HTML, CSS, JavaScript, D3.js

Dataset: Beef and Chicken Consumption, 1909-2017 book.flowingdata.com /vt2/ch6/data/beef-vs-chicken-difference.csv

When comparing meat consumption per capita, beef was the leader for decades, but chicken took over the last decade and seems to be pulling further ahead. When did chicken finally overtake beef? How much more beef did people consume? A difference chart can show the shift over time, using estimates from the United States Department of Agriculture.

We're sticking with D3 for one more example, and we have HTML, CSS, and JavaScript. The HTML and CSS are like the other examples, so you'll focus on the JavaScript portion. I won't show every line of code here, so open the differencechart source to follow along.

The margins and SVG are set like before. This time, though, you use linear scales for x and y. The x-scale represents years, and the y-scale represents pounds per capita consumed each year in the United States.

```
// Scales: x and y
let x = d3.scaleLinear()
    .domain([1909, 2017])
    .range([0, width]);
let y = d3.scaleLinear()
    .domain([0, 100])
    .range([height, 0]);
```

The data is a CSV file with three columns for year, beef consumption in pounds per capita, and chicken consumption in pounds per capita. It looks like this:

```
Year,Beef,Chicken
1909,51.1,10.4
1910,48.5,11.0
1911,47.2,11.1
1912,44.5,10.6
1913,43.6,10.3
1914,42.7,10.3
1915,38.8,10.2
```

After the data is loaded in `differencechart.js`, `initChart()` is called where the x- and y-axes are added. To add lines, you append `<path>` elements using `d3.line()` to define the geometry. Add the line for chicken consumption as shown here:

```
// Chicken consumption line
svg.append("path")
    .attr("class", "line chicken")
    .attr("fill", "none")
    .attr("stroke", "#bf980d")
    .attr("stroke-width", "2px")
    .attr("d", d3.line()
        .x(d => x(d.Year))
        .y(d => y(d.Chicken)));
```

Append another path for beef consumption. It is the same as the chicken consumption line, except the y-coordinate is the `Beef` variable. Figure 6.17 shows the line chart.

```
// Beef consumption line
svg.append("path")
    .attr("class", "line beef")
    .attr("fill", "none")
    .attr("stroke", "#fb470e")
    .attr("stroke-width", "2px")
    .attr("d", d3.line()
        .x(d => x(d.Year))
        .y(d => y(d.Beef)));
```

To fill in the area between the lines, you can use clipping paths. You create an area that fills from the top of the chart to the beef consumption line and another area that fills from the bottom of the chart to the beef consumption line. Then the clipping paths are used to cut out the area above and below the consumption lines. Create the clipping paths first.

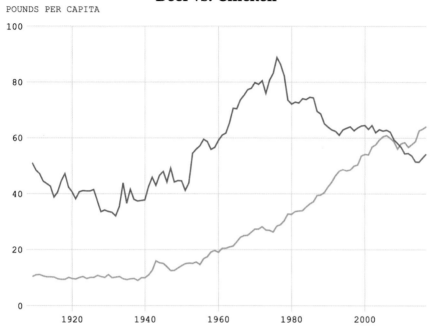

POUNDS PER CAPITA

Beef vs. Chicken

FIGURE 6.17 *Line chart with two lines*

```
// Area clipping paths
svg.append("clipPath")
    .attr("id", "clip-above")
    .append("path")
    .attr("d", d3.area()
        .x(d => x(d.Year))
        .y0(0)
        .y1(d => y(d.Chicken)));
svg.append("clipPath")
    .attr("id", "clip-below")
    .append("path")
    .attr("d", d3.area()
        .x(d => x(d.Year))
        .y0(height)
        .y1(d => y(d.Chicken)));
```

Then create the areas and apply the clipping paths using the `clip-path` attribute. This is probably confusing if you're unfamiliar with JavaScript and SVG clipping paths, but try commenting out the lines that add the `clip-path` attributes to see what the areas look like without the clipping paths versus with.

```
// Area differences
svg.append("path")
    .attr("class", "area above")
    .attr("clip-path", "url(#clip-above)")
    .attr("fill", "#fdad94")
    .attr("d", d3.area()
        .x(d => x(d.Year)).y0(height).y1(d => y(d.Beef)));
svg.append("path")
    .attr("class", "area below")
    .attr("fill", "#f9e59f")
    .attr("clip-path", "url(#clip-below)")
    .attr("d", d3.area()
        .x(d => x(d.Year)).y0(0).y1(d => y(d.Beef)));
```

Note: The difference chart code is adapted from an example by Mike Bostock, the creator of D3. Find it at `https: //datafl.ws/7my`.

In Figure 6.18, you can see beef dominate, but then chicken takes over in 2010. It looks like chicken might stick around for a while.

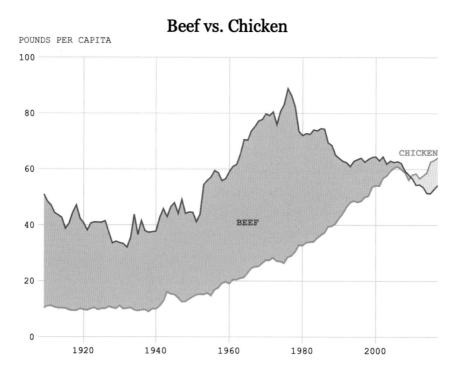

FIGURE 6.18 *Difference chart for beef versus chicken*

HIGHLIGHTING DIFFERENCES

You compared categories with barbell and difference charts. However, you can also highlight differences with charts that are not specifically designed to show gaps and change. Adjust color, scale, and geometry to draw focus to where you need.

Figure 6.19, a line chart sometimes referred to as a *baseline chart*, shows the shift in bachelor's degrees conferred by field of study. Instead of showing totals over the years, percentages change compared to the counts from the first year highlight shifts. Color further directs attention to the fields of study with more change.

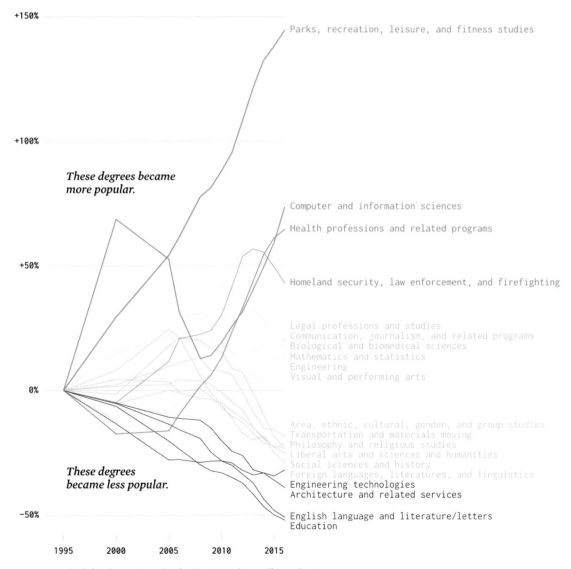

FIGURE 6.19 *"Bachelor's Degree Movers,"* Nathan Yau / 2007-Present FlowingData / https://flowingdata.com/2019/07/10/bachelors-degree-movers / *last accessed February 08, 2024.*

A stacked area chart, shown in Figure 6.20, highlights the contrast between who is older and younger than you, given your age. Usually, the y-axis shows a range from 0% to 100%, but an extension of the axis to show both categories separately draws more attention to the splits.

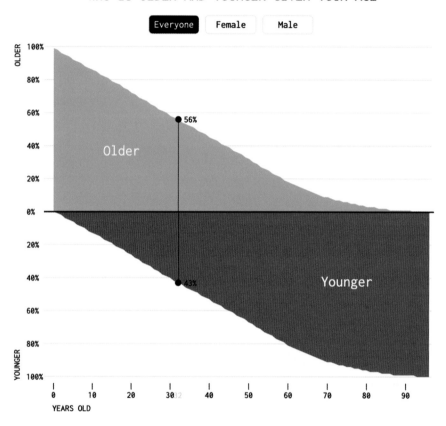

WHO IS OLDER AND YOUNGER GIVEN YOUR AGE

FIGURE 6.20 *"Who is Older and Younger than You,"* Nathan Yau / 2007-Present FlowingData / `https://flowingdata.com/2016/05/10/who-is-older-and-younger-than-you` / *last accessed February 08, 2024.*

Compare categorical values against a reference point, and a bar chart can show differences like a baseline chart. Use a color scheme that represents more than or less than, and you can use a heatmap to show similar data. You can contrast multiple charts with the same geometry but different subsets of the data. Think about the aspects or insights from the data you want to show and let them guide your design and story.

MULTIPLE VARIABLES

The chart types so far show two variables at a time. You showed correlation between two variables. You showed the differences between two categories. Visualizing the relationships between more than two variables is tricky because more variables mean more complexity. To communicate the complexity, you either must explain data concepts or assume your audience already knows how to interpret your results.

However, if the emphasis is more on the individual observations than on overall patterns between all the data points and variables, the charts seem to have a higher success rate. Think of the visualization as a reference or to display a profile.

For example, I occasionally like to bring data out of the screen and into the physical world. In one of those experiments, I brewed beer based on county data, as shown in Figure 6.21. An R script considered population density, race, education levels, healthcare coverage, and household income to define the amounts of hops and grains used in a beer recipe for a given county.

FIGURE 6.21 *"Brewing Multivariate Beer,"* FlowingData / https://flowingdata.com/2015/05/20/brewing-multivariate-beer / *last accessed February 08, 2024.*

I translated multiple variables into a single result: the beer. For more statistically rigorous examples, you might want to check out *principal component analysis* or *multidimensional scaling*, but making beer is also fun.

If beer is of interest, I also visualized all the styles based on multiple variables at `https://datafl.ws/7mv`.

HEATMAP FOR MULTIPLE VARIABLES

You saw how to use a heatmap to visualize data over time in Chapter 4, and the overall structure to show multiple variables is similar, as shown in Figure 6.22. Each row represents a unit or an observation, each column represents a variable, and each cell represents the value of the corresponding observation-variable pair with a color.

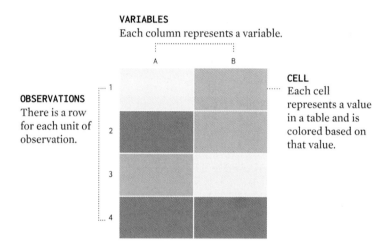

VARIABLES
Each column represents a variable.

A   B

OBSERVATIONS
There is a row for each unit of observation.

1
2
3
4

CELL
Each cell represents a value in a table and is colored based on that value.

FIGURE 6.22 *Heatmap for multiple variables framework*

For multiple variables, the method is useful for a wideout view of your dataset. You can spot missing values or outliers, and you can use it as a reference to look up observations. However, deciphering relationships and patterns is usually more challenging.

MAKING A HEATMAP FOR MULTIPLE VARIABLES

Tools used: R

Dataset: NBA top scorers, 2022-2023 season, `book.flowingdata.com/vt2/ch6/data/nba-top50scorers-2022-23.csv`

I have fond memories of flipping to the sports section in the daily newspaper (delivered to our house!) to see how my favorite basketball teams and players did the night before. We didn't have cable television, and the reception wasn't great all the time, so I rarely watched the games live. The box scores the day after were the next best thing. In this example, you look at the stats for the National Basketball Association's top 50 scores from the 2022–23 season. Are minutes per game, shooting percentages, and points per game related?

Load the data with `read.csv()` and use `head()` to see the first few rows.

```
# Load data
players <- read.csv("data/nba-top50scorers-2022-23.csv")
head(players)
```

The following is a sample of the rows and columns. Each row represents a player, and each column represents a player stat. During the 2022–23 season, Joel Embiid was the leading scorer with 33.1 points per game.

```
> head(players[,c("Player", "FG", "FGpct", "PTS")])
                      Player   FG FGpct  PTS
1               Joel Embiid 11.0 0.548 33.1
2         Luka Don&ccaron;i&cacute; 10.9 0.496 32.4
3            Damian Lillard  9.6 0.463 32.2
4 Shai Gilgeous-Alexander 10.4 0.510 31.4
5   Giannis Antetokounmpo 11.2 0.553 31.1
6             Jayson Tatum  9.8 0.466 30.1
```

For simplicity's sake, subset the first 20 players.

```
# First 20 players
play20 <- players[1:20,]
```

Use the `heatmap()` function, which takes a data matrix and translates the values to filled cells. Set scale to `column` so that the color scale is defined by the range of values in a column, and set `Rowv` and `Colv` to `NA` so that dendrograms linking rows and columns aren't drawn.

```
# Four columns
heatmap(as.matrix(play20[,c("MP", "FG", "FGpct", "PTS")]),
        scale = "column",
        Rowv = NA, Colv = NA)
```

Figure 6.23 shows the output with a structure that resembles the data frame. There are four columns for minutes played per game (`MP`), field goals per game (`FG`), field goal percentage (`FGpct`), and points per game (`PTS`).

Just looking at the heatmap, you don't know which row represents which player. Set `labRow` to the `Player` column for row labels so that the heatmap provides a better reference, as shown in Figure 6.24.

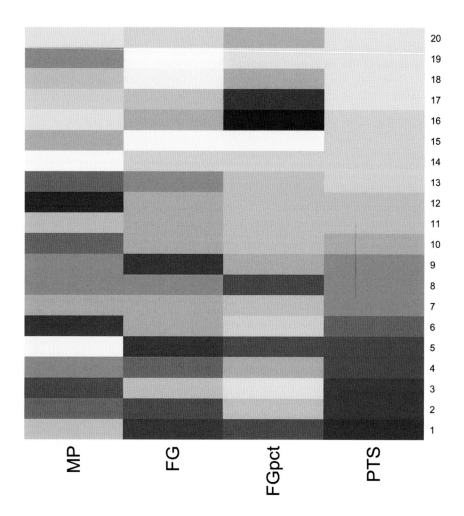

FIGURE 6.23 *Heatmap for NBA players*

```
# Names
heatmap(as.matrix(play20[,c("MP", "FG", "FGpct", "PTS")]),
        scale = "column",
        labRow = play20$Player,
        Rowv = NA, Colv = NA)
```

To reverse the order of the players so that the leading scorer, Joel Embiid, is at the top, you can use order() to rearrange the data.

```
# Reorder
playrev <- play20[order(play20$PTS, decreasing = FALSE),]
```

Then pass playrev to heatmap(). While you're at it, show more columns and change the color scheme away from the default with the col argument.

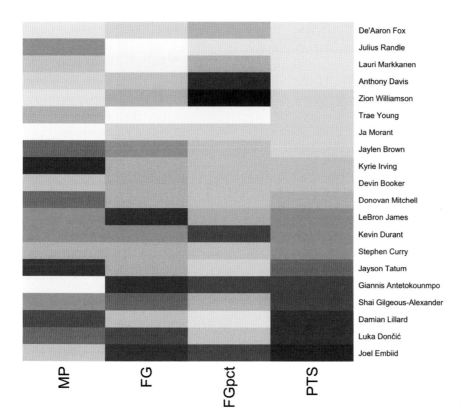

De'Aaron Fox
Julius Randle
Lauri Markkanen
Anthony Davis
Zion Williamson
Trae Young
Ja Morant
Jaylen Brown
Kyrie Irving
Devin Booker
Donovan Mitchell
LeBron James
Kevin Durant
Stephen Curry
Jayson Tatum
Giannis Antetokounmpo
Shai Gilgeous-Alexander
Damian Lillard
Luka Dončić
Joel Embiid

MP FG FGpct PTS

FIGURE 6.24 *Heatmap with row labels*

```
fnames <- c("MP", "FG", "FGpct", "X2Ppct", "X3Ppct", "FTpct",
"PTS")
heatmap(as.matrix(playrev[,fnames]),
        scale = "column",
        labRow = playrev$Player,
        cexCol = 1,
        col = rev(hcl.colors(20, palette = "Blues 3")),
        Rowv = NA, Colv = NA)
```

As shown in Figure 6.25, you get a heatmap with a blue color scheme and more columns of data, with Embiid at the top of the chart.

As you might expect, you can customize the chart more with labels, sizes, and different subsets of the data. Enter `?heatmap` in the R console to check the documentation. Or export the image as a PDF and edit in Illustrator like in previous chapters.

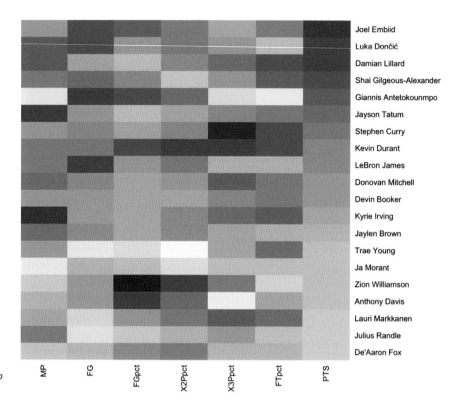

FIGURE 6.25 *Reordered heatmap and a different color scheme*

PARALLEL COORDINATES

Parallel coordinates use positioning and lines to show the relationships between variables. As shown in Figure 6.26, you place multiple axes parallel to each other. The top of each axis represents a variable's maximum, and the bottom represents the minimum. For each unit, a line is drawn from left to right, moving up and down, depending on the unit's values.

A cluster of lines that move up or down together indicates that a correlation between the connecting variables might exist. Lines that cross randomly indicate weak or no correlation.

The challenge is that you can only compare adjacent variables in such a plot and the overall pattern of the lines change depending on the ordering of the axes. So, I tend toward other methods where I can make more comparisons or see patterns more clearly. But maybe you will find a good use for the method.

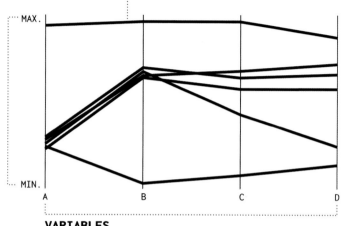

CONNECTING LINES
One line per unit. Look for common
trends across multiple units.

RELATIVE SCALES
Axes span
minimum to
maximum for
each variable.

VARIABLES
Multiple axes placed parallel to each other to find
relationships across variables

FIGURE 6.26 *Parallel coordinates plot framework*

MAKING PARALLEL COORDINATES

Tools used: R

Dataset: NBA top scorers, 2022-2023 season book.flowingdata.com/vt2/ch6
/data/nba-top50scorers-2022-23.csv

Come back to the basketball data from the heatmap example. Maybe it'll be useful to see the data from the parallel coordinates point of view.

Install and load the MASS package in R, which provides a function for parallel coordinates.

```
# Install/load package
install.packages("MASS")
library(MASS)
```

Load the dataset with read.csv(). Remember that the file path is relative to your current working directory.

```
# Load data
players <- read.csv("data/nba-top50scorers-2022-23.csv")
```

Note: The chart can work
as a reference if you're
more interested in each
unit than overall relationships. For example, the
Guardian used a modified
version of parallel coordinates to show athlete rankings https://datafl
.ws/7ms.

If you enter `head(players)`, you'll see that each row of the data represents a player, and 31 columns represent information about each player, such as minutes played, field goal percentage, and points per game. Subset the data to seven of the columns as shown here:

```
fnames <- c("MP", "FG", "FGpct", "X2Ppct", "X3Ppct",
"FTpct", "PTS")
psub <- players[,fnames]
```

The subset is assigned to `psub`. Enter `head(psub)` to see the first few rows. It looks like the following, which shows minutes per game (`MP`), field goals per game (`FG`), field goal percentage (`FGpct`), two-point percentage (`X2Ppct`), three-point percentage (`X3Ppct`), free-throw percentage (`FTpct`), and points per game (`PTS`):

```
    MP   FG FGpct X2Ppct X3Ppct FTpct  PTS
1 34.6 11.0 0.548  0.587  0.330 0.857 33.1
2 36.2 10.9 0.496  0.588  0.342 0.742 32.4
3 36.3  9.6 0.463  0.574  0.371 0.914 32.2
4 35.5 10.4 0.510  0.533  0.345 0.905 31.4
5 32.1 11.2 0.553  0.596  0.275 0.645 31.1
6 36.9  9.8 0.466  0.558  0.350 0.854 30.1
```

It's OK if you don't what these mean in terms of basketball. Just treat them as metrics that may or may not be related.

Pass `psub` to the `parcoord()` function from the MASS package. Figure 6.27 shows the result.

```
parcoord(psub)
```

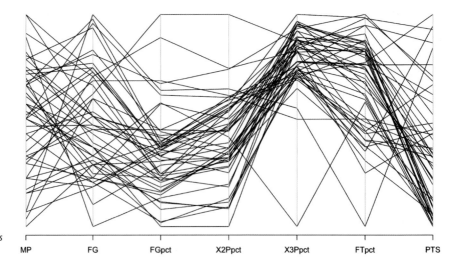

FIGURE 6.27 *Parallel coordinates for basketball players*

There appears to be a positive correlation between two-point percentage and three-point percentage and maybe between three-point percentage and free-throw percentage. The lines tend to move in the same direction as the former but are less tightly paired between the latter. The other metrics appear less related with a lot of crossing lines in between the axes.

You can see how the chart can get messy quickly. When there are a lot of lines that cross each other, the chart looks like scribbles. However, sometimes it's helpful to show one observation at a time, and the rest of the lines provide context.

Try making one chart each for Joel Embiid, Giannis Antetokounmpo, Stephen Curry, and LeBron James. Start with the names.

```
# One player at a time
curr_players <- c("Joel Embiid", "Giannis Antetokounmpo",
                "Stephen Curry", "LeBron James")
```

Use a `for` loop to make each chart in a two-by-two layout.

```
# Chart each player
par(mfrow=c(2,2))
for (pl in curr_players)) {
    col <- rep("gray", dim(players)[1])
    lwd <- rep(.5, dim(players)[1])
    i <- which(players$Player == pl)
    col[i] <- "blue"
    lwd[i] <- 3
    parcoord(psub, col=col, lwd=lwd, main=pl)
}
```

Whereas Figure 6.27 uses equal visual weight to each line, Figure 6.28 gives more visual weight to the current player in blue, and the other lines provide a point of comparison.

Embiid, Curry, and James follow similar patterns, but Antetokounmpo shows a dip at free-throw percentage (FTpct), with the lowest percentage out of the top 50 scorers during the season. The low free-throw percentage stands out compared to the gray lines for the other players.

That said, if you want to compare each variable against the others, a *scatterplot matrix* might work better. Use `plot()` on the player subset.

```
# Scatterplot Matrix
plot(psub)
```

Network graphs are not as popular as they once were, because the novelty wore off, and when you have a lot of vertices and edges, you can quickly end up with an unreadable hairball. Network graph software implements algorithms to minimize overlap and cluster vertices based on number and strength of connections between other vertices, but it has its limitations.

Still, with these limitations in mind, it's not hard to find use cases that let you see connections in a more literal way than abstract metrics.

MAKING A NETWORK GRAPH

Tools used: R

Each network showing the family structures in Figure 6.31 was made in R. This example covers how you might make one of those networks, which you can extrapolate for your own data.

Note: igraph is an open-source collection of tools that, in addition to R, is available for Python, Mathematica, and C. Find more details at `https://datafl.ws/7mw`. The process is similar to the steps outlined here.

In the R console, install the igraph package if you don't have it yet with `install.packages()` and then load the package with `library()`.

```
install.packages("igraph")
library(igraph)
```

Start with an empty graph using `make_empty_graph()`. Set the `directed` argument to `FALSE` since we don't care about the direction of the connections between vertices in this example.

```
# Empty graph
g <- make_empty_graph(directed=FALSE)
```

Add vertices to the empty graph, g, with `add_vertices()`. The following adds one vertex with hexadecimal `color` of `#a3b8a3` and a `size` of 50, which indicates diameter of the circle:

```
# Add vertices
g <- g %>% add_vertices(1, color="#a3b8a3", size=50)
```

Add another vertex with a different `color` but the same `size`.

```
g <- g %>% add_vertices(1, color = "#d7c668", size=50)
```

Then add 10 vertices with a smaller `size` of 20.

```
g <- g %>% add_vertices(10, color = "#cccccc", size=20)
```

Pass g to the `plot()` function to draw the current graph.

```
plot(g)
```

The result, in Figure 6.33, has one large green vertex, a large yellow one, and 10 smaller gray ones for 12 vertices total. The numbers indicate the index and order the vertices were added to the graph.

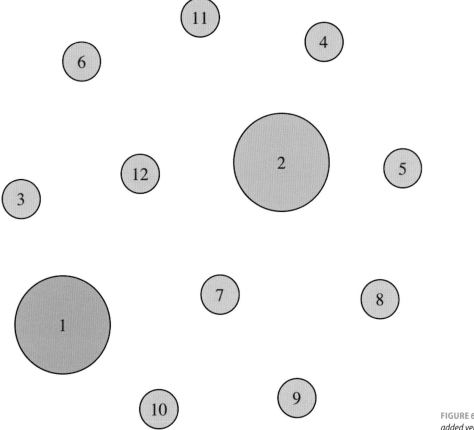

FIGURE 6.33 *Graph with added vertices*

You add edges in a similar way with add_edges(). However, instead of specifying how many to add, you use a vector of indices to define how and what to connect. Pass c(1, 2) to add an edge that connects vertices 1 and 2. You can specify the color of the edge, which will be a line, and the weight, set to 0.01 for now, which indicates how strong the connection is between the vertices.

```
# Connect the two first vertices
g <- g %>% add_edges(c(1,2), weight=0.01, color="#cccccc")
```

You can add multiple edges by adding pairs of numbers to the vector of indices. To connect vertices 8 and 10 and then 8 and 7, try the following:

```
# Connect 8 to 10 and 7
g <- g %>% add_edges(c(8,10, 8,7), weight=0.01, color="#cccccc")
```

Here is how to add three edges between 3 and 1, 4 and 1, and 5 and 1. The
weight and the color are the same.

```
# Connect 3, 4, and 5 to 1
g <- g %>% add_edges(c(3,1, 4,1, 5,1), weight=0.01,
color="#cccccc")
```

Figure 6.34 shows what you have so far. If you're following along, you might
note the placement of the vertices looks different. There is randomness in the
initial placement, so the layout is not always the same.

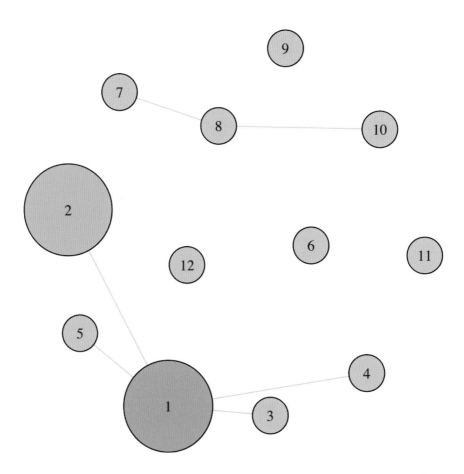

FIGURE 6.34 *Graph with edges
and vertices*

Add two more edges with greater `weight`.

```
# Connect 11 and 12 to 2 with more weight
g <- g %>% add_edges(c(12,2, 11,2), weight=1, color="#cccccc")
```

Call `plot()` again, and you get Figure 6.35. The vertices 11 and 12 are closer to node 2, because the `weight` on the edges were higher than the previous ones.

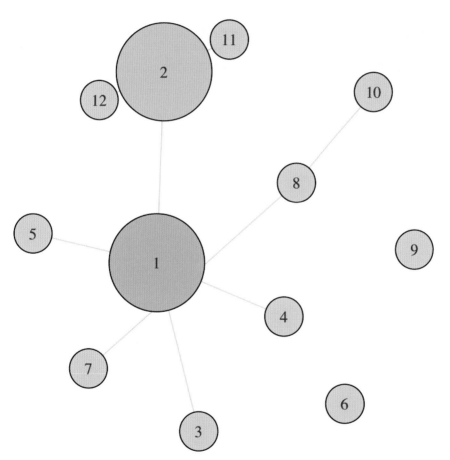

FIGURE 6.35 *Varying weights for the edges*

The igraph package provides various layout algorithms that you can choose depending on your application. The following snippet uses the Fruchterman-Reingold force-directed algorithm, a grid, and a circle, and the last one, `layout _ nicely`, tries to automatically pick for you based on the graph's properties. Figure 6.36 shows the differences.

```
# Layouts
par(mfrow=c(2,2), mar=c(1,0,3,0))
plot(g, vertex.label=NA, layout=layout_with_fr, main="Force-
directed")
plot(g, vertex.label=NA, layout=layout_on_grid, main="Grid")
plot(g, vertex.label=NA, layout=layout_in_circle, main="Circle")
plot(g, vertex.label=NA, layout=layout_nicely, main="Nicely")
```

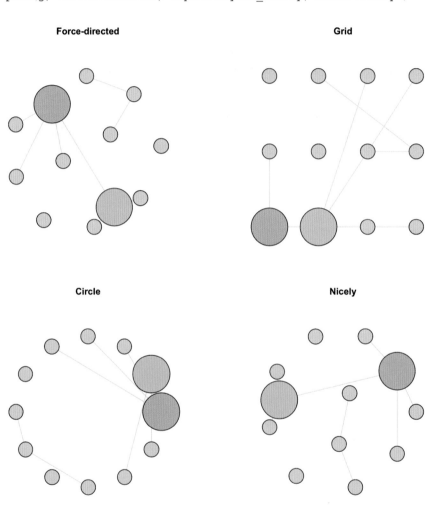

FIGURE 6.36 *Different graph layouts*

You can do more by adding and removing vertices and edges, adjusting sizes, weights, and colors, and using different layout algorithms. However, I tend to avoid more complex networks because I am not fond of the hairball aesthetic. That said, check out `make-network-graph.R` in the chapter source for an example of making a network graph based on a dataset.

WRAPPING UP

Relationships can be complex and messy. They can also be super obvious. So, it's best to consider the context of the data: where it came from, how and why variables appear connected, and how they differ. Use this information to understand data better and help others interpret results.

As you saw in this chapter, various chart types can highlight relationships in different ways. Alternatively, you can design more general chart types to show what you want by adjusting color, geometry, and data choices. Focus more on showing aspects of your data than on just showing data, which typically yields better results with purpose.

You got your first dose of making charts for the Web using the JavaScript library D3.js. There was a little bit of HTML and CSS. If you're new to web development, this might have been tricky because there are more moving parts instead of calling a single function. But if you want flexibility in the browser, it's worth going deeper.

Next up: visualizing space.

Visualizing Space

Location is inherent in many of the things we do. As you read these words, you're aware of where you physically are in the world, and it's increasingly easy to pull out a digital map to find directions to where you want to go. There's an immediate connection to location, which makes maps a great way to visualize geographic data for understanding and communicating spatial patterns.

Mapping spatial data shares much of the process required by visualizing data with charts. However, the added dimension of physical location brings with it different considerations.

For example, a plot that uses abstract x- and y-coordinates can be easily transformed between linear and logarithmic scales to improve readability. Transforming a map that uses latitude and longitude can't just be cropped, zoomed, and stretched without considering the preservation of area, distance, and boundary shapes.

There are separate fields of study to analyze spatial data and to communicate with maps. This chapter focuses on a subset of these fields that uses maps to visualize data. You look at *locations*. Where are people, places, and things in the world? You look at *spatial distributions*. How are the people, places, and things spread out or concentrated within different regions? You look at change over space and time. Does spread change year over year?

WORKING WITH SPATIAL DATA

There are usually two categories when working with spatial data: the geography and the data associated with that geography. You use the former to make the map with boundaries, locations, and features such as bodies of water. The latter tells you about the former, such as who or what lives there.

Sometimes, the data comes bundled together in one set of files. Often, the data that defines the map, and the data about the places in the map come separately, so you have to merge them. In this chapter, you'll learn how to handle this, but first, let's briefly look at working with the geography portion specifically.

GEOCODING ADDRESSES

When your data is a collection of addresses, how do you specify their locations on a map? You can't just open R and tell it to plot 123 Random Street, Some City, USA. You need to know where each address is in terms of latitude, the north-south position of a point on the surface of Earth, and longitude, the east-west position, also known as *geographic coordinates*. *Geocoding* is the process of finding geographic coordinates based on an address. *Reverse geocoding* is the process of finding addresses given geographic coordinates.

There are many services you can use to geocode coordinates, but your results will vary depending on where your addresses are based and their accuracy. Paid services run by companies like Google, Mapbox, and Esri tend to be the most robust. If you have funds and are short on time, you can access their APIs, usually priced by number of queries.

Worthwhile free options do exist, though. Nominatim uses OpenStreetMap data, and you can either search for addresses one by one in the browser or use the API for higher volumes.

For addresses based in the United States, the Census Bureau has a geocoder that you can access via API or upload up to 10,000 addresses and get back coordinates in a batch. It doesn't always find coordinates, though.

Sometimes, the best solution is to use a combination of the geocoding services. For example, you could use free services to get most of your coordinates, and for the addresses that return errors or no results, you could use one of the paid services. The Python library geopy can be helpful here, which lets you try different services at once.

Useful Geocoding Tools

- **Google Maps Platform** (`developers.google.com/maps`): Provides APIs for map, including for geocoding

- **Mapbox**(`mapbox.com`): An alternative to Google Maps that will probably yield similar results

- **Esri ArcGIS Platform**(`esri.com`): Useful if you already use ArcGIS

- **Census Geocoder**(`geocoding.geo.census.gov`): Good for addresses in the United States

- **Nominatum**(`nominatim.openstreetmap.org`): Provides an interactive map and an API

- **geopy**(`github.com/geopy/geopy`): Python library to use multiple geocoding services

MAP PROJECTIONS

With maps, you must compromise when you represent a three-dimensional world with two dimensions on the screen or on paper. *Map projections*, essentially math that places three-dimensional space on a two-dimensional surface, are part of the compromise. They typically try to minimize distortion in area, shape, direction, or distance or a combination of them. Figure 7.1 shows a handful of projections, but some projections are better at things and worse at others, so you choose based on the geography you want to show.

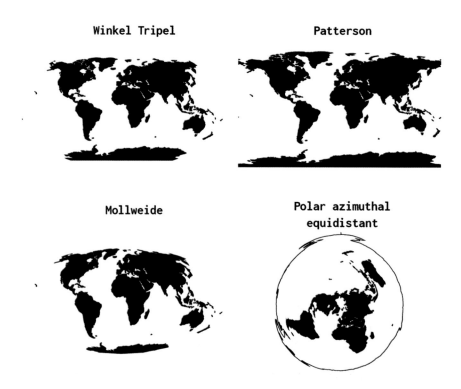

FIGURE 7.1 *Map projections sample*

For example, the Mercator projection provides latitude and longitude lines that are straight, which are good for showing turn-by-turn directions. The popular online mapping services use Mercator for their maps when you need to get from one place to another. The streets appear with right angles. But as shown in Figure 7.2, when you zoom out to show larger areas, the spaces toward the poles appear much larger than they are. This uses Tissot's indicatrix, which uses circles to show the amount of distortion in map projections.

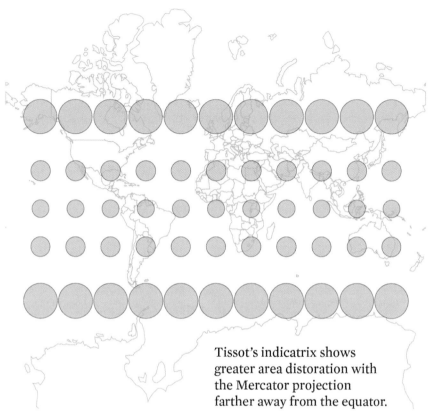

Tissot's indicatrix shows greater area distoration with the Mercator projection farther away from the equator.

FIGURE 7.2 *World map with Mercator projection*

On the other hand, the Albers projection preserves area for regions about the size of the United States or Europe, so many maps of those places use Albers. The Gall-Peters projection distorts shape but preserves area. The Winkel tripel projection minimizes distortion of area, direction, and distance, and it's a common projection for maps of the world.

Many of the projections have parameters for latitude and longitude to define focus on different areas of the world. So, with unlimited options, it can be kind of overwhelming at first. The good news is that you don't have to remember the parameters and customizations most of the time. From a practical standpoint, you can reuse the same projections quite a bit or look up typical projections for a given geography.

Find more demonstrations of the distortion with the Mercator projection at `https://datafl .ws/7n7`.

I can never remember all the parameters for every projection, so I either revisit my old projects or search for the geography of interest to see what is currently standard.

LOCATIONS

Where? It is the most basic question you can ask with a map, but it can take you down many paths. Where are we? Where do we need to go? Where is the nearest pizza place? Where is the best pizza place? From there, you can ask how are locations connected? What is this place like, and how does it compare to others?

For example, one day I wondered about popular coffee chains across the country. My main experience was with Starbucks, which is nearly everywhere, and then I moved to southern California, where I enjoyed The Coffee Bean & Tea Leaf, and then in Buffalo, New York, I saw the dominance of Tim Hortons. I mapped several coffee chains, as shown in Figure 7.3.

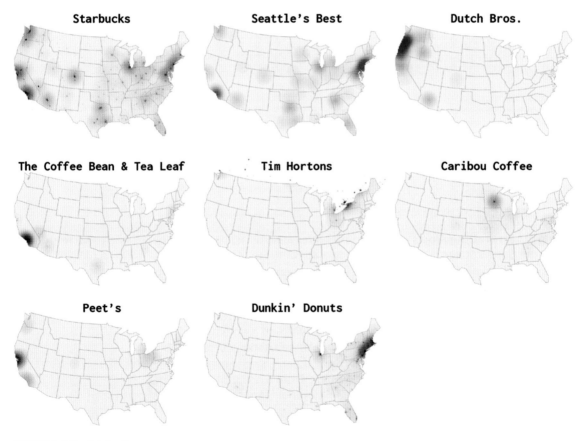

FIGURE 7.3 *Coffee chain locations*

Which coffee chain reigned supreme? As shown in Figure 7.4, I compared number of locations within a 10-mile radius across the country and colored dots by the predominant chain. Starbucks covered the largest geographic area; however, other chains held their own.

FIGURE 7.4 *"Coffee Place Geography,"* https://datafl.ws/coffee

My fascination continued with pizza, grocery stores, sandwich shops, and bars. A simple question about coffee shops led to many more questions and maps, along with playful discussions around the Internet as people chose their favorites.

When looking at location, you want to answer questions about where, the aggregates, and how they might connect. Start with the basics and see where it takes you.

POINTS

The most straightforward way to show locations with latitude and longitude is to draw points on a map. As shown in Figure 7.5, you draw a marker for each location.

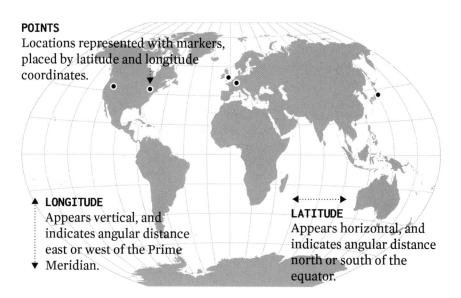

POINTS
Locations represented with markers, placed by latitude and longitude coordinates.

LONGITUDE
Appears vertical, and indicates angular distance east or west of the Prime Meridian.

LATITUDE
Appears horizontal, and indicates angular distance north or south of the equator.

FIGURE 7.5 *Mapping points framework*

Although a simple concept, you can see features in the data such as clustering, spread, and outliers.

MAPPING POINTS

Tool used: R

Datasets:

- State boundaries for the United States, `book.flowingdata.com/vt2/ch7/data/cb _ states.zip`
- Walmart Locations in the United States, `book.flowingdata.com/vt2/ch7/data/walmart-openings-geocoded.csv`

Mapping locations with points is like making a dot plot in R. Set up a visualization area and add dots. However, instead of drawing a blank plot and adding points with x-y-coordinates, you first make a blank map and then use longitude and latitude to define the locations of points.

In this example, you want to see where Walmart locations are in the conterminous United States. So, you will draw a map with state boundary lines and then add the locations.

Load the sf package (i.e., Simple Features for R), which provides functionality specifically for spatial data. Use `install.packages()` if don't have the package yet.

```
Library(sf)
```

The state boundary lines come as a shapefile from the U.S. Census Bureau, which updates boundaries at various geographic levels each year. The shapefiles are available in this chapter's download material. Point to the file path for the `.shp` file and use `st_read()` from the sf package to load the file:

```
# State boundaries
statefp <- "data/cb_states/cb_2022_us_state_20m.shp"
statebnds <- st_read(statefp)
```

Here is a subset of the data, which contains polygons for each state and metadata, such as a unique ID, state abbreviation, and name.

```
Simple feature collection with 6 features and 3 fields
Geometry type: MULTIPOLYGON
Dimension:      XY
Bounding box:   xmin: -124.5524 ymin: 25.84012
    xmax: -80.84313 ymax: 47.05468
Geodetic CRS:   NAD83
    AFFGEOID STUSPS      NAME                     geometry
1 0400000US48    TX      Texas MULTIPOLYGON (((-106.6234 3...
2 0400000US06    CA California MULTIPOLYGON (((-118.594 33...
3 0400000US21    KY   Kentucky MULTIPOLYGON (((-89.54443 3...
4 0400000US13    GA    Georgia MULTIPOLYGON (((-85.60516 3...
5 0400000US55    WI  Wisconsin MULTIPOLYGON (((-86.93428 4...
6 0400000US41    OR     Oregon MULTIPOLYGON (((-124.5524 4...
```

For the sake of simplicity, subset the `statebnds` data to the conterminous United States.

```
# Conterminous United States
inconterm <- !(statebnds$STUSPS %in% c("AK", "HI", "PR"))
conterm <- statebnds[inconterm,]
```

Store locations are in a CSV file, so use `read.csv()`.

There is more than one way to make maps in R. I primarily use the sf package, but you might also want to check out the maps or terra packages to use instead of or in combination with sf.

```
# Store locations
stores <- read.csv("data/walmart-openings-geocoded.csv")
```

Use `head()` to see the first rows of the data and to make sure it loaded correctly.

```
> head(stores)
  store_num year month day      lat       lng   store
1         1 1962     7   1 36.33445 -94.17890 walmart
2         2 1964     8   1 36.25059 -93.11949 walmart
3         4 1965     8   1 36.18320 -94.51260 walmart
4         7 1967    10   1 34.83613 -92.23114 walmart
5         8 1967    10   1 35.16881 -92.72411 walmart
6         9 1968     3   1 36.89540 -89.59512 walmart
```

Each row represents a store with an opening date (`year`, `month`, and `day`), location expressed as latitude (`lat`) and longitude (`lng`), and the kind of store, which can be Walmart or the Walmart-owned Sam's Club. Subset to just the Walmart stores.

```
# Subset to Walmart stores only
walmarts <- stores[stores$store == "walmart",]
```

With data loaded and subset, the mapping part is straightforward with the `plot()` function. The following shows how to draw the original state boundaries from the shapefile. The call to `st_geometry()` on the `statebnds` data is to specify a map of just boundaries rather than several maps of metadata.

```
# States and United States territories
plot(st_geometry(statebnds))
```

Figure 7.6 shows boundaries for the conterminous United States along with Alaska, Hawaii, and Puerto Rico. Because of geographic space in between regions, it is difficult to see everything, which is why in this example you focus on the conterminous United States.

FIGURE 7.6 *Default state boundaries*

Use `plot()` and `st_geometry()` again, but this time use the `conterm` subset.

```
# Conterminous United States
plot(st_geometry(conterm))
```

As shown in Figure 7.7, you can more easily see the boundaries of the states.

FIGURE 7.7 *Conterminous United States*

Use `points()` to add store locations to the map. Treat longitude, which specifies the east-west position on a map, as the x-coordinate and latitude, which specifies the north-south position on a map as the y-coordinate. Make the locations blue for now with the `col` argument.

```
# Draw locations
points(walmarts$lng, walmarts$lat,
       col="blue")
```

Figure 7.8 shows the result. As you might expect, Walmart is located across the country with a higher concentration in areas with greater populations.

To transform the map to an Albers projection, which is commonly used to show the United States, use the *proj-string* assigned to `conterm _ p4s` and apply it to `conterm` with `st _ transform()`.

```
# Project map
conterm_p4s <-
    "+proj=aea +lat_1=29.5 +lat_2=45.5 +lon_0=97.2w"
conterm_albers <- st_transform(conterm, conterm_p4s)
```

You must also transform the store locations, but to use `st _ transform()`, the data must be a compatible data type, which in this case, is an object of

The shapefile stores geographic locations, so if you want to map Alaska, Hawaii, and Puerto Rico in the same view but on different scales, you must add the maps separately. I like to use the `plt` graphical parameter with `par()`, but you can also try using `layout()` or `viewport()`.

Note: The Albers projection, named after Heinrich Albers, is an equal-area map projection, which means it preserves area across geographies.

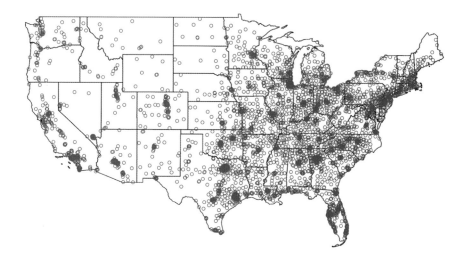

class *sf*. You can change the `walmarts` data frame with `st _ as _ sf()`. Pass the data frame, specify which columns represent the coordinates, and set the proj-string.

```
# Set data
wal_sf <- st_as_sf(walmarts,
                   coords = c("lng", "lat"),
                   crs = "+proj=longlat")
```

Use `st _ transform()` on the new Walmart data, `wal _ sf`, using the same proj-string, `conterm _ p4s`, you used to transform the boundaries.

```
# Transform points
wal_sf_albers <- st_transform(wal_sf, conterm_p4s)
```

Map the store locations the same as before using the projected data. Let's adjust colors and line widths while we're at it when calling `plot()` and `points()`.

```
# Projected points on map
par(mar = c(0,0,0,0))
plot(st_geometry(conterm_albers),
     border = "#cccccc", lwd = .5)
points(st_coordinates(wal_sf_albers),
       col="#30437b", cex = .5)
```

You get a map with an Albers projection, as shown in Figure 7.9, which probably looks familiar shape-wise.

This process of converting data and projecting the boundaries and geographic coordinates typically follows the same steps for other geometries you want to use in maps.

SCALED SYMBOLS

Oftentimes, you don't just have location data. You have data associated with the locations, such as sales for a business or city population. You can still map with points, but you can take the principles of a bubble plot, discussed in Chapter 6, "Visualizing Relationships," and use it on a map. As shown in Figure 7.10, you scale symbols by area and place them on the map by location.

ADDING SCALED SYMBOLS

Tool used: R

Datasets:

- State boundaries for the United States, book.flowingdata.com/vt2/ch7/data/cb _ states.zip
- Walmart Locations in the United States, book.flowingdata.com/vt2/ch7/data/walmart _ addresses.csv

and running paths, or relationships between geographic locations, such as migration and financial aid. As shown in Figure 7.13, lines draw attention to how the locations go together.

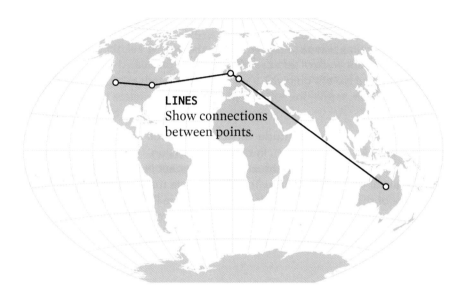

LINES
Show connections
between points.

FIGURE 7.13 *Mapping lines framework*

ADDING LINES

Tool used: R

Datasets:

▨ State boundaries for the United States, `book.flowingdata.com/vt2 /ch7/data/cb_states.zip`

▨ Walmart Locations in the United States, `book.flowingdata.com/vt2 /ch7/data/walmart_addresses.csv`

▨ Brewery Road Trip, `book.flowingdata.com/vt2/ch7/data/brewery-road-trip-path.tsv`

To draw lines that connect locations on a map, you follow the same process as points and symbols. Draw a blank map. Add lines (and other geometries if you like). In this example, you draw a line that connects the first two state centroids from the previous example. It assumes you have boundaries for the conterminous United States and Walmart locations loaded, assigned to `conterm` and `statesdf`, respectively.

Draw a blank map with zero margins using the `mar` argument from `par()` and `st_geometry()` to draw only the boundaries from the shapefile data.

```
# Blank map
par(mar=c(0,0,0,0))
plot(st_geometry(conterm), border="#cccccc")
```

Use `lines()` to draw a single line. The function takes a vector of x-coordinates and a vector of y-coordinates, which in this case, are the first two observations from `statesdf`. Set line width (`lwd`) to 2 and line color (`col`) to the hexadecimal value #30437b.

```
# Draw line
lines(x = statesdf$X[1:2],
      y = statesdf$Y[1:2],
      lwd = 2,
      col = "#30437b")
```

This adds a line to the map, as shown in Figure 7.14.

FIGURE 7.14 *Line connecting two locations*

You can also add other elements to the map, such as points and labels. For example, use `points()` to add end points to the existing line.

```
# End points
points(x = statesdf$X[1:2],
       y = statesdf$Y[1:2],
       pch = 21,
       bg = "#30437b",
       col = "#000000")
```

Note: Think of the addition of more elements to a blank map as layering on top of the other. The blank map is the bottom layer, the line is the second layer, the points are the third, and the labels the top layer.

Add labels for the state abbreviations with `text()`. Use the same x- and y-coordinates from the lines and points, but give the y-coordinates a 0.75 bump up so that the labels appear above the points.

```
# Labels
text(x = statesdf$X[1:2],
     y = statesdf$Y[1:2]+.75,
labels = statesdf$abbrev[1:2])
```

As shown in Figure 7.15, this places two points at the end of the lines and labels on top of each point.

FIGURE 7.15 *Connecting line and points*

This is a simplified example with only two x-y-coordinates, but the same logic applies to add a line with more points. As shown in the following snippet, load `brewery-road-trip-path.tsv`. It is the data for the algorithmically routed road trip through the best breweries in the United States described in Chapter 1, "Telling Stories with Data."

```
# A longer path
roadtrip <- read.csv("data/brewery-road-trip-path.tsv",
                     sep = "\t")
```

The data is assigned to `roadtrip`. Use `head(roadtrip)` to see the first rows of the data frame. There are several columns to the dataset, but you need only the first two for this example to map latitude and longitude.

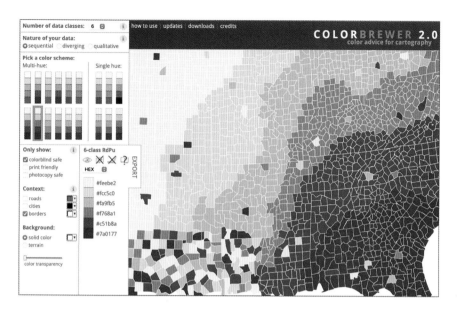

FIGURE 7.20 *Sequential color schemes with ColorBrewer*

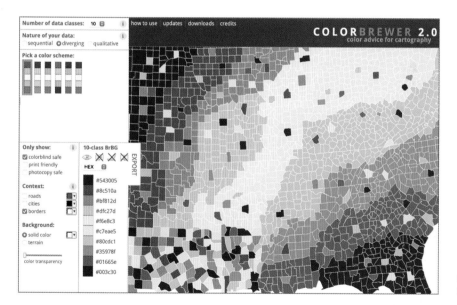

FIGURE 7.21 *Diverging color schemes with ColorBrewer*

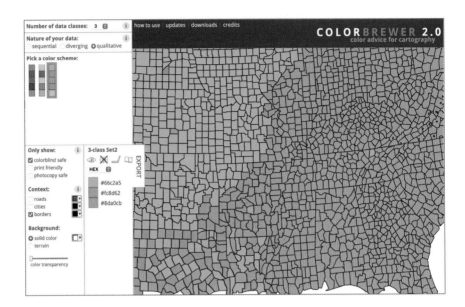

FIGURE 7.22 *Qualitative color scheme with ColorBrewer*

Colorblind-Safe Palettes

When using color as the main visual encoding for your data, such as with choropleth maps and heatmaps, select palettes that are colorblind-safe. About 1 in 12 men and 1 in 200 women have red-green colorblindness, the most common type. This means it is difficult to see the difference between shades of red and green. So, if you make a map that uses only red and green, someone who is red-green colorblind would likely be unable to compare regions. This defeats the purpose of making the map.

Plenty of tools can help with this. ColorBrewer provides a filter to show only colorblind-safe palettes; the Chroma.js Color Palette Helper runs a check to see if your selections are colorblind-safe; Adobe products like Illustrator have options in the View menu to simulate colorblindness in your designs; Microsoft has an Accessibility Checker to analyze spreadsheets; Sim Daltonism is an app that lets you point your camera to see from the perspective of someone who is colorblind. So, it's a lot more straightforward these days to pick colors that everyone can see.

If all else fails, because you're restricted by an existing color scheme or need to use color to match for context, you can use more than one encoding to represent data. This is called *redundant encoding*. You can use text, position, or size to indicate values, along with color. Even if people can't see the contrast between shades, they can still pick up on other cues.

MAKING A CHOROPLETH MAP

Tool used: R

Datasets:

▪ State boundaries for the United States, `book.flowingdata.com/vt2` `/ch7/data/cb_states.zip`

▪ Population Counts, by Race, `book.flowingdata.com/vt2/ch7/data` `/DECENNIALPL2020.P1.zip`

Are there geographic patterns in the distribution of the Asian population in the United States? A choropleth can show what states and regions have high and low rates, based on population estimated from the Census Bureau. Sticking with R, the process should look familiar if you worked through the previous examples.

Load the sf package, which provides functions to work with spatial data.

```
library(sf)
```

Load the shapefile for state boundary lines at a 1 to 20,000,000 scale using `st_read()`.

Note: Remember that file paths are relative to your current working directory in R.

```
# Boundaries
statefp <- "data/cb_states/cb_2022_us_state_20m.shp"
statebnds <- st_read(statefp)
```

Subset to the conterminous United States and transform to Albers.

```
# Conterminous subset
inconterm <- !(statebnds$STUSPS %in% c("AK", "HI", "PR"))
conterm <- statebnds[inconterm,]
conterm_p4s <- "+proj=aea +lat_1=29.5 +lat_2=45.5 +lon_0=97.2w"
conterm_albers <- st_transform(conterm, conterm_p4s)
```

Load state-level population data from the 2020 decennial Census with `read.csv()`.

```
# Load population data
fileloc <- "data/DECENNIALPL2020.P1/DECENNIALPL2020.P1.csv"
pop <- read.csv(fileloc, stringsAsFactors = FALSE)
```

Each row represents a state, and there are 71 columns that represent counts for people who identify as a single race or multiple races. Find the first few rows here:

```
> pop[1:10, 1:5]
           GEO_ID                  NAME   P1_001N   P1_002N   P1_003N
1  0400000US01               Alabama   5024279   4767326   3220452
2  0400000US02                Alaska    733391    643867    435392
3  0400000US04               Arizona   7151502   6154696   4322337
4  0400000US05              Arkansas   3011524   2797949   2114512
5  0400000US06            California  39538223  33777988  16296122
6  0400000US08              Colorado   5773714   5066044   4082927
7  0400000US09           Connecticut   3605944   3273040   2395128
8  0400000US10              Delaware    989948    913430    597763
9  0400000US11  District of Columbia    689545    633468    273194
10 0400000US12               Florida  21538187  17986115  12422961
```

In this example, you want the P1_001N column for total population and P1_006 column for Asian population. You can also look at DECENNIALPL2020. P1_metadata.csv in the same data folder to try other variables later.

Note the first column GEO_ID from pop. It represents a unique ID for each state. Now, look at the first few rows attached to the boundary data conterm_albers.

```
> conterm_albers[1:10, 1:6]
   STATEFP    STATENS      AFFGEOID GEOID STUSPS        NAME
0       48  01779801  0400000US48    48     TX       Texas
1       06  01779778  0400000US06    06     CA  California
2       21  01779786  0400000US21    21     KY    Kentucky
3       13  01705317  0400000US13    13     GA     Georgia
4       55  01779806  0400000US55    55     WI   Wisconsin
5       41  01155107  0400000US41    41     OR      Oregon
6       29  01779791  0400000US29    29     MO    Missouri
7       51  01779803  0400000US51    51     VA    Virginia
8       47  01325873  0400000US47    47     TN   Tennessee
9       22  01629543  0400000US22    22     LA   Louisiana
```

Note: The logic with match() can take some getting used to, because you must keep track of indices, but I like it for the flexibility. You might find merge() more intuitive to join two datasets. Enter ?merge in the console to read the documentation.

The AFFGEOID column from conterm_albers is the same ID structure as GEO_ID from pop. You can use these shared IDs to join the population data to the boundary data with match(). The function returns a vector (the most common data structure in R with elements of the same type) of indices, where the former is located in the latter. The indices are used to get the matching population from pop. For example, the first state in conterm_albers is Texas with an AFFGEOID of 0400000US48. This matches the 44th row in pop. In the following, the 44th value in the P1_006N column, or Asian population, is returned for the first row (for Texas) in conterm_albers.

```
# Join Asian population
conterm_albers$asianpop <-
    pop$P1_006N[match(conterm_albers$AFFGEOID, pop$GEO_ID)]
```

Do the same with the `P1_001N` column to join the total population to the `conterm_albers` boundary data.

```
# Join total population
conterm_albers$totalpop <-
    pop$P1_001N[match(conterm_albers$AFFGEOID, pop$GEO_ID)]
```

Calculate the proportion or rate of Asian population out of the total population for each state.

```
# Calculate rate
conterm_albers$asianrate <-
    conterm_albers$asianpop / conterm_albers$totalpop
```

The `conterm_albers` data has three new columns now: `totalpop`, `asianpop`, and `asianrate`. Check to see if the calculations look right.

```
> conterm_albers@data[1:10,
+     c("NAME", "totalpop", "asianpop", "asianrate")]
        NAME totalpop asianpop  asianrate
0       Texas 29145505  1585480 0.05439878
1  California 39538223  6085947 0.15392566
2    Kentucky  4505836    74426 0.01651769
3     Georgia 10711908   479028 0.04471920
4   Wisconsin  5893718   175702 0.02981174
5      Oregon  4237256   194538 0.04591132
6    Missouri  6154913   133377 0.02167001
7    Virginia  8631393   615436 0.07130205
8   Tennessee  6910840   135615 0.01962352
9   Louisiana  4657757    86438 0.01855786
```

Use `summary()` on the `asianrate` variable to check the quartiles and the range.

```
# Summary statistics
summary(conterm_albers$asianrate)
```

As shown here, the range is about zero to 0.153 with a median of 0.029. That seems about right.

```
    Min.  1st Qu.   Median     Mean  3rd Qu.     Max.
0.007655 0.017695 0.029366 0.038254 0.047825 0.153926
```

With the population data matched to the boundary data, the next step is to define the color scheme. This is when the color tools described in Chapter 2 come in handy. The hexadecimal colors assigned to `shades` in the newly defined function `pickCol()` shown here were generated using the Chroma.js Color Palette Helper:

```
# Define color
pickCol <- function(x) {
    propbreaks <- c(0, .02, .04, .06, .08, 1)
    shades <- c('#d9e0e1', '#acc0c4', '#7fa1a8',
                '#51828c', '#196572')
    i <- max(which(propbreaks <= x))
    return(shades[i])
}
```

The `pickCol()` function takes a value and returns a color based on where it lies on the `propbreaks` scale. The `sapply()` function is used to get the color for each value of `asianrate` in `conterm_albers`.

```
conterm_albers$col <-
    sapply(conterm_albers$asianrate, pickCol)
```

Typically, when you define a color scheme for a choropleth map, the shades should be based on a normalized variable instead of absolute counts. Otherwise, larger regions, such as California, will always have greater counts just because of its size. In this example, the shades are chosen based on proportions, which are normalized by population.

Plot `conterm_albers` and set the `col` argument in `plot()` to define the fill color of each state. Use a white border.

```
# Draw map
plot(st_geometry(conterm_albers),
     col = conterm_albers$col,
     border = "white")
```

This returns a choropleth map with higher rates shown with darker shades, as shown in Figure 7.23.

To add a color legend to the map, I often use Adobe Illustrator to add one manually, but the `legend()` function is a quick way to add one in R. The function is flexible enough so that you can make different types of legends with variation in labels, colors, and geometry. The following snippet adds a legend on the bottom left of the map with a rectangle and corresponding label for each color:

```
# Add legend
legend("bottomleft",
       legend = c("0-.01", ".02-.03", ".04-.05",
                  ".06-.07", ".08+"),
       fill = c('#d9e0e1', '#acc0c4', '#7fa1a8',
                '#51828c', '#196572'),
       title = "Asian Population")
```

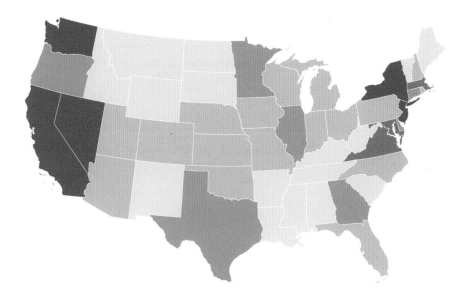

FIGURE 7.23 *Choropleth map colored by rate*

CARTOGRAM

An advantage of choropleth maps is that you can use a familiar map like a contextual anchor for readers. Usually, readers will have at least a sense of the boundary shapes in the areas they've lived. Then you just add color to the shapes for another layer of meaning. However, a trade-off with choropleth maps is that large geographic areas will always get more visual attention than small geographic areas because they fill more space.

Cartograms treat geography more loosely and size areas or symbols by data. So, a large place with few people won't take up so much space when you want to visualize a dataset that is about people.

The example cartogram in Figure 7.24 is a noncontiguous isomorphic cartogram that shifts the size of geographic areas. That is, the cartogram preserves the shape of the boundaries but does not require that the states stay together.

This is one type of cartogram among many that have been devised over the years. A contiguous cartogram keeps neighboring boundaries intact and stretches areas like a sheet of rubber. Dorling cartograms use scaled circles. Mosaic cartograms restrict the layout in a grid.

Each type of cartogram has its merits but, of course, comes with a trade-off that shows geographic areas that are not geographically locked into place. For

SCALED REGIONS
Geographic areas are
proportional to data.

FIGURE 7.24 *Cartogram framework*

many, the trade-off is too much, so they stick to choropleth maps. I'll leave it up to you. I personally have an affinity for Dorling cartograms. I have an aversion to contiguous cartograms because the shapes are usually so warped that it is difficult to compare areas, which makes it difficult to see anything useful.

MAKING A CARTOGRAM

Tool used: R

Datasets:

▦ State boundaries for the United States, book.flowingdata.com/vt2 /ch7/data/cb _ states.zip

▦ Population Counts, by Race and Origin, book.flowingdata.com/vt2 /ch7/data/DECENNIALPL2020.P1.zip

If you made the choropleth map to show Asian population rates in the previous example, then the cartogram package will make the rest straightforward. However, if you didn't make the choropleth map yet, work through the example to load boundary and population data, join the two datasets, and select colors. Then come back to this example.

The goal is to show both Asian rates and total population counts at the same time. Color will represent the former, and circle size will represent the latter in

a Dorling cartogram. Start by loading the cartogram package. Enter `install`
`.packages("0-.01")` if you do not have the package installed yet.

```
library(cartogram)
```

Assuming you have the data from the previous example loaded, pass
`conterm _ albers` to `cartogram _ dorling()`, weighted by `asianpop` to
indicate size.

```
# Cartogram calculations
conterm_dorling <- cartogram_dorling(conterm_albers,
                                     weight = "asianpop")
```

Draw a blank state map with `plot()`.

```
# Blank map
plot(st_geometry(conterm_albers),
     border = "#cccccc",
     lwd = .6)
```

Then add the cartogram circles, also with `plot()`, but with the `add` argument
set to `TRUE`. Use the same color choices from the choropleth map.

```
# Add Dorling cartogram circles
plot(st_geometry(conterm_dorling),
     col = conterm_albers$col,
     add = TRUE)
```

Figure 7.25 shows a cartogram with circles size by Asian population in each
state. The circles, most noticeable in the northeast, do not overlap.

FIGURE 7.25 *Dorling cartogram,
sized by count and colored by rate*

To maintain boundary lines with a noncontiguous cartogram, you follow the same steps, except instead of `cartogram_dorling()`, you use `cartogram_ncont()` to calculate.

```
# Non-contiguous
conterm_ncont <- cartogram_ncont(conterm_albers,
                                 "asianpop")
```

Draw a blank map first, and then add the cartogram shapes.

```
# Blank map and cartogram
plot(st_geometry(conterm_albers),
     border = "#cccccc",
     lwd = .6)
plot(st_geometry(conterm_ncont),
     col = conterm_albers$col,
     add = TRUE)
```

State geometries are sized by Asian population instead of circles, as shown in Figure 7.26.

FIGURE 7.26 *Noncontiguous cartogram, sized by count and colored by rate*

Since you're here, you might as well try a contiguous cartogram that preserves adjacent borders. The steps are similar and made easy with the cartogram package, given you prepared the data. Use `cartogram_cont()` and use `plot()` to draw the results.

```
# Contiguous cartogram
conterm_cont <- cartogram_cont(conterm_albers,
                               "asianpop")
plot(st_geometry(conterm_cont),
     col = conterm_albers$col)
```

You get a blobby result that loosely resembles the United States, as shown in Figure 7.27.

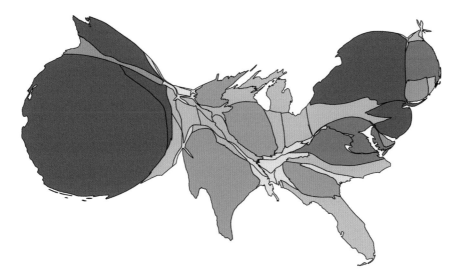

FIGURE 7.27 *Contiguous cartogram, sized by count and colored by rate*

Can you make cartograms for different race populations?

DOT DENSITY MAP

Whereas the cartogram modifies areas to shift visual attention to larger values, a dot density map uses dots instead of a solid fill to represent data. As shown in Figure 7.28, more dots mean greater counts.

Large areas with low counts appear sparse, and smaller areas with high counts appear dense. Dots are usually placed randomly or in a grid, depending on the total counts. The map type is often used to show population density across geographic regions, so the dot metaphor isn't too far off from reality.

The dot density map has been around since the early 1800s, but the method more recently regained popularity with maps by Bill Rankin. In 2009, Rankin mapped race and income in Chicago, Illinois. Dots colored by class shows distinct neighborhood groupings even without government-drawn boundaries.

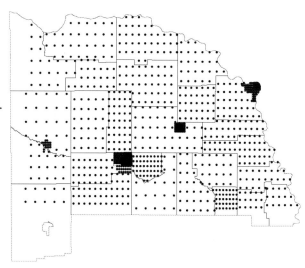

DOTS
Each represents a
unit of count and
distribution shows
density within region.

FIGURE 7.28 *Dot density map framework*

MAKING A DOT DENSITY MAP

Tool used: R

Datasets:

- Block group boundaries for Nevada, `book.flowingdata.com/vt2/ch7` `/data/cb _ 2022 _ 32 _ bg _ 500k.zip`
- Population Counts, by Race, `book.flowingdata.com/vt2/ch7/data` `/DEC2020.P8 _ bg.zip`

See Bill Rankin's dot density maps of Chicago at `https://datafl` `.ws/randots`. I made a national version, which you can find at `https://` `datafl.ws/dotsback`.

For a more granular view of Asian population, you zoom in to Census block groups in Nevada. Views at the state and county level can show general distributions, but as you get closer, you can see more details and variation. Load the sf package, which helps with handling spatial data.

```
library(sf)
```

Load the block groups for Nevada with `st _ read()`.

```
# Load block boundaries
bgfp <- "data/cb_2022_32_bg_500k/cb_2022_32_bg_500k.shp"
nvblocks <- st_read(bgfp)
```

Load block-level population data with `read.csv()`.

```
# Block level population
popfp <- "data/DEC2020.P8_bg/DECENNIALDHC2020.P8-Data.csv"
nvpop <- read.csv(popfp)
```

To get in closer, subset the boundary data to just Clark County in Nevada, which has an ID of 003.

```
# Clark county block groups
clarkblocks <- nvblocks[nvblocks$COUNTYFP == "003",]
```

Subset the population data, `nvpop`, to just Clark County also. The following snippet is different from earlier because the ID in the population data is in a different format than the boundary data.

```
> nvpop[1:5, c("GEO_ID", "P8_001N")]
                GEO_ID P8_001N
1          0400000US32 3104614
2 1500000US320030001011    1293
3 1500000US320030001012    1765
4 1500000US320030001013     644
5 1500000US320030001014    2062
```

We know that the ID for Clark County is 1500000US32003 (with a quick web search or a Census reference). The `GEO _ ID` in `nvpop` is a unique ID for each block group, but the first pass of the block group ID indicates the county. So, use `substr()` to take a substring that is of the length of `clark _ geoid` and subset based on the substrings.

```
# County level ids in nvpop
clark_geoid <- "1500000US32003"
nvpop$countyid <- substr(nvpop$GEO_ID, 1,
                    nchar(clark_geoid))
clarkpop <- nvpop[nvpop$countyid == clark_geoid,]
```

Join the boundary data and population data with `match()` like in previous examples.

```
# Merge population by county
imatch <- match(clarkblocks$AFFGEOID, clarkpop$GEO_ID)
clarkblocks$asianpop <- clarkpop$P8_006N[imatch]
```

Now there's an `asianpop` variable in `clarkblocks`. Use `st _ sample()` to calculate coordinates for one dot per ten population.

```
# Dots
clarkdots <- st_sample(clarkblocks,
    as.integer(clarkblocks$asianpop/10))
```

Draw the map and then add the dots. The hexadecimal color for the points, #19657250, is usually of length six, but the last two digits, 50, indicate an opacity of 50 percent to make the dots semi-transparent. So, when dots overlap, the color becomes darker rather than obscuring everything underneath.

Note: The `st _ sample()` function can take a little while depending on the complexity of your boundaries and how many dots you need.

```
# Map and dot
plot(st_geometry(clarkblocks),
     border = "#cccccc", lwd = .5)
plot(clarkdots, pch=19, cex=0.1,
     col="#19657250",
     add = TRUE)
```

As shown in Figure 7.29, there is a much higher population density in the center, and then population is sparser as you move away from the city centers.

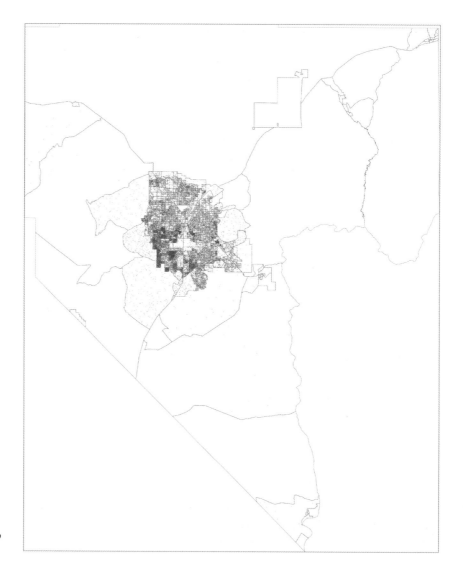

FIGURE 7.29 *Dot density map to show population*

Experiment with different colored dots, sizes, and number of dots per population to see how the map changes. With your own data, you'll want to look for the balance between image size and dot counts. If there are too many dots in a small space, the filled boundaries will look solid. If there are only a few dots in a big space, then the map will look almost blank.

I mapped one dot per person for all the races at `https://datafl.ws/dotsback`.

SPACE AND TIME

You've seen the different types of data and visualization methods separated by chapters, but as you saw in Chapter 5, data types can go together to form an interesting story. The passing of time lends itself well to creating a narrative that moves forward. Looking at space and time together works the same.

Think of each map you make as a snapshot in time. The data is collected during a period to estimate what the area was like then. So, if you make more than one map, you can show several snapshots in time. Create a sequence of maps spread over a significant time span, and you can see changes, stability, and irregularities.

Figure 7.30 shows a sequence of state grid maps that show obesity rates from 1985 through 2015, based on body mass index estimates from the Centers for Disease Control and Prevention (CDC).

Each square represents a state. Each grid represents a year. The colors represent the average rates in each state during a year. The color scale was chosen based on historical CDC maps and to show an inflection point in the 2000s, with a shift from green to purple, In the 1980s, obesity rates were mostly less than 15%, but by 2015, rates were mostly greater than 30%. Maybe this means that diets should adjust. Maybe this means we need to adjust the definition of healthy weight. Maybe it's both.

By placing the maps in a sequence over the years, you can see the shifts for individual states and how the nation changed overall. Spatial and temporal data go well together.

SEQUENCE OF MAPS

If you know how to make a single map, then you can make more than one map. Make maps for different periods of time, line them up, and you can show changes over space and time, as shown in Figure 7.31.

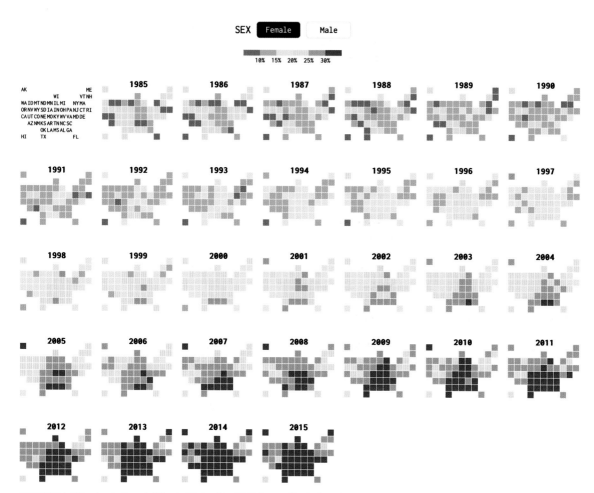

FIGURE 7.30 *"Mapping the Spread of Obesity,"* Nathan Yau / 2007-Present FlowingData/https://flowingdata.com/2016/09/26/the-spread-of-obesity / *last accessed February 08, 2024.*

MAP SEQUENCE
Placing maps together can show patterns over time.

FIGURE 7.31 *Sequence of maps framework*

START   MIDDLE   END

Usually, the main challenge is to make the changes noticeable between maps. Try a color scheme that emphasizes changes and differences. Use encodings that don't get lost when you make smaller maps.

Making a Sequence of Maps

Tool used: R

Datasets:

▓ State boundaries for the United States, `book.flowingdata.com/vt2/ ch7/data/cb_states.zip`

▓ Walmart Openings in the United States, `book.flowingdata.com/vt2/ ch7/data/walmart-openings-geocoded.csv`

The first Walmart location opened in 1962, then called Wal-Mart Discount City. Since then, thousands of locations opened around the world. How did they get to where they are now? You can map the Walmart location dataset you looked at already to see the growth over time.

You already made a map of all the locations. You can build on that previous example to make a sequence of maps. There will be one map per year to show the cumulative number of stores opened each year since 1962.

Load the sf package like before. It is the workhorse package for dealing with spatial data.

```
library(sf)
```

Read in state boundaries with `st_read()`, subset to the conterminous United States, and load the Walmart openings dataset with `read.csv()`. The dataset contains observations for both Walmart and the Walmart-owned Sam's Club, but you just need the Walmart locations.

```
# State boundaries
statefp <- "data/cb_states/cb_2022_us_state_20m.shp"
statebnds <- st_read(statefp)

# Conterminous United States
inconterm <- !(statebnds$STUSPS %in% c("AK", "HI", "PR"))
conterm <- statebnds[inconterm,]

# Store locations
stores <- read.csv("data/walmart-openings-geocoded.csv",
                   sep=",")
walmarts <- stores[stores$store == "walmart",]
```

Use the Albers projection to transform the state borders. Project the location data too with `st_transform()`.

```
# Project map
conterm_p4s <-
    "+proj=aea +lat_1=29.5 +lat_2=45.5 +lon_0=97.2w"
conterm_albers <- st_transform(conterm, conterm_p4s)

# Project points
wal_sf <- st_as_sf(walmarts,
                   coords = c("lng", "lat"),
                   crs = "+proj=longlat")
wal_sf_albers <- st_transform(wal_sf, conterm_p4s)
```

You've done everything up to this point in previous examples. Now, you get into the time component. Check the time span with `range()`.

```
> range(walmarts$year)
[1] 1962 2010
```

The data goes from 1962 to 2010. Set a sequence of numbers using the colon (:) notation for the year range.

```
# Year range
years <- 1962:2010
```

Set a seven-by-seven grid with the `mfrow` argument in `par()`. Set margins with `mar`, which is the space around each map, and the outer margins with `oma`, which is the space around the full grid.

```
# Seven rows, seven columns, with set margins
par(mfrow = c(7, 7),
    mar = c(2,0,1,0), oma = c(2,2,2,2))
```

Use a `for` loop to iterate through the years. On each iteration, you draw a map for the current year with points showing all the stores that have opened on or before that year.

```
for (yr in years) {
    curr <- wal_sf_albers[wal_sf_albers$year <= yr,]
    plot(st_geometry(conterm_albers),
         border = "#cccccc", lwd = .2,
         main = yr)
    points(st_coordinates(curr),
           col="#30437b", pch=20, cex = .2)
}
```

The `curr` line subsets the data, `plot()` line draws a blank map, and `points()` adds the stores based on the subset. This produces Figure 7.32.

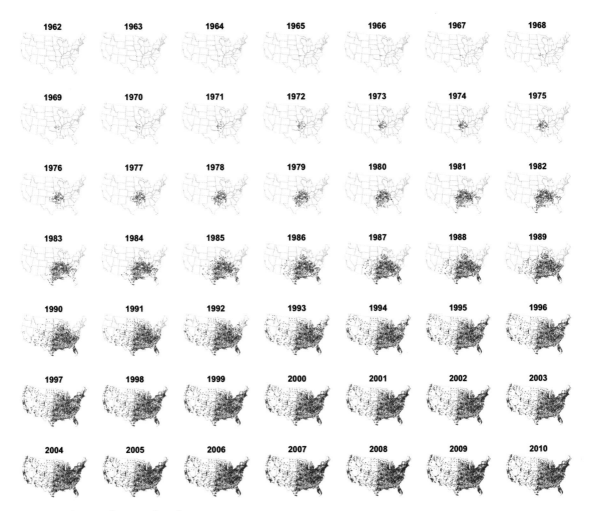

FIGURE 7.32 *Sequence of maps, one for each year*

Annotating

You see the first location open in 1962. There is relatively slow growth for about a decade, and then openings pick up in an organic-like way out of Arkansas until there are Walmart locations across the country.

The passage of time lends itself to annotation to highlight the changes. Figure 7.33 shows a lightly annotated version of Figure 7.32 rearranged for size.

Data folks often assume that patterns in maps and charts are obvious, so they don't annotate. They don't want to get in the way of the data. However,

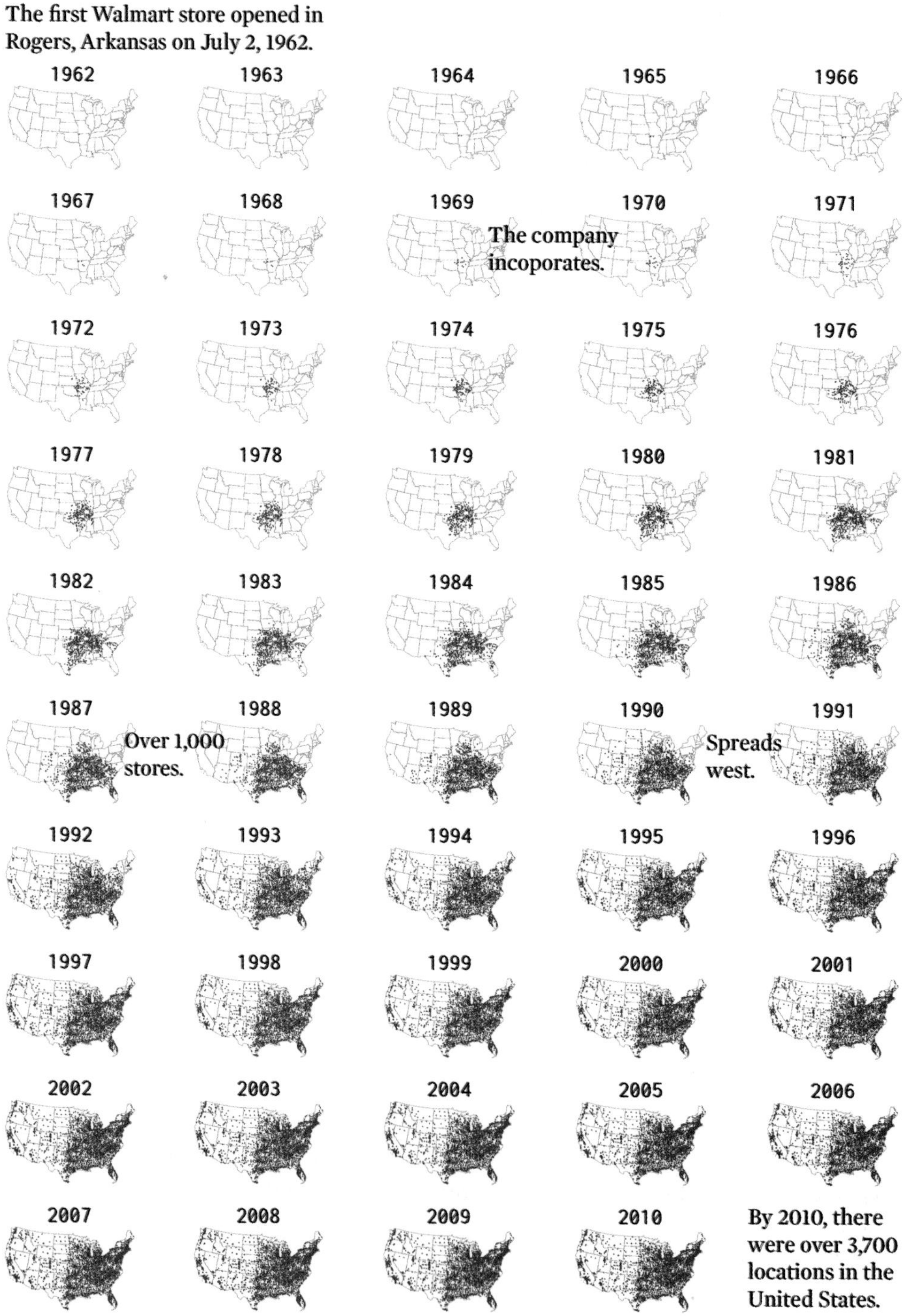

The first Walmart store opened in
Rogers, Arkansas on July 2, 1962.

1962	1963	1964	1965	1966

1967	1968	1969	1970	1971

The company incoporates.

1972	1973	1974	1975	1976

1977	1978	1979	1980	1981

1982	1983	1984	1985	1986

1987	1988	1989	1990	1991

Over 1,000 stores.

Spreads west.

1992	1993	1994	1995	1996

1997	1998	1999	2000	2001

2002	2003	2004	2005	2006

2007	2008	2009	2010	

By 2010, there
were over 3,700
locations in the
United States.

FIGURE 7.33 *Annotated sequence of maps*

when there's a pattern that stands out is when you should annotate the most. Bring attention to the changes, reinforce text, and verify what the readers think they see.

It is better to annotate too much than to not annotate enough. Despite my best efforts, I have received many notes that a chart didn't make sense. I have never received a complaint that there was too much explanation.

ANIMATED MAP

One of the more fun ways to visualize changes over space and time is to animate your data. As shown in Figure 7.34, instead of showing slices in time with individual maps, you can show the changes as they happen frame by frame.

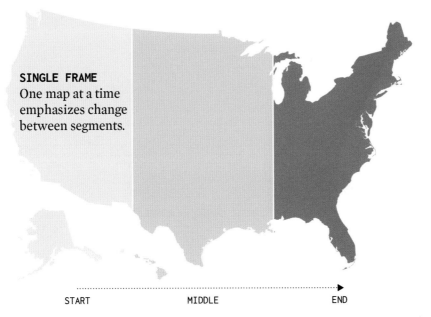

SINGLE FRAME
One map at a time
emphasizes change
between segments.

START   MIDDLE   END

FIGURE 7.34 *Animated map framework*

The trade-off with animation is that viewers must watch the whole thing and wait for things to play out. Some will be impatient and wish you just showed everything at once. Why make a bar chart that updates over time when you can show an entire time series as a line chart? With maps, why animate when you can show a sequence of maps to show an overall pattern?

Note: The Internet is full of visualization critics, which can be intimidating for beginners. But if you want to communicate data to an audience, you must put it in front of eyeballs. Don't take feedback personally and consider the context of the critiques. Filter out the insincere ones.

It's fun to watch data dance on the screen. It might take more time to interpret, but many times, you need people to stay and watch. When the data moves, people tend to watch. That is a good thing.

One of my first experiences with animation and audience came when I was poking at the Walmart dataset that you've been looking at in this chapter. Shown in Figure 7.35, dots appeared on a map in a grow-then-shrink animation, starting in 1962 through 2010. The growth is slow at first, and then Walmart locations spread across the country almost like a virus. It keeps growing, with bursts in areas where the company makes large acquisitions. Before you know it, Walmart is everywhere.

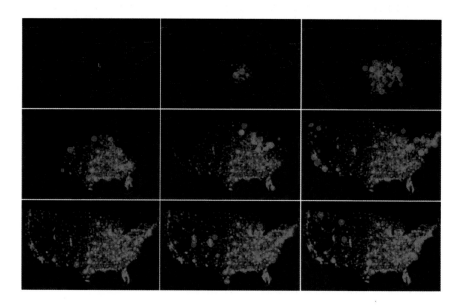

FIGURE 7.35 *"Growth of Walmart,"* `https://datafl.ws/wmt`

At the time, in 2010, I was just trying to learn the now-defunct Flash and Action-Script, but the map was shared across the Web and viewed millions of times. This was before social media was commonplace. Although I've made things since that were more popular, the quick experience sticks with me as when I learned that visualization is sometimes better even when it is not the most visually efficient. Data can be fun.

For what it's worth, the most popular things on FlowingData, over almost two decades, move in some way. I'm not saying you should animate all your charts, because balance in life is also a good thing, but making things that are fun can help people consider a dataset more seriously.

MAKING AN ANIMATED MAP

Tool Used: R

Datasets:

- State boundaries for the United States, book.flowingdata.com/vt2 /ch7/data/cb _ states.zip
- Walmart Openings in the United States, book.flowingdata.com/vt2 /ch7/data/walmart-openings-geocoded.csv

You made a sequence of maps in the previous example. Imagine you made a flip book out of each map in the sequence. You would show one map at a time instead of all of them at once in a grid. The animation package makes this straightforward. Load the package with library().

```
library(animation)
```

The package provides a saveGIF() function that pieces together an animated GIF, given a sequence of plots or maps. Specify the animation width (ani .width), animation height (ani.height), the time in between each frame in seconds (interval), and the filename to save it as (movie.name). Every new plot made in the first bracketed part of saveGIF(), the expr, creates a new frame in the animation.

```
saveGIF({

    # Use for-loop like with map sequence
    # to draw frames.

}, ani.width = 800, ani.height = 500,
interval = 0.1, movie.name = "walmart-growth.gif")
```

Like the sequence of maps, you use a for loop to iterate through each year, as shown in the following snippet. You don't use mfrow in par() to make a grid this time.

```
saveGIF({
    years <- 1962:2010

    par(mar = c(2,0,5,0))
    for (yr in years) {

        # Wal-Mart locations open on or before this year
        curr <- wal_sf_albers[wal_sf_albers$year <= yr,]
```

```
# Blank map
plot(st_geometry(conterm_albers),
     border = "#cccccc",
     lwd = .2,
     main = yr)

# Previous years
prev <- curr[curr$year != yr,]
points(st_coordinates(prev),
       col = "#dbe1f1", pch=20, cex = .3)

# This year
thisyear <- curr[curr$year == yr,]
points(st_coordinates(thisyear),
       col = "#30437b", cex = 1)
   }
}, ani.width = 800, ani.height = 500,
interval = 0.1,
movie.name = "walmart-growth.gif")
```

To make the openings each year more obvious, the stores opened in previous years are colored light gray (col = "#dbe1f1") and made smaller (cex = .3) than the points for the current year, which are dark blue (col = "#30437b") and made larger (cex = 1). Figure 7.36 shows one frame from the animated GIF.

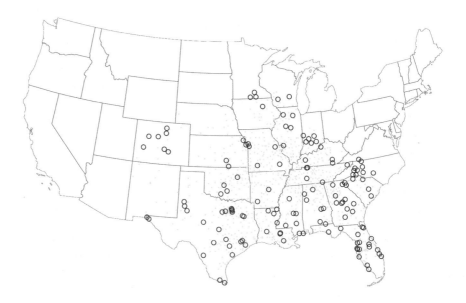

FIGURE 7.36 *One frame from animated map*

The animated version of the sequence of maps better shows the growth pattern over the years because you can see which stores open each year. This could be further refined by introducing more frames per year, annotating, or adding a counter.

You can also venture outside of R and use a hybrid approach to animate. For example, I have used R to generate images and then used the command-line tool ImageMagick to string together the images as frames in an animation. The advantage was that I had more control over how the frames played. I could make the animation speed up, slow down, and pause.

If you have a lot of frames, GIF files can grow quickly, especially if you have higher-resolution images. In this case, it might be better to use a tool like FFmpeg, which generates video files. Then, you can use video-editing software to make further edits with text overlays, music, and speed.

See more about ImageMagick at `imagemagick.org` and more about FFmpeg at `ffmpeg.org`. I used the latter alongside R to show the growth of Target locations at `https://datafl.ws/target`.

WRAPPING UP

There are a lot of possibilities for what you can do with spatial data. With just a few basic skills, you can map geographic datasets and tell all sorts of interesting stories. Draw a blank map. Add features. Explain. Repeat.

While the examples in this chapter used R, you can apply similar steps with other tools, such as the ones described in Chapter 2. The good news is that it continues to get easier to map data, especially online. Design custom maps for the web with point-and-click interfaces. Make them interactive. Animate. Make them responsive for mobile phones.

In the first edition of this book, I explained how to make an interactive map with Flash and ActionScript. It felt like a lot of work. It also felt like it could easily break if one of the services stopped working or one of the components grew outdated. I just didn't realize the part that would die would be Flash. But if you know the process of making maps and visualizing data, it's a lot easier to apply the steps to other tools.

It's time to shift attention toward *what* to visualize. You've learned *how* to visualize data up to this point. You can make different charts and handle different types of data. In the next chapter, you use what you've learned to ask questions about data and find the interesting spots in the infinite set of options. It's like learning to write and type. Once you can type without stopping to search for every letter, you can shift attention to the words you want to say and just write.

Analyzing Data
Visually

Visualization reveals patterns in data that you might not have seen otherwise, but there are infinite choices for how you can visualize a single dataset. What you see depends on what you look for. Data analysis helps you filter through noise, answer questions, and guide you toward interesting areas. You can use the tools and methods you've learned so far in this process.

GATHERING INFORMATION

For those new to visualization, it's easy to see finished graphics and appreciate the power of displaying patterns. A generic spreadsheet of numbers transforms into obvious insights. It can seem automatic. Plug a dataset into a tool, and the truth reveals itself. Sometimes, this happens, but more often, there is a not-so-elegant process of gathering information that leads to insight.

A question or a curiosity kickstarts the process. You gather data. Check to see if the data is worth digging into with quick charts and *overviews*. If there's something there, then you spend time *exploring details*. You ask more questions, maybe gather more data, filter out noise (or focus on it), and repeat the process until you reach *conclusions*.

Practitioners walk through this process in different ways, depending on the data, the application, the field of study, the available resources, the tools on hand, and the questions they're asking. Some use statistical tests. Some run simulations. Some use visualization. Some use heavy computing. Go with what suits your needs.

I take a hybrid approach, but as you might have guessed, I tend strongly toward visualization. I spend more time making charts to gather information than I do on the charts that I publish.

Tukey called it "graphical detective work" in *Exploratory Data Analysis* (Pearson, 1977). You kind of know what you're looking for, but you don't know what you're going to find yet. You work with your bag of tools through the available resources. In spending time with the dataset and making charts, you generate knowledge about the numbers, and ideally you glean something useful.

OVERVIEWS

Before you spend a lot of time and resources analyzing a dataset, get a general sense of what you're working with. Is the data trustworthy? Is there a lot of noise? Are there a lot of gaps or missing data? Do overall aggregates match your expectations? Do you need to adjust your expectations?

These first steps of analysis are a gentle way of getting to know your data. It's like when you meet someone on a first date or at a party with an unfamiliar crowd. It's the small talk. There are common questions, and conversation points that you use to decide if you want to get to know someone better. Instead of talking about the weather, asking where someone is from and what they do for a living, or seeing how they react to certain jokes, you ask data questions about structure, sources, and distributions.

It's during this stage when you can quickly decide if you want to pursue the gathering process further. It's no fun getting to know a dataset only to find out deep into the analysis that the numbers don't represent what you thought they did. Sometimes, it's impossible to know what the data is about until you've looked at it deeply, but it's good to at least get a feel for things early on if you can.

Look at the summary statistics that you might have learned about in an introductory statistics course, plot distributions to see the spread of observations, perform quick checks for quality, and adjust your questions based on what you find.

SUMMARIES

Some summary statistics provide a quick look at the range of a dataset: mean, median, mode, minimum, and maximum. Any software designed to help you understand data provides functions to find these values. Here's a quick rundown of what each statistic represents.

- **Mean:** Statistically, it is the sum of observations divided by the number of observations. It provides an idea of where the collection of numbers tends toward. More commonly, when people refer to an "average" from a numeric point of view, they usually are talking about the mean.

- **Median:** Imagine arranging a group of five people by height, from shortest to tallest. The middle point, or the third person's height, would be the median. It represents the middle of a dataset and is less prone to getting pulled lower or higher by extreme values than the mean.

- **Mode:** What value occurs the most in a dataset? That is the mode. For example, if in the group of five people, two of them were 60 inches tall and the other three were 55, 57, and 59 inches, respectively, the mode would be 60. It is helpful to find what is most common.

- **Minimum:** It is the lowest value.

- **Maximum:** It is the highest value and, with the minimum, indicates the full range.

▦ **Percentiles:** Order the data and mark where a percentage of the data is below. For example, 90th percentile is where 90% of the data is less than the corresponding value, median is 50th percentile, and 10th percentile is where 10% of the data is less than the value.

Calculate the summary statistics. Check to see if they make sense. This might mean comparing to estimates from previous years or a known calculation from a different data group. Maybe you have prior knowledge about what it should be. Do the values seem too high or low? Were there miscalculations because of missing data? Look for anything that seems off.

While the calculations themselves might be enough to judge, it can help to visualize them with a box plot, as shown in Figure 8.1. The ends of the box introduce two more values for the 25th percentile and the 75th. The distance

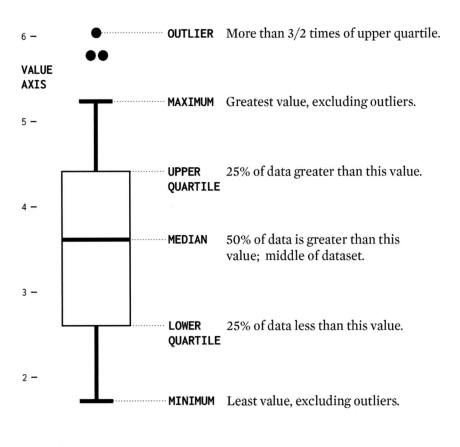

FIGURE 8.1 *Box plot framework*

between the two marks is known as the *interquartile range*. The lines that extend from the box, known as the *whiskers*, represent the minimum and maximum values within 1.5 the interquartile range of the 25th and 75th percentiles, respectively.

A box plot on its own isn't especially useful, though, unless you have prior knowledge about the data. They're more useful when you have multiple ranges to compare, such as in Figure 8.2. During several speed dating sessions, people were asked to score their partners on various attributes and say if they wanted to go on an actual date with that person. You can see increasing yes rates with higher scores, as one might expect.

You don't have to use a box, of course. It's the values that each spot in the box plot represents that are important. Figure 8.3 shows a different version that represents the age of workers in different occupations. It's from an interactive graph that lets you search for an occupation to see the summary statistics. Dots show the summary statistics, a thicker line shows the interquartile range, and a dotted line extends to the minimum and maximum ages.

You can see that even though the summary statistics are basic and show limited details, they can provide a useful overview. At this point in the game, that is all you need.

MAKING A BOX PLOT

Tool used: R

Dataset: NBA Players, 2013-14, book.flowingdata.com/vt2/ch8/data /nba-players-2013-14.csv

How tall are players in the National Basketball Association? Probably tall. The dataset provides players' names, positions, and heights, along with other information from the 2013–2014 season. Start by loading two packages in R: readr and dplyr. If you haven't installed them yet, use `install.packages()`, as shown here:

```
# Load package
install.packages(c("readr", "dplyr"))
library(readr)
library(dplyr)
```

The readr package provides functions to load files, and dplyr provides functions for data manipulation. You could use `read.csv()` and bracket notation like in previous chapters, but like I've said, there are various methods and tools to get you where you need to go. Even within R, you can use different packages, functions, and data structures to produce the same results.

THE HIGHER THE BETTER

Generally speaking, people wanted to date others who had higher ratings across all attributes.

Attractiveness

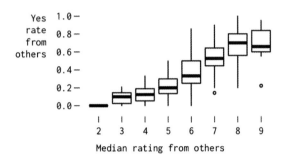

Median rating from others

Fun

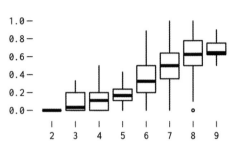

Intelligence

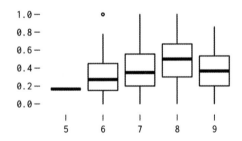

Ambition

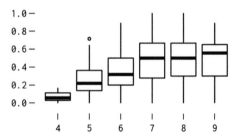

Sincerity

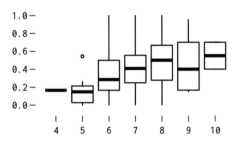

SOURCE
Raymond Fisman, et al. (2005)

FIGURE 8.2 *"What the Sexes Want, in Speed Dating,"* https://datafl.ws/dating

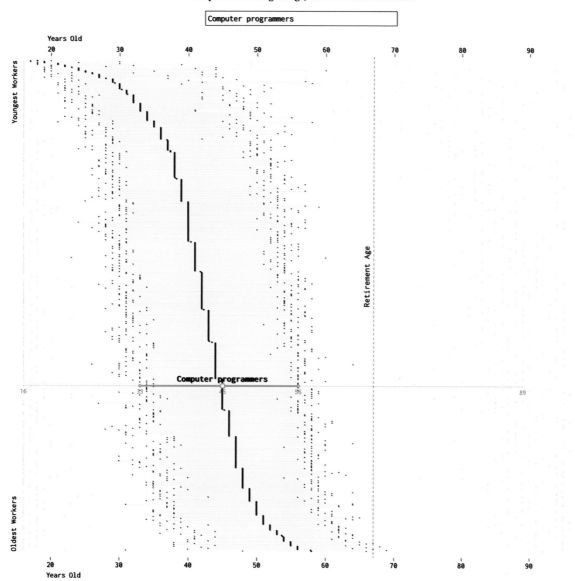

Jobs by Age of Workers

Sorted by youngest workers to oldest. Hover over each
occupation to see age range, minimum and maximum.

FIGURE 8.3 *"Age and Occupation,"* Nathan Yau / 2007-Present FlowingData / `https://flowingdata.com/2021/09/30/age-and-occupation/` *last accessed February 08, 2024.*

Learn more about the tidyverse at tidyverse.org.

readr and dplyr belong to a collection of packages called the *tidyverse* that "share an underlying design philosophy, grammar, and data structures." The collection grew in popularity since the first edition of this book, and it provides a unified way of programming in R. Some people use tidyverse packages exclusively.

You get a sampling in this chapter, but we won't lean on the tidyverse completely. Instead, you'll use some functions and see how it works with what you've learned in previous chapters. Start by loading the CSV file with `read_csv()` instead of `read.csv()`. The NBA dataset is relatively small, but for larger files in hundreds of megabytes or gigabytes, `read_csv()` tends to load data more efficiently.

```
# Load data
players <- read_csv("data/nba-players-2013-14.csv")
```

The function returns a data structure known as a *tibble*, which is a modified version of a data frame. You can treat it like a data frame. The first rows of the dataset look like the following. There is one row per player for 528 rows total.

```
> players %>% select(Name, POS, Ht_inches)
# A tibble: 528 × 3
   Name                POS    Ht_inches
   <chr>               <chr>      <dbl>
 1 Gee, Alonzo         F             78
 2 Wallace, Gerald     F             79
 3 Williams, Mo        G             73
 4 Gladness, Mickell   C             83
 5 Jefferson, Richard  F             79
 6 Hill, Solomon       F             79
 7 Budinger, Chase     F             79
 8 Williams, Derrick   F             80
 9 Hill, Jordan        F/C           82
10 Frye, Channing      F/C           83
# … with 518 more rows
```

The previous code uses `%>%`, which is known as a *pipe* and is provided by the dplyr package. The output from the left side of the pipe is passed to the right side of the pipe. If you're familiar with piping in Unix, this is like using the pipe character, |. (If not, no need to worry.) So, the player data is passed to `select()` to show specific columns: `Name`, `POS` (player position), and `Ht_inches` (player's height in inches). You can still use the dollar sign notation to access columns, as shown next. Call `summary()` to get summary statistics for height.

```
> summary(players$Ht_inches)
   Min. 1st Qu.  Median    Mean 3rd Qu.    Max.
  69.00   77.00   80.00   79.12   82.00   87.00
```

The minimum is 69 inches, and the maximum is 87 inches. The median is 80 inches. Maybe this is all you need to know, but you can see this in box plot form with the `boxplot()` function. The graphical parameter `las` is set to 1 so that all axis labels are set horizontally.

```
# Box plot
par(las = 1)
boxplot(players$Ht_inches,
        main = "NBA Player Height, Inches")
```

This gives you a box plot, as shown in Figure 8.4. The y-axis represents height. The maximum height of 87 inches is represented by the top bar, and the minimum height is represented by the dot at the bottom, as it falls outside 1.5 times interquartile range of the 25th percentile. This is the default behavior of the `boxplot()` function, but you can modify these marks if you want to make custom box plots with your own software.

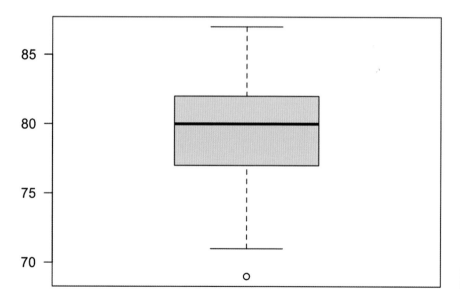

FIGURE 8.4 *Box plot showing NBA player heights*

Basketball players tend to vary in height by the position they play. Centers tend to be taller, guards tend to be shorter, and forwards are usually somewhere in the middle. Does this check out with the data?

Find the positions classified by `POS` in the `players` data using the `unique()` function.

```
# Player positions
ppos <- unique(players$POS)
```

Alternatively, if you were sticking with the tidyverse, you could use the following with `distinct()`:

```
> players %>% distinct(POS)
# A tibble: 5 × 1
  POS
  <chr>
1 F
2 G
3 C
4 F/C
5 G/F
```

We'll stick with the first option. There are five player positions in the dataset. Set `mfrow` with `par()` to make five charts, one for each position. Set margins, outer margins, and the bordering box type to `none` while you're setting graphical parameters.

```
# Graphical parameters
par(mfrow = c(1, length(ppos)),
    mar = c(2, 2, 2, 2),
    oma = c(1, 3, 2, 2),
    bty = "n")
```

Use a for-loop to make a box plot for each position, as shown next. The pipe notation is used again, along with `filter()` to subset the players with the current position in the loop. This is the equivalent of using `players[players$POS == pos,]` with bracket notation. The `boxplot()` function is called on the heights in `curr`. The y-axis limits are set explicitly to the range of the full dataset so that each chart covers the same range, which makes it easier to compare positions.

```
# Box plot for each player position
for (pos in ppos) {
    curr <- players %>%
        filter(POS == pos)
    boxplot(curr$Ht_inches,
            ylim = range(players$Ht_inches),
            main = pos)
}
```

As shown in Figure 8.5, you get five box plots side-by-side. Centers, noted with "C" appear highest and are, therefore, the tallest. The guards are the shortest. So, the values appear to verify the initial expectation.

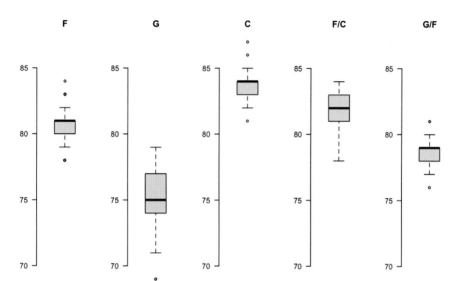

FIGURE 8.5 *Several box plot side-by-side*

There is a more straightforward way to make multiple box plots by using formula notation, as shown next. The formula with the tilde (~) specifies that box plots should be drawn by POS.

```
# Using the tilde notation
boxplot(Ht_inches ~ POS,
        data = players,
        ylab = "",
        main = "NBA Player Height by Position")
```

All the box plots are drawn in the same plotting space instead of five separate charts, as shown in Figure 8.6.

When making comparisons, it's often helpful to sort categories in a useful way. In this case, you can sort the positions by height. The following sets the order of the positions explicitly with `levels` in `factor()`:

```
# Reorder
players_fact <- players
players_fact$POS <-
    factor(players_fact$POS,
           levels = c("C", "F/C", "F", "G/F", "G"))
```

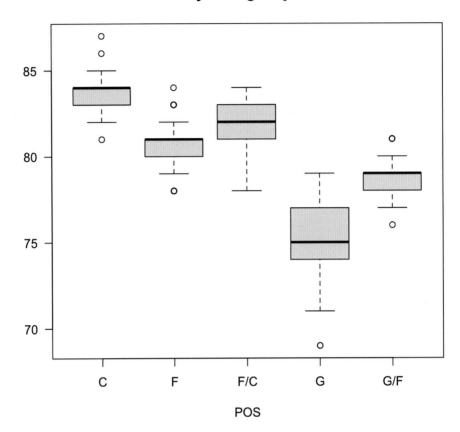

FIGURE 8.6 *Box plots in the same chart*

Use the formula notation again but with the ordered data `players_fact`.

```
boxplot(Ht_inches ~ POS,
        data = players_fact,
        ylab = "",
        main = "NBA Player Height by Position,\nOrdered")
```

From left to right, the positions are ordered from tallest to shortest (Figure 8.7).

DISTRIBUTIONS

In statistics, distributions can be expressed with mathematical formulas, and they have formal names and specific shapes. But more generally, you can think of distribution as how the data is spread out across a range or multiple ranges.

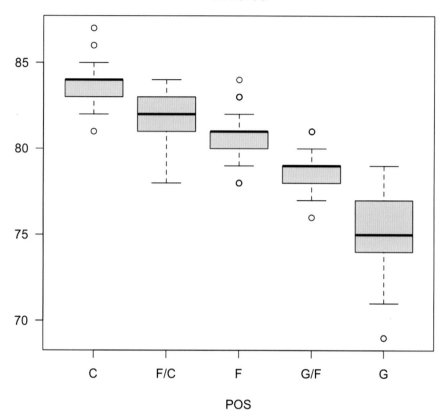

FIGURE 8.7 *Ordered box plots, specified with factored positions*

Summary statistics are a simplification of distributions. Look at the data more closely, and you can find more detail.

As shown in Figure 8.8, sometimes plotted data looks like a bell curve (*unimodal*), has a couple of peaks (*bimodal* or *multimodal*), or has multiple peaks (*multimodal*). The tapered ends of the distributions are the *tails*. Peaks indicate where the data tends to or the spots in the data that are more common.

You might also have heard of *skewness,* or which way a distribution leans. With unimodal distributions, there can be negative skew or positive skew. As shown in Figure 8.9, the former shows a tail that seems to pull further left, and the latter shows a tail that pulls further right.

While distributions can be closely studied, I typically look for a shape that doesn't look random and a modality that makes sense for a given dataset

UNIMODAL
It looks like a bell curve with a single peak.

MULTIMODAL
A distribution with multiple peaks.

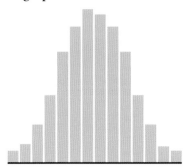

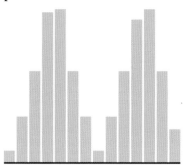

FIGURE 8.8 *Distribution modality*

NEGATIVE SKEW
A tail that seems to pull further left.

POSITIVE SKEW
A tail that seems to pull further right.

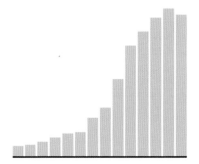

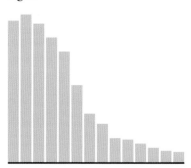

FIGURE 8.9 *Distribution skewness*

when I am in the early stages of analysis. The histogram, shown in Figure 8.10, comes in handy.

The histogram looks like a bar chart initially. There are bars that sit next to each other along a value axis. Height represents frequency. However, the value axis is continuous, and each bar width, or *bin*, represents the covered range of values. So, taller bars mean higher frequency or that a given range is more common than the others.

For example, Figure 8.11 shows a simple timeline for the median age American females and males experience relationship milestones for the first time in their lives. This is based on 2013 to 2015 data from the National Survey of Family Growth by the Centers for Disease Control and Prevention.

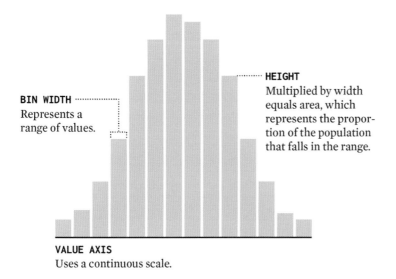

BIN WIDTH
Represents a
range of values.

HEIGHT
Multiplied by width
equals area, which
represents the propor-
tion of the population
that falls in the range.

VALUE AXIS
Uses a continuous scale.

FIGURE 8.10 *Histogram
framework*

MEDIAN AGE FOR THE FIRST TIME

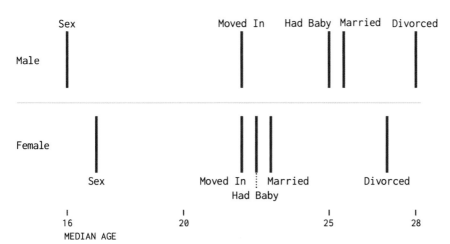

FIGURE 8.11 *Relationship
timelines*

The median age when females had sex for the first time was 17 years old. The
median age for males was 16. However, the median ages tell only part of the
story. As shown in Figure 8.12, the ages that things happen in people's lives
are spread across a range.

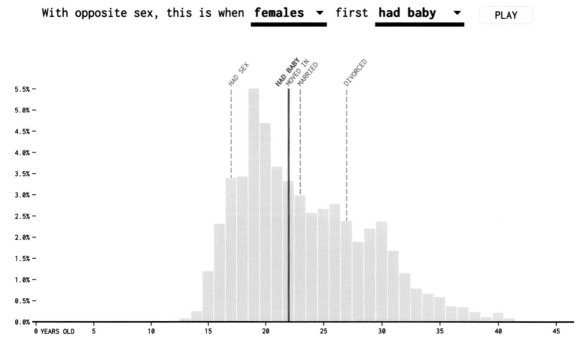

With opposite sex, this is when **females** ▾ first **had baby** ▾   PLAY

FIGURE 8.12 *"Relationships: The First Time…,"* FlowingData / `https://flowingdata.com/2017/02/23/the-first-time` / *last accessed February 08, 2024.*

We often refer to the peaks of these distributions as what is normal, but the peaks can be a small percentage of a wider distribution. It's worth getting an overall sense of the distributions so that you can make more detailed conclusions later.

Making a Histogram

Tool used: R

Dataset: NBA Players, 2013-14, `book.flowingdata.com/vt2/ch8/data/nba-players-2013-14.csv`

Use a histogram to see more details in the distribution of NBA player heights. Load the readr and dplyr packages again for loading and handling data, respectively.

```
library(readr)
library(dplyr)
```

Use `read_csv()` to load the dataset. This is the same dataset as the box plot example where each row represents a player.

```
# Load data
players <- read_csv("data/nba-players-2013-14.csv")
```

Pass the `Ht_inches` data to `hist()` for a default histogram. As shown in Figure 8.13, each bin covers two inches, and while the median is 80 inches overall, there appears to be a quicker drop-off in the taller ranges.

```
# Default histogram
hist(players$Ht_inches,
     xlab="inches",
     main="NBA Player Heights")
```

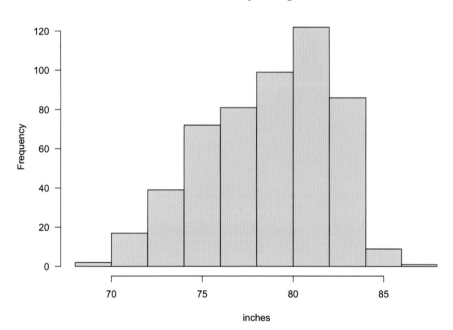

FIGURE 8.13 *Default histogram*

You can specify the bin breaks for more detail. The `breaks` argument in `hist()` takes a vector of values or passes a single value to define the number of total bins. The following creates one-inch bins from 65 to 90 inches:

```
# Histogram
hist(players$Ht_inches,
     breaks=seq(65, 90, 1),
     xlab="inches",
     main="NBA Player Heights")
```

There is a spike at 80 inches, as shown in Figure 8.14, and while the shape is similar to Figure 8.14, you can see more variation with the one-inch bins.

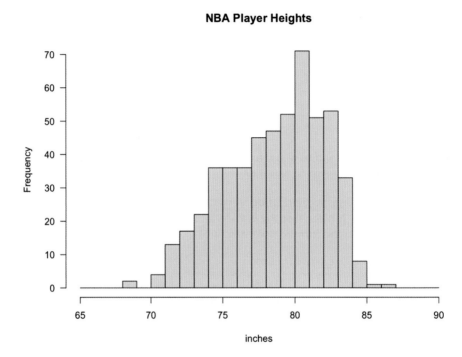

NBA Player Heights

FIGURE 8.14 *Histogram with smaller bins*

Try more bin sizes to see how this affects the shape of the histograms.

```
# Vary bin sizes
par(mfrow=c(1,3), mar=c(5,3,3,3))
hist(players$Ht_inches,
     breaks=seq(65, 90, 1),
     xlab="inches", main="One-inch bins")
hist(players$Ht_inches,
     breaks=seq(65, 90, 3),
     xlab="inches", main="Three-inch bins")
hist(players$Ht_inches,
     breaks=seq(65, 90, 6),
     xlab="inches", main="Six-inch bins")
```

Figure 8.15 shows the difference between one-, three-, and six-inch bins. The smaller bins show the most variation, and the larger bins show the least detail. In this case, the smaller bins are useful, but this might not be the case with your own datasets. Smaller bins might just be a bunch of noise or larger

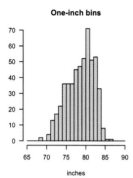
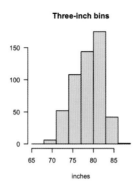
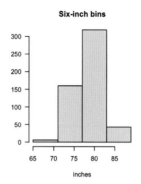

FIGURE 8.15 *Varying bin size for more granular or broader ranges*

bins might be too broad to show any shape, so I'll leave bin size to you. It's up to you to adjust.

How about comparing height distributions across player positions? The process is like that of the box plots. Get the unique position classifications and iterate with a `for` loop. For the former, use `unique()`.

```
# Comparison between positions
ppos <- unique(players$POS)
```

Instead of placing charts side-by-side with one row and five columns, define a layout with five rows and one column. Set `mfrow` with `par()` to `c(5, 1)`. On each `for` loop iteration, use `filter()` to subset to the players with the current position and explicitly define `breaks` so that each histogram is on the same horizontal scale.

```
# Plot
par(mfrow=c(5,1))
for (pos in ppos) {
    curr <- players %>% filter(POS == pos)
    hist(curr$Ht_inches,
        breaks=seq(65, 90, 1),
        xlab="inches", main=paste0(pos, " Heights"))
}
```

Guards are the shortest overall, but they also have the widest range. You can see this easily, because the histogram for the guards has the most bins. On the other hand, the height of centers appears to be more restricted to tall, as shown in Figure 8.16.

Sorting usually makes it easier to compare distributions, so try the previous using an order from shortest to tallest position. The following snippet also calculates the mean height for each position with `mean()` and draws a blue reference line with `abline()`.

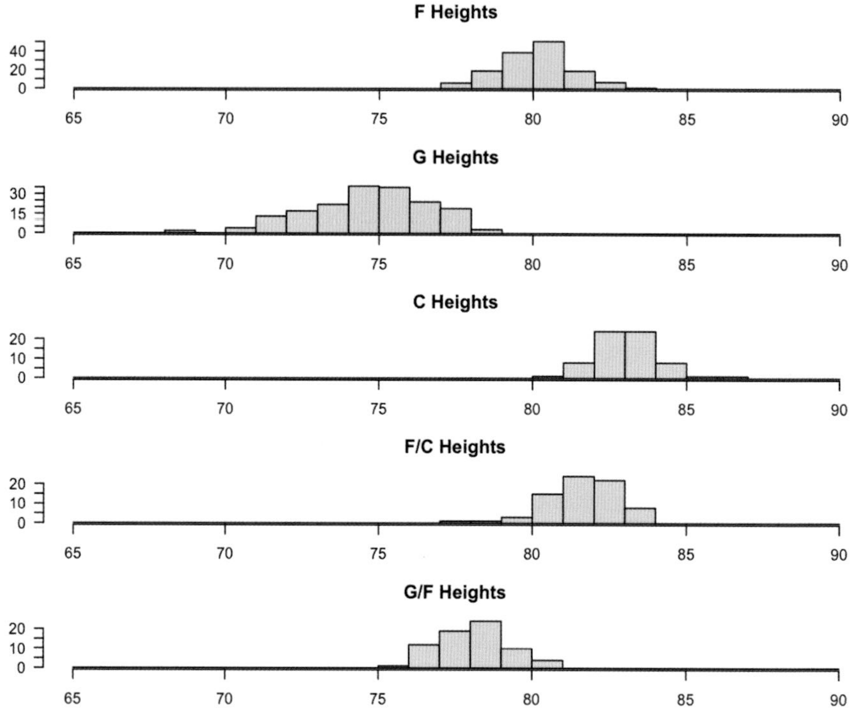

FIGURE 8.16 *Comparing distributions by category*

```
# Reordered histograms
ppos2 <- c("G", "G/F", "F", "F/C", "C")
par(mfrow=c(5,1))
for (pos in ppos2) {
    curr <- players %>% filter(POS == pos)
    curr_mean <- mean(curr$Ht_inches)

    hist(curr$Ht_inches,
        breaks=seq(65, 90, 1),
        border = "white",
        xlab="inches",
        main=paste0(pos, " Heights"))
    abline(v = curr_mean,
        col = "blue",
        lwd = 2)
}
```

This lets you make the straightforward comparison between means. The light gray bars, as shown in Figure 8.17, are like background information to provide context.

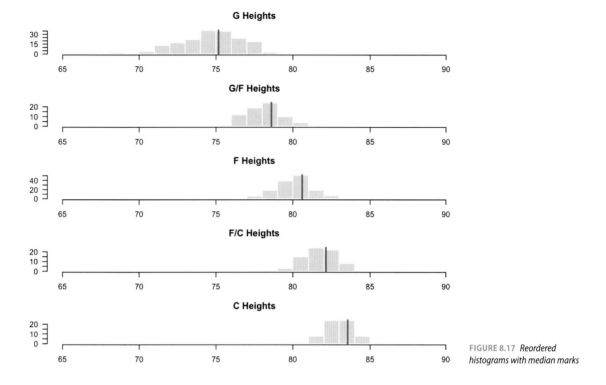

FIGURE 8.17 *Reordered histograms with median marks*

Making a Density Plot

Tool used: R

Dataset: NBA Players, 2013-14, book.flowingdata.com/vt2/ch8/data /nba-players-2013-14.csv

The bins in a histogram are discrete. However, sometimes you might want a continuous version because your data is on a continuous scale, or you need to a see a smoother view. A density plot is a solution, as shown in Figure 8.18. Like the histogram, the x-scale is continuous without breaks, and the y-scale is the proportion of the data that falls in the corresponding range. The difference is that the data is smoothed to make one shape instead of separate bins.

Load the readr and dplyr packages and then load the data with `read_csv()` like in previous examples.

```
library(readr)
library(dplyr)

# Load data
players <- read_csv("data/nba-players-2013-14.csv")
```

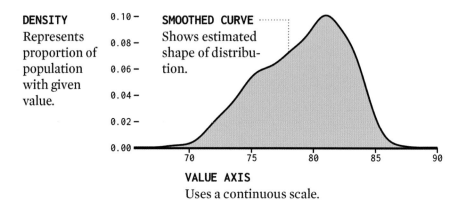

FIGURE 8.18 *Density plot framework*

Use density() on the Ht_inches variable to calculate smoothed coordinates. The function provides different smoothing options, which you can read about in the documentation (Enter **?density** in the console), but the defaults will do fine for this example.

```
# Calculate density coordinates
pdens <- density(players$Ht_inches)
```

Pass the calculations to plot().

```
# Plot
par(las = 1)
plot(pdens, lwd = 2,
     main = "NBA Player Height")
```

As shown in Figure 8.19, you get a smoothed version of Figure 8.13 in line form.

Add a fill under the smoothed curve with polygon() to which you can pass the same pdens coordinates. Think of it as layers. Use plot() to draw the initial view and use polygon() to add to the view.

```
# Plot
par(las = 1)
plot(pdens, lwd = 2,
     main = "NBA Player Height")
polygon(pdens,
        col = "lightblue")
```

While you're adding to the plot, use abline() and points() to mark the peak of the curve.

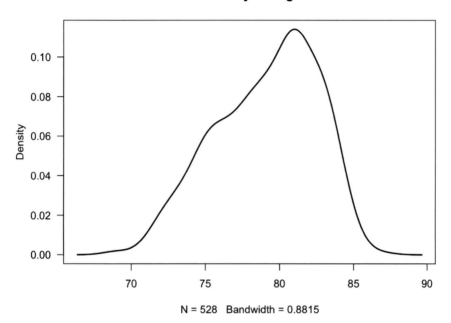

NBA Player Height

N = 528   Bandwidth = 0.8815

FIGURE 8.19 *Simple density plot*

```
# Max point
i <- which.max(pdens$y)
abline(v = pdens$x[i],
       lty = 2)
points(pdens$x[i], pdens$y[i],
       pch = 21,
       bg = "black")
```

This gives you the density plot in Figure 8.20 with a filled light blue polygon.

Like in the histogram example, it would be helpful to see the density plots for different positions. I'll leave that for you as an exercise, but you can use the same logic with a `for` loop, subset to a player position, and draw the plot on each iteration.

Making a Beeswarm Chart

Tool used: b

Dataset: NBA Players, 2013-14, book.flowingdata.com/vt2/ch8/data /nba-players-2013-14.csv

Whereas the histogram and density plot show distributions by aggregating and smoothing, the beeswarm chart shows every data point individually as a

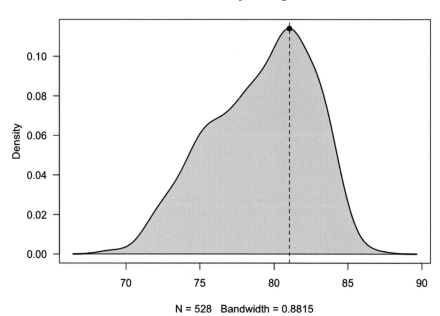

FIGURE 8.20 *Density plot with annotation*

dot (or bee). The clustering of the dots reveals an overall distribution, as shown in Figure 8.21.

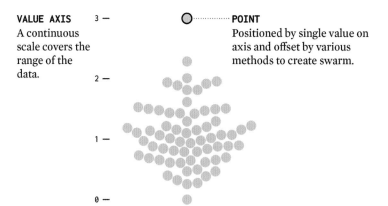

FIGURE 8.21 *Beeswarm chart framework*

The chart type is relatively new. The name didn't exist when I wrote the first edition of this book, but the beeswarm is commonplace these days. I see it in use every day. At the trade-off of using more space and often showing more noise, the beeswarm chart is less abstract and less aggregated than other chart types.

It's easier to see when an event occurred or where a person, place, or thing belongs compared to the full population.

When I started using beeswarm charts, before they had an established name, I had to construct them from scratch. However, the process is a lot more straight-forward now. In R, the beeswarm package provides a single function.

Load the readr and beeswarm packages. As usual, you can use `install .packages()` or a package installer via RStudio or the R GUI to install the packages if you don't have them yet.

```
library(readr)
library(beeswarm)
```

Load the NBA player data with `read_csv()`.

```
# Load data
players <- read_csv("data/nba-players-2013-14.csv")
```

Pass `Ht_inches` to `beeswarm()` to look at the distribution of player heights.

```
# Beeswarm
par(las = 1)
beeswarm(players$Ht_inches,
         main = "NBA Player Heights")
```

Height in this dataset are integers, so there are players with the same height, which you can see in Figure 8.22. The dots, each one representing a player, are centered on the x-axis and placed on the y-axis by height. You're probably familiar with this distribution shape by now, with a peak around 80 inches and quicker drop off at the taller heights.

With the same formula notation you used to make separate box plots for each position, you can make beeswarms separately, too. Set the swarm method to `swarm` and the dot size (`cex`) to 0.7. The `corral` argument specifies what to do with dots that would stretch past boundaries and overlap with other player positions. Setting it to `random` sets the x-position randomly. Set point type (`pch`) to 21, which is a filled circle with a border, and the fill color (`bg`) to black with 50% transparency.

```
# By position
beeswarm(Ht_inches ~ POS,
         method = "swarm",
         cex = .7,
         corral = "random",
         pch = 21,
         bg = "#00000050",
         data = players,
         main = "NBA Player Heights, by Position")
```

Note: Enter `?beeswarm` to see all the chart options.

NBA Player Heights

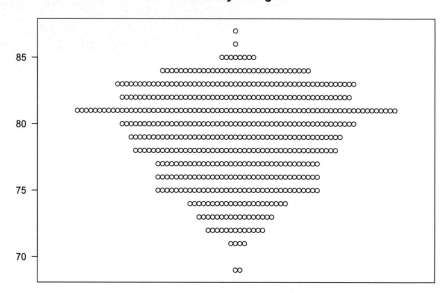

FIGURE 8.22 *Beeswarm chart showing player heights*

There is a swarm for each position, as shown in Figure 8.23.

NBA Player Heights, by Position

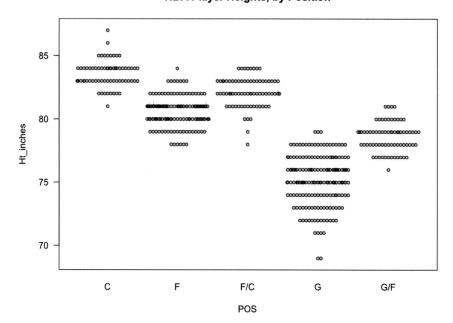

FIGURE 8.23 *Beeswarm chart by category*

Because the heights round to whole numbers, the dots line up horizontally. However, beeswarm charts tend to be more useful when values aren't so even. For the sake of demonstration, add random noise to the heights with `runif()`, which generates random numbers from a uniform distribution within a specified range, 0 to 1 in this case. Assign the heights with noise added to `Ht_inches_rand` in the `players` data.

```
# Add noise
players$Ht_inches_rand <- players$Ht_inches +
    runif(dim(players)[1], 0, 1)
```

Make a beeswarm chart with the new data.

```
beeswarm(Ht_inches_rand ~ POS,
         method = "swarm",
         pch = 21,
         bg = c("red", "blue", "black", "purple", "darkgreen"),
         data = players,
         main = "NBA Player Heights, by Position")
```

With less space in between dots and tighter clustering, as shown in Figure 8.24, the charts look more like full distributions instead of a bunch of dots in a row.

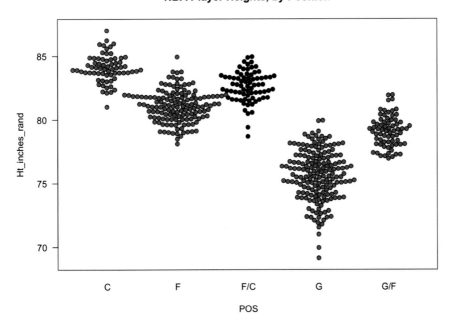

FIGURE 8.24 *Beeswarm chart with more variation*

Like I said, one of the advantages of the beeswarm is that each data point gets a symbol. In this case, each dot represents a player. The `beeswarm()` function lets you set colors and sizes pointwise, which means you can call out individual data points.

For example, highlight the player Rudy Gobert by using a different color and size so that the point for Gobert stands out from the rest. Start with the color. All points will be gray, except the point for Gobert, which will be purple.

```
# Color for each player
players$col <- "#cccccc"
players$col[players$Name == "Gobert, Rudy"] <- "purple"
```

Define the size of all the points as 1, except the point for Gobert, which will get a `cex` size of 3.

```
# Circle size for each player
players$cex <- 1
players$cex[players$Name == "Gobert, Rudy"] <- 3
```

Use `beeswarm()` like before, but set the `pwcol` and `pwcex` arguments to the `col` and `cex` columns in players, respectively.

```
# Beeswarm
beeswarm(Ht_inches_rand ~ POS,
         method = "swarm",
         pch = 20,
         pwcol = players$col,
         pwcex = players$cex,
         data = players,
         main = "NBA Player Heights, by Position")
```

As shown in Figure 8.25, the point for Gobert stands out from the rest. Can you figure out how to add a name label with `text()`?

The `beeswarm()` function provides a lot of flexibility so that you can customize charts for your own data. Try changing the method for arranging points, adding labels, or using different color schemes.

QUALITY OF THE DATA

Like distributions, there are formal methods to assess data quality, but the eyeball test again works well in the early stages of gathering information. Make quick charts without worrying about aesthetics and readability.

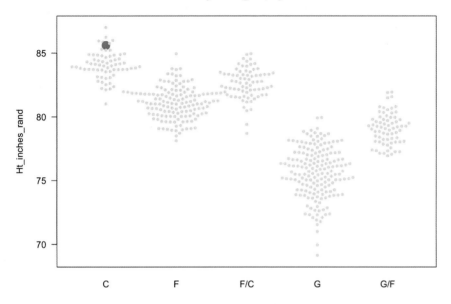

NBA Player Heights, by Position

FIGURE 8.25 *"One point highlighted in the swarms,"* Nathan Yau / 2007-Present FlowingData/`https://flowingdata.com/2016/03/03/marrying-age`/ *last accessed February 08, 2024.*

If you have time series data, make a line chart. If you have categorical data, make a bar chart. If you have spatial data, make a map. Is there a trend? Does it match expectations? Does the line or bars go up and down randomly suggesting that the data is a bunch of noise? Do you have to aggregate the data into wider time bins or broader categories to capture a signal? Answer these questions early so you don't have to suffer through analytical regret later.

Consider the source of the data and how the files you have on your computer came to be. Is the source reliable? What was the methodology behind the estimates? For example, once a pornography site analyzed their traffic data to find which state watched the most. Kansas appeared to be a strong outlier with many more pageviews per capita. The Internet did its thing for a few days where it gawks and points without much context. However, traffic location was based on IP addresses, and if the software could not define the state, it defaulted to the center of the United States. The geolocation defaulted to Kansas, which inflated the state's per capita count.

In another example, news outlets reported on what appeared to be important research on changing people's minds. The research concluded that you could change a person's mind with a 22-minute conversation, which carried implications in how you might shift thought and voting on political and social issues. It turns out the data behind the research was fake.

See other examples of mistaken data at `https://datafl.ws/miss`.

As of this writing, AI-generated images and text are at a peak. It's gotten easier to generate and edit media, and it's getting more difficult to decipher what is real and not. I can only imagine that fake datasets will grow more readily available with time.

When I work with data, my main method to judge quality is to compare against previous estimates from a source that I trust. I often work with microdata, or individual survey responses instead of aggregates, to make my own calculations. To verify, I might use my methodology with a previous year's microdata to match with known estimates. If they aren't equal, then I probably made an error, or the microdata is not right.

Do what works for you, but keep an eye out throughout the process. Ask yourself if what you're seeing makes sense. Sometimes the numbers lie, intentionally and unintentionally. If the data seems overly shocking or the trends seem to be oddly clear, look closer.

ADJUSTING QUESTIONS

Once you have a sense of data quality and what the data is about, you can decide what questions you'll be able to answer. Oftentimes, you need to adjust when the data is too noisy, doesn't represent what you thought, or more interesting things popped up as you were summarizing.

I find it's best to treat initial curiosities as a jumping-off point. Rarely do I end up answering the exact questions that I had to start, but they often lead to something else that is worth analyzing more deeply. The alternative, posing a question and leaving it unanswered or providing data that provides zero information, isn't much fun for you or the reader.

EXPLORING DETAILS

You have a good feel for the data. Now, get in closer to see the details. This stage of the gathering process is less mechanical and more context-specific. It depends on how much data you have, the structure of the data, how granular the data is, and what you're looking for in the data.

Looking for what is best in your dataset? Define what is "best." Are the estimates reliable enough to make a judgment? Are there unexpected trends, and if so, do you need to adjust your own expectations, or is there something interesting going on here? Is there variation within groups and stagnation in others?

Do any people, places, or things jump out from the rest of the distributions, and are they measurement errors or real-life outliers?

This is a third or fourth date conversation. You've done the small talk and found out a little bit about the person. You know their hometown, what food they like, gotten a feel for their humor, and what movies they've seen lately. Now, it's time to find out who this person truly is, which is more complex but vastly more interesting.

COMPARISONS

When I was a kid, sometimes I earned a good grade or scored well on a test. I would excitedly tell my parents the news. After giving me the kudos that I craved, they almost always followed by asking how others did. It bothered me, because I didn't want to be compared to anyone else.

But my parents were just trying to figure out the scale of my scores. Me saying that I got an 85 doesn't mean a lot if you don't know the minimum and maximum. Did everyone get an 85? Is an 85 good or was the test out of a possible 200? I understand my parents' queries better now that I have young children who come home with similar sentiments.

Comparisons provide meaning to your data. They provide context, whether something is good or bad, high or low, and top or bottom. There is a genre of visualization that specifically gives you a sense of scale by starting with something familiar and then scaling up or down toward the unfamiliar.

You can look at variation across a full population, and you can look at variation across and within subgroups of a population. Figure 8.26 shows income distributions by age group, as education levels and work experience play a role in how much you make. An annual income of $43,000 was the median overall in 2020, but it's on the lower side if you're older than 60 and impressive if you're a teenager.

Find examples of scale comparisons that range from the practical to the ridiculous at https://datafl.ws/scale.

In Chapter 4, "Visualizing Time," you saw how comparing data over days, months, and years can show change, trends, and cycles. In Chapter 7, "Visualizing Space," you saw how to compare cities, countries, and regions. The most straightforward method to make visual comparisons is to use a common scale across all categories, time, or space. Have multiple charts? Use the same x- and y-scales with each chart. Scaled symbols? Size with the same area scale across categories.

To compare marrying age across demographics, Figure 8.27 shows percentages for males and females with age on the x-axis and percentage of marriages on

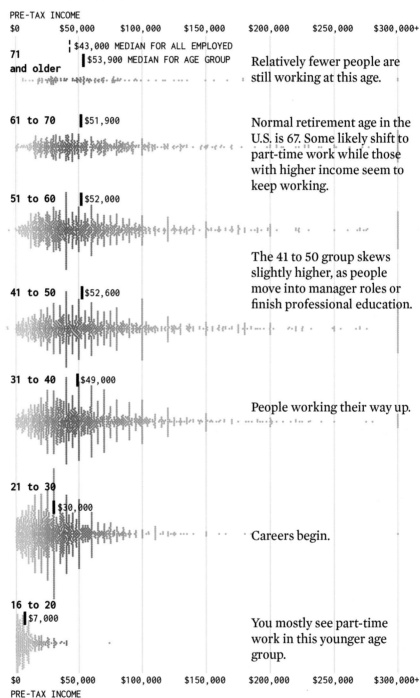

INCOME BY AGE

PRE-TAX INCOME

| $0 | $50,000 | $100,000 | $150,000 | $200,000 | $250,000 | $300,000+ |

71 and older
¦ $43,000 MEDIAN FOR ALL EMPLOYED
▌ $53,900 MEDIAN FOR AGE GROUP

Relatively fewer people are still working at this age.

61 to 70 ▌$51,900

Normal retirement age in the U.S. is 67. Some likely shift to part-time work while those with higher income seem to keep working.

51 to 60 ▌$52,000

The 41 to 50 group skews slightly higher, as people move into manager roles or finish professional education.

41 to 50 ▌$52,600

31 to 40 ▌$49,000

People working their way up.

21 to 30 ▌$30,000

Careers begin.

16 to 20 ▌$7,000

You mostly see part-time work in this younger age group.

| $0 | $50,000 | $100,000 | $150,000 | $200,000 | $250,000 | $300,000+ |

PRE-TAX INCOME

FIGURE 8.26 *"How Much Americans Make,"* https://datafl.ws/ageinc

SOURCE: American Community Survey, 2020

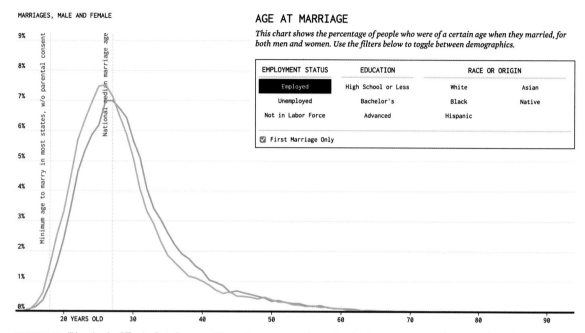

MARRIAGES, MALE AND FEMALE

AGE AT MARRIAGE

This chart shows the percentage of people who were of a certain age when they married, for both men and women. Use the filters below to toggle between demographics.

EMPLOYMENT STATUS	EDUCATION	RACE OR ORIGIN	
Employed	High School or Less	White	Asian
Unemployed	Bachelor's	Black	Native
Not in Labor Force	Advanced	Hispanic	

☑ First Marriage Only

FIGURE 8.27 *"Marrying Age,"* FlowingData / `https://flowingdata.com/2016/03/03/marrying-age` / *last accessed 08 February, 2024.*

the y-axis. The chart is interactive with demographic toggles, and the lines update as you click. As you look at different groups, you see the lines shift up and down.

Use comparisons to better understand your data, and then keep the good ones with you for later when you need to communicate the unfamiliar to an audience.

PATTERNS

Throughout this book, you have looked for patterns. The volume of traffic crashes tends to repeat itself on a weekly basis. People with certain jobs tend to marry others with certain jobs. Household types have moved toward smaller families and dual incomes with no kids.

Data trends upwards and downwards, like the whims of a teenager on social media (Figure 8.28). By the time you read these words, there will probably be a social media platform that I've never heard of sitting on top, or maybe social media will disband, and we'll return to a more peaceful time on the Internet where independent websites roamed free.

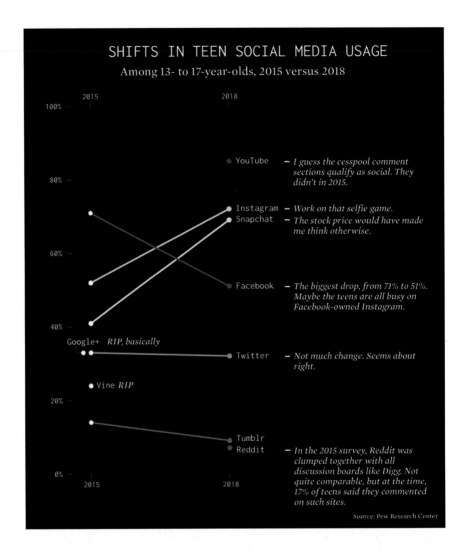

FIGURE 8.28 *"Shifted Social Media Usage, Among Teens,"* `https://datafl.ws/7nj`

In some places, as shown in Figure 8.29, there are more bars than grocery stores based on data from the Google Maps API. From a per-capita perspective, Wisconsin has the third highest rate with about 8 bars per 10,000 people. North Dakota and Montana take the one and two spots at 9.9 and 8.6 bars per 10,000 people, respectively. Delaware, Maryland, and Mississippi have the lowest rates, all with fewer than 1.5 bars per 10,000 people.

According to estimates from the Bureau of Labor Statistics, those in higher income groups tend to spend differently than those in lower income groups.

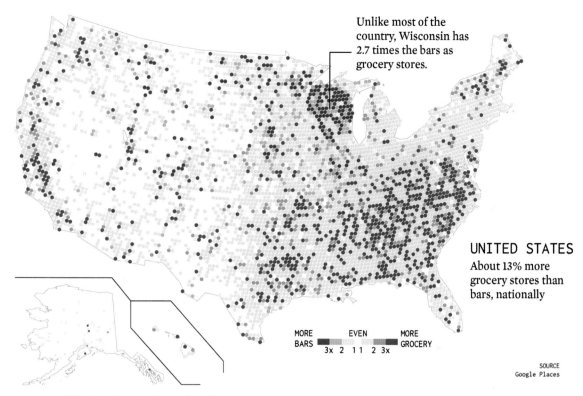

Unlike most of the country, Wisconsin has 2.7 times the bars as grocery stores.

UNITED STATES
About 13% more grocery stores than bars, nationally

MORE BARS — EVEN — MORE GROCERY
3x 2 1 1 2 3x

SOURCE
Google Places

FIGURE 8.29 *"Where Bars Outnumber Grocery Stores,"* https://datafl.ws/bars

When the essentials are paid for, there is greater flexibility for spending in other categories, as shown in Figure 8.30.

Look for the tendencies in the data. Note the patterns. When you find something, zoom in closer to see if there's more to note in the smaller details.

UNCERTAINTY

We want the simple answer. We want the concrete, definitive answer, and data is supposed to supply that, but usually, it doesn't work that way. Instead, we have estimates with margins of error, probabilities for possible outcomes, and ranges that the true answer might fall in. There is almost always uncertainty attached to the data, so when you visualize and analyze, you should treat it like it is not concrete.

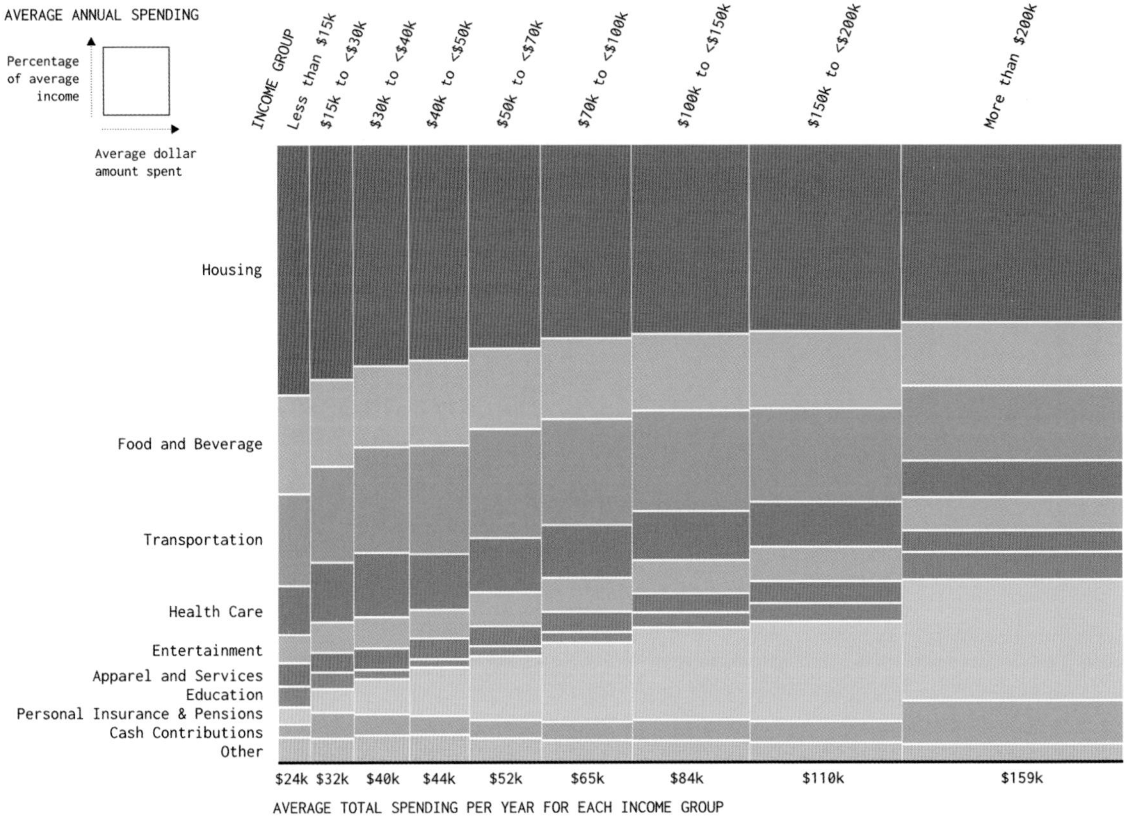

FIGURE 8.30 *"How Different Income Groups Spend Money,"* Nathan Yau / 2007-Present FlowingData /https://flowingdata.com/2018/02/08/how-different-income-groups-spend-money / *last accessed February 08, 2024.*

In statistics, we use a lot of "maybe" and "possibly" and "likely." There is less use of "definitely" and "absolutely certain." Even when a pattern in a chart looks obvious, I still feel the need to qualify the pattern with "it appears that" instead of "it is that."

For example, with a curiosity about the variation of dinner time between states, I used the American Time Use Survey, the dataset that keeps on giving, to calculate peak dinner time for each state. Figure 8.31 shows the results.

The peak times are highlighted in the middle, but as a parent with young children, I am attuned to much earlier, off-peak dinner times. I couldn't just leave it as single data points per state. There's a range of dinner time possibilities, so I calculated when eating tends to pick up and when it tends to slow down. The start and end times are noisy, but they're closer to reality.

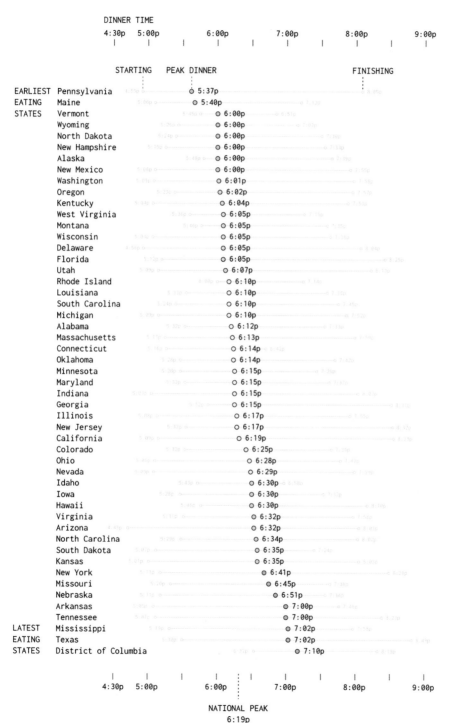

DINNER TIME

| | 4:30p | 5:00p | | 6:00p | | 7:00p | | 8:00p | | 9:00p |

STARTING   PEAK DINNER   FINISHING

EARLIEST	Pennsylvania	◉ 5:37p
EATING	Maine	◉ 5:40p
STATES	Vermont	◉ 6:00p
	Wyoming	◉ 6:00p
	North Dakota	◉ 6:00p
	New Hampshire	◉ 6:00p
	Alaska	◉ 6:00p
	New Mexico	◉ 6:00p
	Washington	◉ 6:01p
	Oregon	◉ 6:02p
	Kentucky	◉ 6:04p
	West Virginia	◉ 6:05p
	Montana	◉ 6:05p
	Wisconsin	◉ 6:05p
	Delaware	◉ 6:05p
	Florida	◉ 6:05p
	Utah	◉ 6:07p
	Rhode Island	◉ 6:10p
	Louisiana	◉ 6:10p
	South Carolina	◉ 6:10p
	Michigan	◉ 6:10p
	Alabama	◉ 6:12p
	Massachusetts	◉ 6:13p
	Connecticut	◉ 6:14p
	Oklahoma	◉ 6:14p
	Minnesota	◉ 6:15p
	Maryland	◉ 6:15p
	Indiana	◉ 6:15p
	Georgia	◉ 6:15p
	Illinois	◉ 6:17p
	New Jersey	◉ 6:17p
	California	◉ 6:19p
	Colorado	◉ 6:25p
	Ohio	◉ 6:28p
	Nevada	◉ 6:29p
	Idaho	◉ 6:30p
	Iowa	◉ 6:30p
	Hawaii	◉ 6:30p
	Virginia	◉ 6:32p
	Arizona	◉ 6:32p
	North Carolina	◉ 6:34p
	South Dakota	◉ 6:35p
	Kansas	◉ 6:35p
	New York	◉ 6:41p
	Missouri	◉ 6:45p
	Nebraska	◉ 6:51p
	Arkansas	◉ 7:00p
	Tennessee	◉ 7:00p
LATEST	Mississippi	◉ 7:02p
EATING	Texas	◉ 7:02p
STATES	District of Columbia	◉ 7:10p

| | 4:30p | 5:00p | | 6:00p | | 7:00p | | 8:00p | | 9:00p |

NATIONAL PEAK
6:19p

SOURCE: Bureau of Labor Statistics / BY: FlowingData

FIGURE 8.31 *"When is Dinner, by State,"* https://datafl .ws/dintime

When pondering how many years we have left to live, it's impossible to know the exact date and time. But using mortality data, we can guess the possible outcomes, as shown in the interactive in Figure 8.32. The range of possibilities is more interesting than average life expectancy.

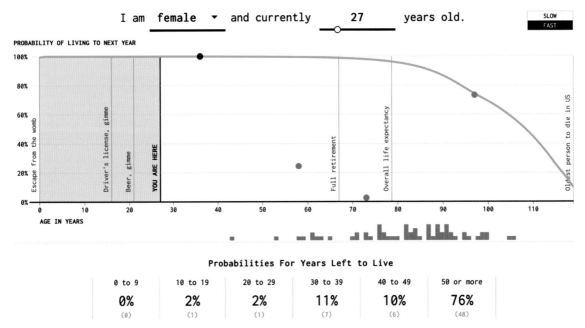

FIGURE 8.32 *"Years You Have Left to Live, Probably,"* FlowingData / `https://flowingdata.com/2015/09/23/years-you-have-left-to-live-probably` / *last accessed 08 February, 2024.*

Even when we have a lot of data, it can be difficult to provide an exact answer. How much do people have saved for retirement, given their age? The Survey of Consumer Finances asks people every two years, but when you look at the survey data, you see a lot of noise. Then there are more questions, such as what you should consider retirement savings. Should it just be money marked as retirement savings, or do you count all financial assets? What about home equity? Figure 8.33 is from an interactive graphic that shows a range of values for different types of savings using median, 25th and 75th percentiles, and individual data points.

While basic summary statistics are the simple answer, sometimes the more accurate solution is the more uncertain one. Favor ranges and possibilities over single values.

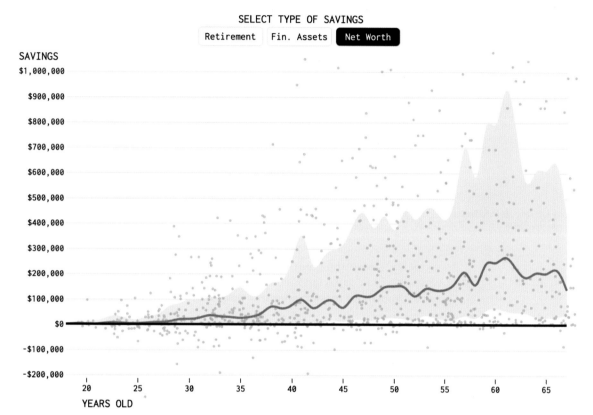

HOW MUCH SAVINGS GROW WITH AGE

As we get older, savings tend to grow, but so does the range.

SELECT TYPE OF SAVINGS

Retirement   Fin. Assets   Net Worth

FIGURE 8.33 *"How Much Savings Growth with Age,"* Nathan Yau / 2007-Present FlowingData / https://flowingdata.com/2019/11/08/ saving-for-retirement-and-age / *last accessed February 08, 2024.*

OUTLIERS

Outliers are data points that stand out from the rest. There are methods and criteria to detect outliers, but in the end, finding outliers is a subjective task. The context of your data dictates what you do with the outlier.

For example, Figure 8.34 shows subscribers to FlowingData over a 30-day period. There are two days when subscriber counts suddenly dipped. These two points are outliers in the context of the rest of the data points, but what do you do with them? Was there a server error that led to incorrect measurements? Did I make an offensive chart that made a bunch of people hate me

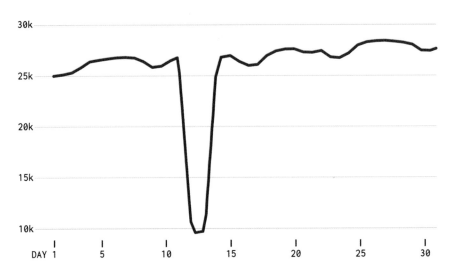

FLOWINGDATA SUBSCRIBERS OVER 30-DAY PERIOD

FIGURE 8.34 *Line chart showing subscribers over time*

suddenly? Given the counts rise back quickly, it's most likely the former, in which case you could ignore the errant estimates. However, if I were a content creator known for making offensive videos, you might treat the dip differently.

In some cases, you can treat outliers as something to highlight. It is a standout or something unique rather than something to ignore. Figure 8.35 is a still from an animated scatterplot that shows the distribution of births by age. Using data from the National Survey of Family Growth, there was one respondent who had 12 kids by age 30. At the time, my two kids were a handful, and the data point resonated for me.

When looking at relative job popularity across the country (Figure 8.36), the most interesting data points were the outliers. They were the ones that were, compared to the national average, much more popular in a given state or region. For example, economists and budget analysts are many times more popular in Washington, D.C., whereas actors are more common in California and New York. Fishing and hunting workers are more popular in Alaska, Maine, and Louisiana. The outlier jobs help define a state by showing what is unique.

There are ingredients that are unique to certain cuisines. As shown in Figure 8.37, soy sauce, sesame oil, and Szechwan peppercorns are relatively more common in Chinese cuisine, based on the percentage of recipes the ingredients appear in. In Italian recipes, the most cuisine-specific ingredients were parmesan cheese and fresh basil; in French recipes, it was shallots and unsalted butter; in Mexican recipes, it was corn tortillas, black beans, and avocado.

GROWING FAMILY

How many kids do women give birth to and when do they have them? Farther right means older and farther down means more kids.

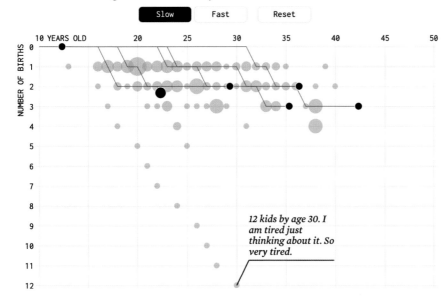

12 kids by age 30. I am tired just thinking about it. So very tired.

FIGURE 8.35 *"How Many Kids We Have and When We Have Them,"* Nathan Yau / 2007-Present FlowingData / https://flowingdata .com/2019/02/01/how- many-kids-we-have-and- when-we-have-them / *last accessed February 08, 2024.*

JOB POPULARITY IN EACH STATE
Search for a job below.

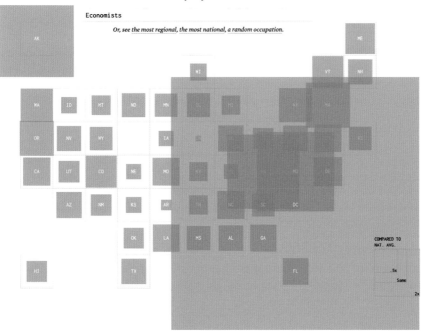

FIGURE 8.36 *"Where Your Job is Most Popular,"* Nathan Yau / 2007-Present FlowingData / https://flowingdata .com/2019/02/27/where- your-job-is-most- popular / *last accessed February 08, 2024.*

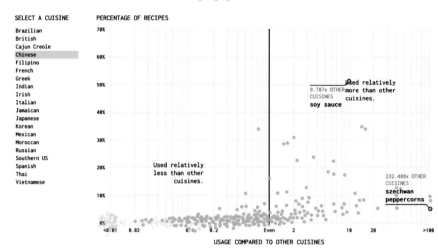

FIGURE 8.37 *"Cuisine Ingredients,"* Nathan Yau / 2007-Present FlowingData / https://flowingdata .com/2018/09/18/ cuisine-ingredients / *last accessed February 08, 2024.*

To find outliers, look for what sticks out. What you do with the outlier depends on what you're looking at, what you're looking for, and the questions you ask.

DRAWING CONCLUSIONS

With findings in hand from your data explorations, the process of telling stories with data is more straightforward. It's no longer just, "Here's the data. Look at it." You've answered questions through data and explored the details so that you can say, "Here's the data. This is what it says. Here is what we learned and why it's important." You move beyond an audience of one (yourself) and think about who you must communicate to.

The visualization process is about taking data, which is an abstract view of something more complex. The data is usually a simplification, but it is the best way to measure how things are going, so you analyze and explore. Then, in telling stories with data, you highlight what you found in the process to help others connect the abstract to reality.

I scribbled this process some years ago, as shown in Figure 8.38. It's not perfect, but the steps still hold. A lot of people get stuck between data and visualization. They never make it all the way around, which leads to charts that don't do much other than take up space.

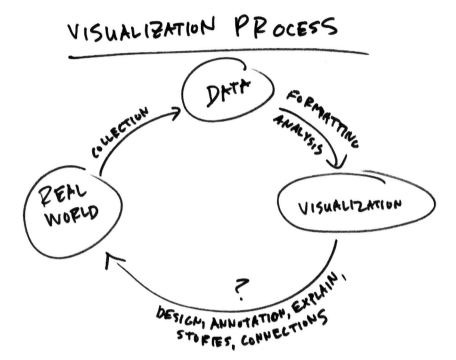

FIGURE 8.38 *Visualization process flowchart*

When you analyze data, think about where it came from, why it exists, what it is supposed to represent, and what it actually represents. Let the context inform your questions and answers. The context makes for meaningful visualization that tells you more than how numbers were converted to shapes and colors.

WRAPPING UP

In school, analyzing data can feel automatic and mechanical. Generate a hypothesis test. Calculate statistics. Consult table and make pseudo-decision. However, in a practical setting, analysis is more fluid. You ask questions, try to answer them, and adjust. You can move back and forth between steps as one finding informs another.

The analysis phase of visualization is my favorite part of the process because it's when you learn about the data. You get to take a spreadsheet or a data file that might as well be gibberish to most, and you find new things and create insights. With the new information, you can tell stories that communicate complexity to a wider audience. The information you gather during the analysis phase makes decisions a lot easier when you design your final graphics.

I tend to couple more traditional analysis with visual analysis equally. It provides me with the right balance of precision and exploration. The balance might look different for you. The key is not the balance, though. The key is to keep asking and answering questions about the data until you are satisfied with the findings.

In the next chapter, you figure out how to design graphics with these findings in mind. You design with a purpose. A lot of people just copy and paste the output from their software, which is the easy thing to do, but you can do better than that.

Designing
with Purpose

When you explore your own data, you don't need to do much in terms of storytelling. You are, after all, the storyteller, so you probably don't need to narrate to yourself. However, the moment you use visualization to present information—whether it's to one person, several thousand, or millions—a stand-alone chart is no longer good enough.

Sure, you want others to interpret results and perhaps form their own stories, but it's hard for readers to know what questions to ask when they don't know anything about the data in front of them. It's your responsibility to set the stage. Think about who and what your visualization is for and design with the purpose in mind.

GOOD VISUALIZATION

Although people have been visualizing data for centuries, only in the past few decades have researchers been studying what works and what doesn't. In that respect, visualization is a relatively new field. For a while, there was no consensus on what visualization actually is. Is it an analysis tool? Is it a form of communication? Is it art? Those who believed visualization was one thing would disagree with others who felt visualization was another thing because a chart that is good for communication might not be good for analysis, and vice versa.

However, visualization is not a single thing with a single set of rules and standards. Visualization is a medium that can serve different purposes.

Martin Wattenberg and Fernanda Viégas used book genres to describe the various forms of visualization, and Eric Rodenbeck related visualization to movies and photography, which you can see at https://datafl.ws/genre and https://datafl.ws/med, respectively.

For example, those who analyze data often use traditional statistical charts in their explorations. If a graphic or interactive chart doesn't help in analysis, then it's not useful. On the other hand, those who use visualization to communicate data to others require ways to highlight insights more than they need to discover insights. Those who use visualization for data art require flexibility in visual encodings and ways to piece together components. Some people use all the resources that visualization provides.

Imagine if we expected movies to follow the same structure, flow, and style across all genres. Dramas, comedies, action movies, and documentaries would all be the same, which defeats the purpose of making and watching movies. An action movie shouldn't have to make you laugh, and every comedy shouldn't need a great car chase. With visualization, you don't always need speedy precision or beautiful aesthetics. What you need depends on the who, what, and why of your work.

When you approach visualization as a medium instead of just a tool, you're allowed to ask better questions about your data and produce better work. Instead of asking what a tool can do and then adjusting your statistical questions to fit within the tool's capabilities, you start with the data and purpose and then use the visualization to achieve your goal. If the visualization fits the purpose, then it's good. If it does not, then you try something else.

For those new to visualization, it can be easy to be fooled into what makes a good chart. People are quick to assume what a chart is for, what it should look like, and the motives behind it. If the work does not check their boxes, which usually stem from analytics or from some "expert" opinion article, they deem it a failure. So, while criticism can be useful, consider where it comes from and if it's worth absorbing in the context of the visualization's purpose.

INFINITE OPTIONS

It's common to learn about visualization in terms of restrictions and rules, as if you must limit your possibilities to make charts the right way. This approach is important in the beginning. It works in the same way you must learn how to write. Learn to spell words correctly, what punctuation is for, how to structure sentences, and how to break up ideas into paragraphs and sections.

Learn how charts work so that you don't accidentally make a misleading chart that says the opposite of what you want. A bar chart value axis should start at zero because the length of the bar represents the data. Pie chart percentages should sum to 100 because the sum of the parts represents the whole.

Once you set up foundations, the maximum fun begins. You get infinite options with visualization as a medium. Adjust colors and geometries. Add layers of context through annotation and visual metaphors. Use the insights that you found during data exploration and analysis to guide your choices.

VISUALIZATION COMPONENTS

All the choices at once can be overwhelming, like kids in a candy shop allowed to get whatever they want. It can help to think of visualization as components that fit together. Instead of imagining a single chart full of data, you split it up into smaller pieces to figure it out.

There are various ways you can split up a visualization. Jacques Bertin, in *Semiology of Graphics* from 1967, described (based on the 1983 English translation by William S. Berg) a "plane" and the "retinal variables." The former is like the coordinate system that defines how geometries are placed in a space. The latter defines how to encode data into visuals.

William S. Cleveland, in his 1994 book *The Elements of Graphing Data*, lists the "basic elements of graph construction" as "scales, captions, plotting symbols, reference lines, keys, labels, panels, and tick marks." In *The Grammar of Graphics*, published in 2005, Leland Wilkinson more formally defined the components of a statistical graphic as data, variable transformations, scale transformations, coordinate system, visual elements, and guides.

For example, Figure 9.1 shows the components of a simplified bar chart using Wilkinson's classifications. The data and transformations are not shown, but with the coordinate system (time on the x-axis and a linear numeric scale on the y-axis), visual elements (the bars), and the guides (axes, title, and source), the components make the bar chart.

THIS IS A BAR GRAPH
It's a standard chart that uses length to encode data.

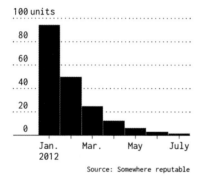

COORDINATE SYSTEM
Time on the horizontal and numeric on the vertical.

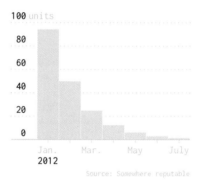

VISUAL ELEMENTS
Bars are sized by the data they encode.

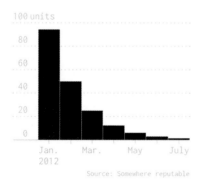

GUIDES
The axes, labels, and this text show how to read the chart.

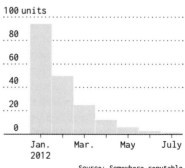

FIGURE 9.1 *Bar chart components*

This breakdown is useful when you want to experiment with form and aesthetics because you can adjust the parts instead of making every chart from scratch. For example, if you change the visual elements in Figure 9.1 but keep everything else the same, you get different charts, as shown in Figure 9.2.

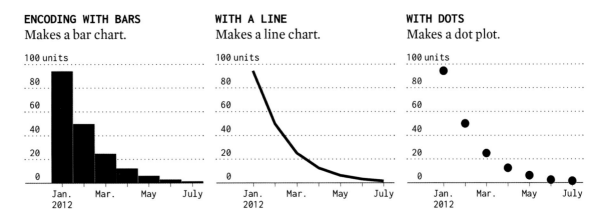

FIGURE 9.2 *Changing visual elements*

From an implementation point of view, this reduces the amount of work you have to do to make different charts, as various code libraries make direct use of the approach. The JavaScript library D3, the Python library Altair, and the R package ggplot2 let you define charts as components. Make one chart and modify parts of your code to get new charts. With point-and-click tools, using components as a way of thinking about visualization can help you navigate through the options.

Load the data. Define a coordinate system. Draw the axes with defined scales. Draw the data based on visual encodings. Customize the components along the way.

As you've seen throughout this book, you can get a lot done working with charts without splitting them into components. There are packages and applications that put things together for you once you supply the data. A single function call can get you almost all the way to where you need to go for a finished chart. However, when you want to customize results or make your own ad hoc visualizations that are specific to a dataset, think of a visualization as pieced together components.

INSIGHT FOR OTHERS

Once you shift jobs from data detective to data designer, your task is to communicate what you know to the audience. They most likely haven't looked at the data in the same way you did, so they won't see the same thing that you see if there's no explanation or setup. My rule of thumb is to assume that people are showing up to graphics blindly because usually they are. They come from social media, a link in a random article, or a mention in a talk.

When people get to your charts, you want to tell them the story of the data or at least give them a guided tour. You don't have to write an essay to accompany every graphic, but a title and a little bit of explanation are always helpful. Otherwise, it can quickly become like a game of Telephone, and before you know it, the graphic you carefully designed is explained with the opposite meaning you intended. The Web is weird like that.

VISUAL HIERARCHY

You went over visual hierarchy in Chapter 4, "Visualizing Time," but it's worth mentioning again, as it should be a consistent goal when you visualize data for an audience. The defaults in most software use equal visual weight for many components because the areas that deserve more attention should be decided by you.

If you want to focus on specific data points, make them more visually prominent to direct reader attention. Make the important bits jump out. You can use contrasting colors to highlight subsets of the data and make others fall into the background. You can make data points appear larger, and because they take up more space on the screen, they demand more attention. Use position to separate points. Provide annotation to explain interesting areas.

At the least, figure out the elements that you want to highlight the most and the elements that are there for context. Then you can decide the visual weights in between.

AESTHETICS

Aesthetics inherently refers to beauty, which is subjective. To some, a minimalist chart represents beauty. To others, bright colors with decorations represent beauty. Some might argue that making charts pretty is an unnecessary effort because it gets in the way of the data and inhibits clarity.

It's the other way around, though. Aesthetics can improve clarity. Put effort into aesthetics, and it can help readers understand your charts better by providing readability through visual hierarchy, a common identity across a broader theme, and a signal that time and effort was spent on the visualization. Plus, it's fun to make nice things. People like nice things. I like nice things. Default settings are no fun.

I have ongoing projects that I like to separate visually with differing aesthetics. *Data Underload* is a more analysis-focused project that I use to answer data curiosities. Many of the charts you've seen throughout this book come from the project. They vary in complexity, but they typically use a healthy amount of whitespace, a monospace typeface for labels, and a serif typeface for explanations. My color preferences have shifted over the years between saturated and unsaturated colors.

On the other hand, my *Statistical Atlas* project is meant to resemble previous atlases produced by the Census Bureau in the 1800s. As shown in Figure 9.3, the colors are more washed out, there are decorative borders, and the text layout is template-like.

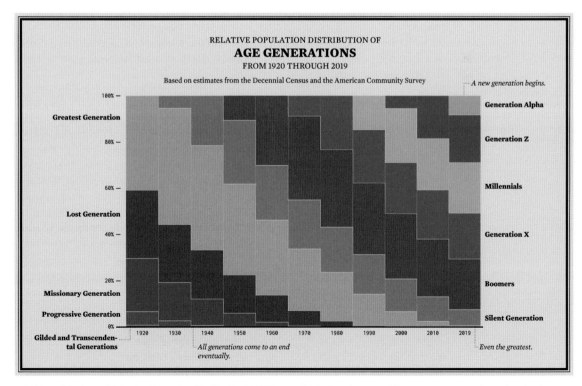

FIGURE 9.3 *"Coming and Going Age Generations,"* Nathan Yau / 2007-Present FlowingData / https://flowingdata.com/2021/05/18/change-in-age-generations / *last accessed February 08, 2024.*

Sometimes I go with the use-the-nearest-drawing-tool-available aesthetic, such as in Figure 9.4. There were crayons nearby, and I tried to visually explain the importance of filling out surveys for the decennial count.

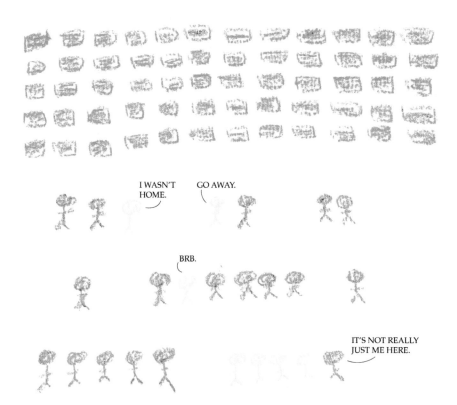

FIGURE 9.4 *"Making the Count,"* 2007-Present FlowingData / `https://flowingdata.com/2018/03/05/making-the-count/` *last accessed February 08, 2024.*

If you make graphics for a publication, you likely will need to match existing aesthetics. Maybe you have to make company dashboards that need to use a common theme across platforms. If you're doing your own thing, it might be beneficial to develop your own aesthetic so that your work is specific to you. Whatever it is, working on aesthetics in your charts is worth the extra effort.

VISUAL METAPHORS

Statistical charts are often abstract representations of data whittled down to bare geometries. They look like computer output with no connection to what the data is about. That's fine when you are in the data. Barebones gets you quick charts that can be applied to various datasets, regardless of context. However, the abstraction can make it a challenge for readers to connect.

Tip: If you're not sure where to begin, it can help to copy a graphic pixel-by-pixel, which forces you to look closely at the details.

It's hard to feel or interpret anything beyond quantitative measurements when all you have is a barebones dot plot. Visual metaphors can help.

Use elements in your visualization to represent the context of the data. This can be straightforward, such as selecting colors that are relevant. Figure 9.5 shows the percentage of people who still smoke by demographic. The categories in the stacked bar charts use common cigarette colors.

SEX

A higher percentage of males smoke than females do. The difference between the two increased during this time period.

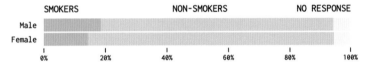

EDUCATION

College smokers decreased by almost half, but those with only some high school went down by a few percentage points.

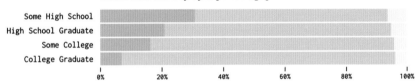

HOUSEHOLD INCOME

Similar to education, lower household income is related to higher smoker rates. The trend is more evident in recent years.

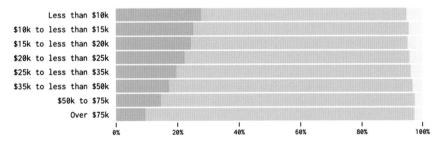

FIGURE 9.5 *"Who Still Smokes?"* Nathan Yau / 2007-Present FlowingData / `https://flowingdata.com/2016/06/20/who-still-smokes` / *last accessed February 08, 2024.*

Figure 9.6 is a screenshot from an interactive visualization that shows rising incomes with an elevator metaphor. A person icon in each elevator makes the choice more obvious. The visualization represents a "rise to the top." The higher the income, the higher the percentile, and it varies by age.

At a younger age, it takes a lot less to stand at the top. As you get older, it takes a lot more.

Enter your net worth to see the percentiles in different age groups.

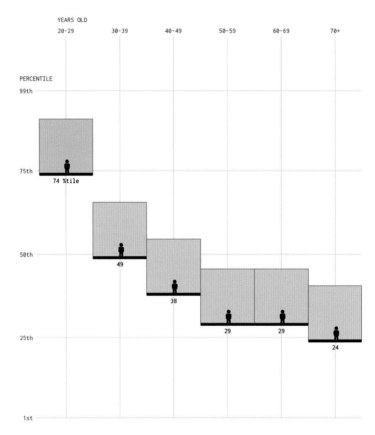

YOUR NET WORTH

$100,000

FIGURE 9.6 *"Rising to Top Net Worth, by Age,"* Nathan Yau / 2007-Present FlowingData / `https://flowingdata.com/2023/10/26/rising-to-top-net-worth-by-age` / *last accessed February 08, 2024.*

To show what makes people happy over a lifetime, I used force-directed happy faces that varied by area, color, and smile size, as shown in Figure 9.7. It might not be the most perceptually accurate visualization, but it was fun to make. That's bonus points.

Nigel Holmes' work epitomizes the use of visual metaphor in charts, often intertwining illustration and data patterns into a single graphic. The combination is often playful and entertaining as it informs. Mona Chalabi uses visual metaphors to great effect. She won a Pulitzer Prize showing the ridiculous scale of Amazon founder Jeff Bezos' wealth with a series of growingly outrageous comparisons.

Funny illustrations might not work for your next company report, but you can adopt the sentiment. Your visualization is about something. Use visual elements to represent that something alongside the quantitative insights.

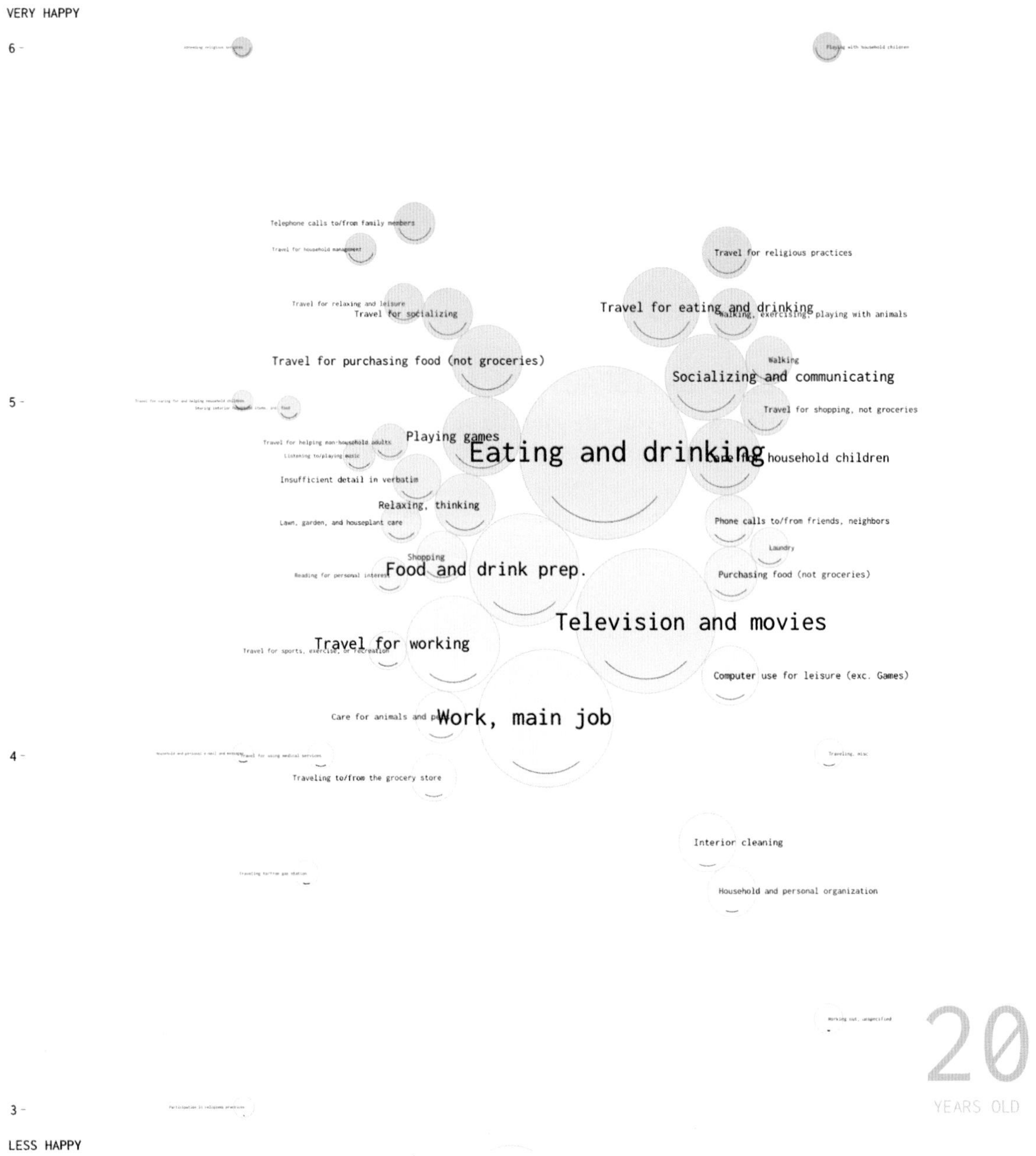

VERY HAPPY

6 –

5 –

4 –

3 –

LESS HAPPY

20 YEARS OLD

FIGURE 9.7 *"When Americans are Happiest,"* Nathan Yau / 2007-Present FlowingData / https://flowingdata.com/2023/01/04/when-americans-are-happiest / *last accessed February 15, 2024.*

ANNOTATION

Visualization is great for revealing patterns, but they're not always obvious to those who haven't looked at the underlying data. Words are a straightforward solution to improve this readability issue. They can help set expectations, explain encodings, direct readers' eyes to the insights, and provide narrative. Err on the side of too much annotation rather than too little because a reader can always skip words, but if a reader gets lost because you didn't explain enough, then the visualization is a sunk effort.

Direct annotation, as shown in Figure 9.8, works best if you have the space. It's more straightforward to make a chart separately and write the words

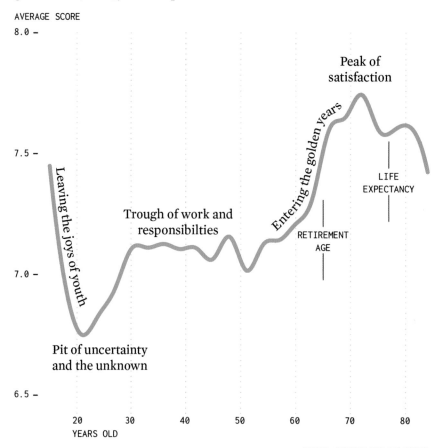

LIFE SATISFACTION AND AGE

How would you rate your life on a scale from 0, your worst possible life, to 10, your best possible life?

AVERAGE SCORE

FIGURE 9.8 *"Life Satisfaction and Age,"* Nathan Yau / 2007-Present FlowingData / https://flowingdata.com/2022/11/10/life-satisfaction-and-age / *last accessed February 15, 2024."*

SOURCE: AMERICAN TIME USE SURVEY

somewhere else, but an annotation layer on top of the chart keeps the words and encodings more tightly coupled. This is especially useful when you might traditionally use a legend to describe categories. You don't have to scan back and forth to remind yourself what each color represents, and instead you can keep your eyes on the patterns.

Imagine you're giving a talk, and your chart appears on a large screen. You might use a pointer to direct attention to a specific area of the chart and then explain why that area is relevant. To explain the chart when you're not in the room, place words in the area you would point to and explain the area with text.

ACCESSIBILITY

If your goal is to help people understand data, it's in your best interest to make your charts accessible to everyone. Use colors that most people will likely see. The color tools listed in Chapter 2 should help. Supplement visual encodings with text to explain the patterns and insights. Adding text is relatively straightforward, and researchers are working on ways to automate the annotation process. Provide computer interaction that is accessible via key presses.

Some have experimented with the nonvisual senses to communicate data. There are sonification tools to turn data into sound. There are tangible objects through 3-D printing or just everyday things like balls and boxes that are off the computer screen.

At the time of this writing, accessibility is relatively new in visualization, but I hope that when I revisit this text in another decade, there will be a lot more in this area. For that to happen, we must actively design with accessibility in mind.

WRAPPING UP

Many people see design as just a way to make your graphics look pretty. That's part of it, but design is also about making your graphics readable, understandable, and usable. You can help people understand your data better than if they were to look at a default graph. You can clear clutter, highlight important points in your data, or evoke an emotional response. Data graphics can be entertaining, fun, and informative. Sometimes, it'll just be the former, depending on your goal, but no matter what you try to design—visualization, information graphic, or data art—let the data guide your work.

When you have a lot of data, and you don't know where to begin, the best place to start is with a question. What do you want to know? Are you looking for seasonal patterns? Relationships between multiple variables? Outliers? Spatial relationships? Differences between categories? Then, look back to your data to see if you can answer your question. If you don't have the data you need, then look for more.

When you have your data, you can use the skills you learned from the examples in this book to tell an interesting story. Don't stop here, though. Think of the material you worked through as a foundation. At the core of all your favorite data visualization projects is a data type and a method that you now know how to work with. You can build on these for more advanced and complex graphics. Add interactions, combine plots, or complement your graphics with photographs and words to add more context.

Remember, data is simply a representation of real life. When you visualize data, you visualize what's going on around you and in the world. You can see what's going on at a micro-level with individuals or on a larger scale spanning the universe. Learn data, and you can tell stories that most people don't even know about yet but are eager to hear. There's more data to play with than ever before, and people want to know what it all means. Now you can tell them. Have fun.

Index